Environmental chemical analysis

Environmental chemical analysis

Iain L. Marr, M.Sc., Ph.D.,
Lecturer in Chemistry
University of Aberdeen

and

Malcolm S. Cresser, D.I.C., Ph.D.,
Lecturer in Soil Science
University of Aberdeen

International Textbook Company

Distributed in the United States by
Chapman and Hall
New York

Published by International Textbook Company
a member of the Blackie Group
Bishopbriggs, Glasgow G64 2NZ, and
Furnival House, 14–18 High Holborn, London WC 1V 6BX

Distributed in the USA by
Chapman and Hall
in association with Methuen, Inc.
733 Third Avenue
New York, N.Y. 10017

British Library Cataloguing in Publication Data

Marr, Iain L.
   Environmental chemical analysis.
   1. Chemistry, Analytic
   I. Title   II. Cresser, Malcolm S.
   543   QD75.2

   ISBN 0-7002-0282-X

For the USA, International Standard Book Number is 0-412-00201-9

Printed in Great Britain by Thomson Litho Ltd, East Kilbride, Scotland

Preface

There is a very real need both to teach analytical chemistry in relation to the jobs it has to do, and also to show how chemical analysis can yield reliable data which are valuable to other scientists. There is also a need to explain the difficulties facing the analyst, and to show how he chooses methods and techniques appropriate to the situation. The methods developed and the results obtained by analytical chemists will be used by many other scientists, and some background knowledge and appreciation of the subject is a prerequisite to avoiding possible pitfalls and errors.

I hope that teachers in universities, technical colleges and even schools will find in this book the inspiration to try a new approach to teaching analytical chemistry. When the coverage of this text falls short of what they need, the references will guide them to the specialist literature. Senior undergraduates should be encouraged to follow up some of these references, but younger students should find the text reasonably complete in itself.

The book would be little more than a seedling still had it not been for the generous and enthusiastic assistance and encouragement of my colleague Malcolm Cresser. After eleven years of teaching analytical chemistry to undergraduates and postgraduates in a university Soil Science department, he was as convinced as I was that this text would meet a real need. Our fields of experience have been largely complementary, and the balance has improved greatly under his influence. The final text, however, has been very much a combined effort.

There are of course still areas outwith our experience, and we have not hesitated to ask friends and experts for assistance—help has always been willingly and generously given, and to these people we owe special thanks. We would like to mention here Steve Black (art work), David Bullock (lead in blood), Bob Chalmers (prompt answers to all sorts of awkward questions), Brian Clark (environmental impact analysis), Peter Brown, Ian Davidson and Sam Frazer (costing of analytical services), Dieter Klockow and Jan Slanina (analysis of air and rain), Eric Lachowski (electron microscopy), Jim Marr (X-ray diffraction), Andrew Morrison (LIDAR), Alistair Smith (GC/MS of fatty acids), Gunther Tölg (problems in ultra-trace analysis), Richard Weddle (analysis of food) and various commercial firms mentioned in the text. Many students deserve thanks too, for trying out all the experiments as well as many more besides. Finally, we wish to thank our respective wives Eva and Louise, who have both waited patiently a very long time for alterations to kitchens to be completed, and the publishers, who have also been very patient and given much encouragement.

We are grateful to the literary executor of the late Sir Ronald A. Fisher, FRS, to Dr Frank Yates, FRS, and to the Longman Group Ltd, London, for permission to reprint the data on page 18 from Table III of their book *Statistical Tables for Biological, Agricultural and Medical Research* (sixth edition, 1974, previously by Oliver and Boyd, Edinburgh).

I.L.M.

Contents

1 THE NATURE AND SCOPE OF ENVIRONMENTAL
CHEMICAL ANALYSIS   1
1.1 Introduction   1
1.2 A typical analytical study—lead in the environment   4
1.3 Environmental impact assessment   7
1.4 The philosophy underlying this text   8

2 PERFORMANCE AND STRUCTURE OF
ANALYTICAL METHODS   9
2.1 Choosing a method   9
2.2 A statistical view of analytical procedures   9
    2.2.1 Standard deviation
    2.2.2 Errors
    2.2.3 Limits of detection and determination
    2.2.4 Calibration graphs and regression analysis
    2.2.5 Comparison of results
2.3 Criteria for selecting a method   19
    2.3.1 Accuracy and precision
    2.3.2 Sensitivity
    2.3.3 Selectivity
    2.3.4 Interferences
    2.3.5 Speed
    2.3.6 Cost and facilities
    2.3.7 Operator skills
    2.3.8 Scale of working
2.4 Sources of error in trace analysis   24
    2.4.1 The laboratory environment
    2.4.2 Containers
    2.4.3 Volatilization
    2.4.4 Reagents
2.5 Sampling   33
    2.5.1 Heterogeneity
    2.5.2 The time factor
    2.5.3 Errors arising during sampling
    2.5.4 Storage and preparation of samples
2.6 Dissolution and decomposition of samples   35
    2.6.1 Dissolution
    2.6.2 Fusion in melts
    2.6.3 Heating in a gas stream
2.7 Separation   37
    2.7.1 Separation by phase change
    2.7.2 Partition between two liquid phases
    2.7.3 Practical separation techniques

2.7.4   General problems associated with separation techniques
2.7.5   Apparent separations
2.8   Determination   46
2.8.1   Errors in determination
2.8.2   Speed of response
2.9.   The complete analytical procedure—a survey of sources of error   47

3   THE ATMOSPHERE   50

3.1   Composition of the atmosphere   50
3.2   Common air pollutants and their sources   50
3.3   Gases, vapours and particles   52
3.4   Odour thresholds   53
3.5   Air pollution and health   54
        3.5.1   Legislation in the UK
        3.5.2   Monitoring the environment
        3.5.3   Working atmospheres: the Health and Safety at Work Act, 1974
3.6   Sampling of airborne solids   57
        3.6.1   Smoke and dust
        3.6.2   High-volume air samplers
        3.6.3   Portable "personal" air samplers
        3.6.4   Where to sample
        3.6.5   Units for measurement of airborne dust
        3.6.6   General background
3.7   Examination of airborne solids   60
        3.7.1   Total weight and particle size distribution
        3.7.2   Identification of minerals—optical microscopy
        3.7.3   Identification of minerals—X-ray diffraction
        3.7.4   Quantitation by X-ray diffraction
        3.7.5   Interconversion of solid species on filters
        3.7.6   Non-destructive elemental analysis—X-ray fluorescence
                and emission
        3.7.7   Chemical analysis for individual elements
        3.7.8   Toxic organic compounds
        3.7.9   Radioactivity of airborne dust
        3.7.10 Results for an urban dust sample
3.8   Direct instrumental methods for gaseous pollutants   70
        3.8.1   Infrared spectrophotometry
        3.8.2   Non-dispersive infrared analysers
        3.8.3   Infrared emission spectroscopy
        3.8.4   UV laser remote sensing—LIDAR
        3.8.5   Mass spectrometry
        3.8.6   Draeger detector tubes
3.9   Sampling of gases and the atmosphere   78
        3.9.1   Containers
        3.9.2   Solid absorption systems
        3.9.3   Cold traps
        3.9.4   Small "personal" diffusion samplers
        3.9.5   Liquid absorption systems
        3.9.6   Efficiency of absorption
3.10 Gas chromatography   82
        3.10.1 Partition between a moving phase and a stationary phase
        3.10.2 The gas chromatograph
        3.10.3 The carrier gas flow control system
        3.10.4 The sample injection system

3.10.5   The column
3.10.6   The detector
3.10.7   Optimizing performance
3.10.8   Temperature programming
3.10.9   Quantitation in gas chromatography
3.10.10 Determination of aromatic hydrocarbons in exhaust, in petrol and in air
3.10.11 Determination of low levels of carbon monoxide—catalytic conversion

3.11   Some chemical methods for determining trace gases   94
    3.11.1   Sulphur-containing gases in the atmosphere
    3.11.2   Determination of H_2S
    3.11.3   Determination of SO_2
    3.11.4   Oxides of nitrogen in the atmosphere
    3.11.5   Determination of NO_x
    3.11.6   Oxides of carbon in the atmosphere
    3.11.7   Determination of CO_2
3.12   Some case studies of air pollution   101

4   THE HYDROSPHERE   104
4.1   The hydrological cycle and pollution   104
4.2   The oxygen balance in natural waters   106
4.3   River quality   107
4.4   Legal aspects of water pollution in the UK   108
4.5   The need for legislation on water quality   109
4.6   Programmes for monitoring water quality   110
4.7   Observations on sampling   111
4.8   Storage of samples and prevention of contamination   112
4.9   The analysis of water—what is required?   114
4.10   Selected analytical methods for water quality control   115
4.11   pH measurement—the glass electrode   115
4.12   Conductivity   116
4.13   Dissolved oxygen (DO)   116
    4.13.1   Winkler method
    4.13.2   Electrochemical method—polarography
    4.13.3   The Mackereth oxygen cell
4.14   Biochemical oxygen demand (BOD)   121
4.15   Chemical oxygen demand (COD)   121
4.16   Methods for the determination of inorganic nitrogen   122
    4.16.1   Determination of ammonia
    4.16.2   Determination of nitrite
    4.16.3   Determination of nitrate
4.17   Determination of phosphate   126
4.18   Automation of colorimetric procedures   127
4.19   The determination of chloride by titrimetry (visual)   130
4.20   Ion-selective electrodes   131
    4.20.1   Glass membranes
    4.20.2   Single-crystal membranes
    4.20.3   Determination of fluoride
    4.20.4   Polymer membranes
    4.20.5   Liquid membranes
    4.20.6   Selectivity
    4.20.7   Potentiometric titrations
4.21   Ion chromatography   136

4.22 The determination of heavy metals 136
    4.22.1 Photometric methods with dithizone
    4.22.2 Polarographic determination of heavy metals
    4.22.3 Anodic stripping voltammetric determination of metals
    4.22.4 Differential pulse stripping analysis
4.23 The importance of chemical species—speciation 144
4.24 Trace organics in water—total organic carbon (TOC) 145
    4.24.1 Outline of method for TOC determination
4.25 Determination of some individual compounds or groups of compounds 146
in polluted waters
    4.25.1 Photometric determination of phenols
    4.25.2 Determination of hydrocarbons
4.26 Gas chromatography/mass spectrometry (GC/MS) 151
4.27 The EPA survey procedure: priority pollutants 152

5 THE LITHOSPHERE 155
5.1 Introduction 155
5.2 The need for chemical analysis of soils and rocks 155
5.3 Available elements 157
5.4 Particle size distribution in soils 158
5.5 Soil analysis versus visual symptoms shown by plants 159
5.6 Sampling problems with rocks and soils 160
5.7 Subsampling 161
5.8 Dissolution for total elemental analysis 162
5.9 Some selected chemical methods in soil analysis 163
    5.9.1 The determination of soil pH
    5.9.2 The assessment of lime requirement
    5.9.3 Determination of available phosphorus
    5.9.4 Determination of available nitrogen
    5.9.5 Determination of total nitrogen
5.10 Flame atomic absorption spectroscopy 168
    5.10.1 Interferences in AAS
    5.10.2 Applications of flame AAS to soil and rock analyses
    5.10.3 The determination of exchangeable cations by AAS
5.11 Flame emission spectroscopy 176
5.12 Other emission techniques 179
5.13 Identification of minerals 180
    5.13.1 X-ray diffraction
    5.13.2 Thermal methods of analysis

6 THE BIOSPHERE 183
6.1 The nature of the biosphere 183
6.2 The need for plant analysis 183
    6.2.1 Deficiency problems
    6.2.2 Toxicity problems
    6.2.3 Pasture analysis
    6.2.4 Biogeochemical prospecting
6.3 The need for analysis of zoological specimens 186
6.4 The merits of treating the biosphere as a whole 187
6.5 Sampling problems 187
    6.5.1 Plants
    6.5.2 Animals, etc.

6.6   Sample preparation problems   189
        6.6.1   To wash or not to wash?
        6.6.2   Drying
        6.6.3   Grinding
        6.6.4   Homogenization
        6.6.5   Sample preparation for plant pigment determinations
6.7   Sample dissolution   192
        6.7.1   Scope for digestion of multi-element analysis
        6.7.2   Acid digestions for trace analysis
        6.7.3   Problems with dry ashing
        6.7.4   Fusion techniques
6.8   Analysis of plant tissue for N, P, K, Ca and Mg   194
        6.8.1   Digestion procedure
        6.8.2   Nitrogen by distillation/titration
        6.8.3   Phosphorus by spectrophotometry
        6.8.4   Potassium by flame photometry
        6.8.5   Calcium and magnesium by AAS
6.9   Boron in plant tissue   194
        6.9.1   Spectrofluorimetry
        6.9.2   Dissolution procedure for boron determination
        6.9.3   Fluorimetric determination
6.10   Cobalt in plant tissue   198
        6.10.1 Ashing procedure
        6.10.2 Dissolution and solvent extraction
6.11   Sulphur in plant tissue   199
        6.11.1 Oxygen flask combustion: procedure
        6.11.2 Turbidimetric determination of sulphate
6.12   Simultaneous multi-element analysis   200
        6.12.1 Emission spectrography
        6.12.2 Plasma emission spectroscopy
6.13   The role of trace elements in living systems   201
        6.13.1 The nature of enzymes
        6.13.2 Rates of enzyme-controlled reactions
        6.13.3 Deactivation of enzymes
        6.13.4 Inhibition of enzymes
6.14   Trace element determinations on very small samples   204
        6.14.1 Electrothermal atomization
6.15   Cold vapour and hydride generation systems in AAS   206
        6.15.1 Determination of mercury in urine

7   FOOD   209
7.1   Introduction   209
7.2   Food legislation   209
7.3   The composition of food   211
7.4   Preservatives   212
        7.4.1   Determination of fungicides on citrus fruit peel
        7.4.2   Identification of the chromatographic peaks by GC/MS
7.5   Anti-oxidants   215
        7.5.1   Determination of BHA in fats by spectrofluorimetry
7.6   Vitamins   215
        7.6.1   Determination of vitamin C
7.7   Volatiles in foods: head-space analysis   217
7.8   Pesticides   219
        7.8.1   Organochlorine pesticides

        7.8.2   Organophosphorus pesticides
        7.8.3   Columns for gas chromatography of pesticides
        7.8.4   Standards for pesticide residue analysis
7.9   Fatty acids: derivatization in gas chromatography   223
        7.9.1   Determination of fatty acids in edible fats and oils
        7.9.2   Other derivatization reactions
        7.9.3   Capillary gas chromatography
7.10   Chromatography of non-volatiles: HPLC   226
        7.10.1   The high-pressure liquid chromatograph
        7.10.2   Preconcentration procedures for HPLC
7.11   Some natural poisons: the mycotoxins   230
        7.11.1   Thin-layer chromatography
        7.11.2   Detection of aflatoxins in peanuts
7.12   Trace metals in food   232
        7.12.1   Determination of total trace metals
        7.12.2   Determination of trace organometallic compounds

8   COMPETITIVE ANALYTICAL CHEMISTRY   237
8.1   The lunar rocks   237
8.2   Trace elements in fly ash   238
8.3   The 100 % fallacy—analyses of an amphibole   239
8.4   An extensive programme to study igneous rocks   240
8.5   New methods for old   241
8.6   Trace elements in sea water   242
8.7   Analysis in archaeology   242
8.8   Practical limits of methods—trace iron in tungsten   243
8.9   Ethanol in pharmaceutical preparations   244
8.10   Mercury in the environment   245
8.11   Lead in blood—success at last   246

Appendix 1   TWA-TLV's for some gases and vapours   249

Appendix 2   Quality of water for human consumption   251

Appendix 3   EPA priority pollutants   252

Index   255

1 The nature and scope of environmental chemical analysis

1.1 Introduction

Almost everybody has some idea of what is involved in environmental chemical analysis. Indeed, other people's preconceived notions might well come to be regarded by the environmental analyst as one of the main occupational hazards of his work. Mere mention of an association with soils or plants as an analyst can all too quickly prompt the typical response: "Oh, how interesting! You must come and look at my gooseberry bushes. I'm sure there's something wrong with the soil as they've all gone a funny colour." On the other hand, if you admit to working in a laundry, rarely does someone say: "Oh, how interesting! You must come and help me with my dirty washing." So to the general public the environmental analyst, like the doctor or veterinary surgeon, is a potential source of highly valuable knowledge and information—in short, he holds the key to many of life's little mysteries.

To the analyst, on the other hand, the general public, and indeed even those members of it who might be expected to know better, often appear to have a surprisingly naïve concept of environmental analysis. While the gooseberry bushes may well be exhibiting symptoms of some deficiency or toxicity in the soil, it is equally likely that they may be under attack from any one of a number of pests or diseases or a neighbour's stray herbicide. In this instance, chemical analysis of a soil sample, however careful and comprehensive, will take up a good deal of time but may throw no light at all upon the malaise of the bushes. Chemical analysis in isolation, then, should never be regarded as a panacea, but rather as a powerful tool which may be used to provide the answer to highly specific questions. In many instances the analyst has a reasonable idea of what chemical species he is likely to find in his samples and what their approximate concentrations are likely to be before he starts any laboratory work. Analysis is then used to confirm or refute a diagnosis. Although in some instances he may be confronted by a complete "unknown", fortunately such events are rare.

Nevertheless the general public's concept of an analysis and that of the analytical chemist would, if reduced to terms of fundamental definitions, probably lead to similar end products. Qualitative analysis is the name given to the identification of elements or compounds which are present in a sample, while quantitative analysis is the process of measurement of the amount or concentration of any one or more of the species present in a sample. In practice this division into qualitative and quantitative analysis, whilst convenient, does not stand up to close scrutiny. The analyst may well establish that a particular species is present, but he cannot normally establish its absence. Rather, he shows that, if it is present, it is at a level below that which may be detected by the particular test he has used to look for its presence. This level may be considered as totally insignificant and therefore effectively zero, but in as many other cases the low level which may still just be detected lies well above those levels which may occur in the environment and give rise for concern. It might therefore be more satisfactory to develop concepts of quantitative and semi-quantitative analysis, which would at least save the environmental scientist from having to face the apparently miraculous appearance and disappearance of elements in ecological systems. In practice, by far the greater part of the analyst's work is quantitative.

The curious may wonder why the authors should feel the need to stress that environmental analytical chemistry is capable only of answering very specific questions. The reason is that all too often the scientist requesting the analysis may do so in very vague terms: "The fish are dying at a fish farm north of here. We think it's something in the water. Do you think you can tell us what it is?" A very reasonable question—or is it? Are the fish disease-free? Is their diet adequate? Have the deaths suddenly started? Has there been a change in the diet recently? Is the food from a reasonable supplier? Is any pollution suspected and is it likely to be organic or inorganic? Is there any reason to suspect a change in the level of pollution? And so on.

Note that the analyst does not need to be an expert in fish husbandry. The questions he is asking are commonsense, but if he gets satisfactory answers he may at least have some clues as to what to start looking for. At least he would have a rational basis for deciding if dead (and live) fish, or water, or the fish food would be the most suitable sample to commence work on. Note also that, unless he has much experience of a particular type of sample, chemical analysis may tell him nothing at all. He must first establish suitable reference levels, for example, for the composition of the fish which were, until taken for analysis, swimming about quite happily. It may be, of course, that the person posing the problem has sufficient knowledge and experience to interpret the numerical results of particular analyses, in which case the analyst's problem is alleviated to some extent.

It is worth considering here a further example of a problem associated with obtaining suitable reference levels for comparative purposes. Suppose soil analyses are to be carried out to ascertain the levels of zinc and cadmium contamination in the vicinity of a smelter. With the wisdom of hindsight it is easy to suggest that soil samples should have been collected and either analysed or stored under suitable conditions before the smelter became operational. Because soil is very variable in composition, collecting samples a few kilometres away does not provide a satisfactory alternative. In this instance it may be necessary to collect samples from under old buildings in the hope that they will have been protected from contamination, and will therefore provide natural background levels for zinc and cadmium in the area.

In this example, the analyst is answering a specific question, namely, "What are the total levels of zinc and cadmium contamination in the soils?" He provides the answer by determining the total levels of the two elements in contaminated and uncontaminated soil (note, by the way, that we speak of the elements as being *determined* and the soil as being *analysed*). He could equally well have been asked; "Are these elements in a form in which they can be taken up by vegetables grown in the area, to reach a dangerous level?" This is a different question altogether, and would require different analyses to be done to provide the answer. When selecting a method of analysis, it is important that the analyst be quite clear about the precise question he is being asked and is trying to answer.

It would be quite misleading to create the impression that *every* analysis completed by a competent analyst will have involved a substantial amount of painstaking interrogation and detective work before the start of the laboratory investigation. This approach is necessary when some particular one-off problems have to be solved, it is true, but much of the everyday work of the environmental analytical chemist may involve the determination of the same species in a number of samples on a routine basis, i.e. by the same analytical procedure. In this case much original thought may go into the selection and specification of procedures for sample collection and analysis, but the final procedure, once established as reliable, becomes simple routine— much like following instructions in a cookery book. Environmental analyses in this category generally fall under one of two broad headings: quality control, or routine testing.

In *quality-control* analysis the analyst is answering the question, "Is the customer receiving a product whose chemical and/or physical composition falls within clearly defined limits?" This may involve establishing that a metal alloy does not contain levels of impurities which would weaken its strength, or that a pharmaceutical preparation does contain a certain minimum level of active ingredient. It may involve checking the protein content of a food product or confirming that a fertilizer will give a farmer at least as much of a specified plant nutrient element as the bag indicates. Sometimes it may involve checking that undesirable elements are present only at levels below some extremely low specified concentration, as is often the case in the semiconductor industry.

In most of the examples cited, the determinations do not need to be completed with great precision, but there are instances where even a small error in the result of a determination may be important. In the case of nuclear fuels or precious metals, for example, quite a small error could correspond to a very substantial financial loss (or enough plutonium going "missing" to make a small nuclear weapon).

In *routine testing* on the other hand, the analyst compares samples with suitable control standards to provide a quantitative evaluation of the extent of a problem, and possibly of the extent of the treatment which is necessary to rectify the problem. This may sound complicated, but is really very simple. He is answering questions such as, "How much fertilizer does this soil need?" or, "Does the analysis of this patient's blood or urine indicate that he is suffering from lead poisoning?" or, "Is the zinc level in these apple tree leaves so low as to suggest that zinc deficiency may be a problem in the orchard they came from?" Routine testing, then, is concerned with providing the answer to specific problems, and not with guaranteeing the quality of a marketable product.

This division is rather arbitrary, since the same method of analysis may be applied in routine testing, in quality control, and in solving one-off problems. It is, however, useful in that it gives an indication of the vital role played by the analytical chemist in so many spheres of human activity. Sometimes analytical procedures are borrowed directly (or after slight modification) from quality control or routine testing laboratories in order to solve one-off problems. Is the sliver of glass in the pocket of the arrested man really from a beer glass, as he suggests, or could it be from the broken window at the scene of a crime? Do the levels of phosphorus in soil samples taken from the archaeological excavation indicate the type or extent of human activity on the site? Can we tell from looking at the scrapings of paint on bits of wreckage from this aircraft exactly how it broke up? These three questions all pose a further question to the analyst, namely, "What determination will give the most useful information?" Once answered, the resulting method is likely to be drawn from an appropriate routine procedure as used in the glass industry, in agriculture, or in the paint industry.

1.2   A typical environmental study — lead in the environment

One aspect of environmental chemical analysis makes it rather different from many of the examples just quoted: one is dealing with the environment as a whole, the ecosystem. One of the reasons for carrying out chemical analysis of environmental samples is to be able to understand biological pathways or cycles, particularly those involving harmful materials. This assists the environmental health specialist in deciding what levels can be tolerated, what levels exist, and whether the materials are in a form which makes them readily available to plants and animals. These analyses may be followed by others to see whether man accumulates the harmful substances or simply excretes them, possibly without change. This should become clearer if we look at a specific example. Figure 1.1 shows some data for daily lead throughput for a

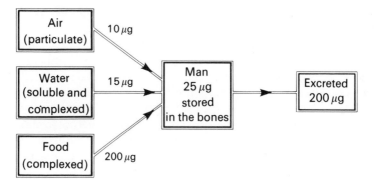

Figure 1.1   Daily lead balance for a typical city dweller.

typical urban dweller in a developed country.[1] It shows why it is essential to investigate many different components of the environment before attempting to draw conclusions from the results. In this case samples of air, airborne dust, drinking water and a large variety of foods must be analysed for their lead content, care being taken to determine the total lead, not just the water-soluble species. From the individual results it will then be possible to estimate the lead content of the "weekly shopping basket" and interpret that in terms of the total burden in the diet per person.

It is clear that any two sets of results for these analyses will probably show large discrepancies, depending on where and when the samples were collected, so very many samples from many sources will have to be analysed at many times over a prolonged period so as to make it possible to construct the simple diagram shown in Fig. 1.1. Indeed, one might argue that such gross bulking of analytical data (applicable perhaps to the 1971 average Scottish man with 0.83 of a wife and 1.20 children) does not make any sense, and that one should rather subdivide the population into groups living, say in the towns and in the country, or in areas with hard or soft water, and then make comparisons between these groups.

Having arrived at figures such as those shown in Fig. 1.1, one would then ask where the body stores the lead accumulating at 25 µg per day, and to answer this many different parts of the body will have to be analysed. Blood and urine are easily obtained from living people, and most surveys are based on analyses of the former. But there is reason to believe that the lead is stored in the bones, and is only released into the blood in times of stress. So do blood-lead levels give a true picture? Other workers have analysed teeth extracted by dentists from live patients, and others have analysed milk teeth lost by children. How do these results fit in?

It is particularly unfortunate that in the case of lead in the environment the analyses are not easy, and it now seems that some of the results published in the literature are subject to serious errors. But such results can and do attract the attention of the media and are brought to the notice of the public who are not in a position to discriminate between good results and bad. Thus results quoted in a 1974 publication[1] compared a mean blood-lead level of $230 \mu g l^{-1}$ for UK inhabitants with one of $220 \mu g l^{-1}$ for mountain dwellers in New Guinea and concluded that both must represent a "natural" and therefore safe value. More recent work, discussed by Grandjean[2] quotes figures of only $30 \mu g l^{-1}$ and $50 \mu g l^{-1}$ for blood-lead in children in remote areas, while yet another study suggests that the lead levels in the environment in ancient Egypt were only one-hundredth of present-day levels in developed countries. This ties in with the changes of lead concentration found at varying depth in polar ice corresponding to atmospheric deposition from different historical periods, the levels increasing significantly at depths laid down since the beginning of the industrial revolution 200 years ago (see p. 53).

Possibly even more difficult than the chemical analyses are the sociological and psychological surveys which are needed together with the chemical work to show at what levels the lead in the various sections of the environment begins to present a hazard. It is therefore not surprising that one report concluding that current levels of lead exposure in the UK do not present a significant health hazard[3] should be followed a year later by one finding that there is a definite correlation between blood-lead level and intelligence in children at school.[4]

However difficult it may be to carry out these investigations with sufficient care and skill to be able to obtain reliable results and to be able to draw significant conclusions from them, it does not take much effort to show that a problem does indeed exist. Just as one can attempt to draw up a mass-balance for lead in the ordinary citizen, so one can try to do it for the whole country. The annual demand for lead in the UK is around 4×10^5 tonnes, of which some 10 000 tonnes are consumed as additives in petrol, and therefore find their way into the air and on to the land near our roads and cities. The high levels of lead in airborne street dust (around 0.1 % or more, see 3.7.10) are then not very surprising.

More surprising are the claims that swans are being killed by lead poisoning arising from lead weights lost in rivers and lakes by anglers, amounting in the UK to some 250 tonnes per year. The lead pellets are swallowed by the swans as they scavenge for food in the sediments of the rivers, and are not discharged by the digestive system, but remain to be slowly dissolved and absorbed into the blood stream.[5]

1.3 Environmental impact assessment

A law of physics states that for every action there is an equal and opposite reaction: a similar law can be said to exist in the case of man's actions on the environment. It reacts to disturbance by assimilation or by transformation of factors which may ultimately degrade the ecological stability of the environment as well as the quality of life of man. It is with these changes in mind that environmental scientists seek to understand the physical and chemical responses of the environment to external influences. Environmental impact assessment (EIA) is a procedure which attempts to define and assess the effects of a proposed project, policy or product so that better-informed decisions can be made. It is generally recognized that EIA must consider the following:

   (i) The environmental impacts of the proposed action
  (ii) Any adverse impacts which cannot be avoided
 (iii) An analysis of alternatives to the action, including the "no-go" alternative
 (iv) Identification of monitoring schemes
  (v) Suggestion of mitigating measures to reduce environmental impact.

Within these broad considerations, impacts must be identified, measured, interpreted and communicated to decision-makers and the public. In the UK, EIA has so far been developed to assess the potential impacts of major new projects such as power stations, petrochemical complexes and mineral workings. In other countries it is seen as a tool to encourage better control of pollution and to develop integrated environmental management.

It is useful to distinguish between EIA methods, which are concerned with the identification of impacts and the organization of results, and EIA techniques, which are concerned with predicting impacts, such as mathematical models for predicting concentrations of air pollutants at varying distances from a source. Such techniques provide the data which are classified, interpreted and organized by the EIA methods. Techniques are available for a number of topics, such as risk and hazard assessment, air and water pollution, waste disposal, health, and ecological and visual impacts. Environmental chemistry in all its aspects has a very important role to play in the provision of information on environmental processes. Pollutants which enter the environment from human actions require detailed chemical analysis in order to identify the mechanisms and pathways by which the effects occur. Environmental chemistry not only contributes to the general level of knowledge of environmental processes, but also plays an important role in the design of monitoring programmes established to identify environmental trends and to provide data which assist the mitigation of potentially harmful effects.

Environmental chemistry plays an important part in the identification of Threshold Limit Values for toxic substances (see section 3.5.3) and also in defining emission levels for various pollutants. Without an understanding of the chemical processes, attempts to minimize the harmful effects of development would be futile. Environmental analytical chemistry is, then, one component of the multi-disciplinary subject of EIA, but environmental chemists should be aware of the various uses to which their skills can be applied in EIA. EIA is not an exact science: it involves the interpretation of the significance of many different impacts and thus also the use of "objective" science as well as subjective value judgements in decision making.[6,7]

1.4 The philosophy underlying this text

In the following chapters the authors have tried to give some insight not just into the working tools of the environmental analyst, but also into the types of problem he may be called upon to help in solving—the *raison d'être* for his labours. They have also tried to indicate why a certain line of approach or choice of method may be needed for attacking the problem in hand, and to give a brief resumé of the difficulties the analyst may face along the way.

References

1 Great Britain: Department of the Environment (1974) *Lead in the Environment and its Significance to Man.* Pollution Paper No. 2, HMSO, London.
2 Grandjean, P. (1981) *Nature*, **291**, 188.
3 Great Britain: Department of Health and Social Security (1980) *Lead and Health* (The Lawther Report). HMSO, London.
4 Yule, W., Lansdown, R., Miller, I. B. and Urbanowicz, M. A. (1981) *Develop. Med. Child Neurol.*, **3**, 567.
5 Birkhead, M. (1981) *New Scientist*, 2nd April, p. 14.
6 Clark, B. D., Bisset, R. and Wathern, P. (1980) *Environmental Impact Assessment*, Mansell, London.
7 Canter, L. (1977) *Environmental Impact Assessment*, McGraw-Hill, New York.

2 Performance and structure of analytical methods

2.1 Choosing a method

The customer requesting the analysis of a sample is often interested not so much in the numerical results themselves as in their relation to other values for other samples. These values may have been obtained in other laboratories by operators using different procedures and instruments: is the customer then justified in making any comparisons at all? His faith in analytical chemistry is much to be applauded, but it is a stern reminder to the analytical chemist that he must not only produce results, but also be able to demonstrate his confidence in them. Success here will depend on his having made the right choice at the outset of the project.

Without wishing to insult his client, the analyst will do well to start by assuming that his client does not really know what samples should be analysed, or for what constituents. A discussion of the background to the problem may lead to suggestions of an alternative approach, perhaps easier, cheaper, more reliable or more informative. A visit to the site or the laboratory may prove worthwhile at this stage, and familiarity with the samples—their expected composition and their stability for example—will assist the analyst in choosing a suitable method and avoiding at least some of the possible pitfalls.

Next, the literature should be consulted: *Analytical Abstracts* is a helpful starting point which is quickly surveyed, while specialist publications from government agencies and other organizations will draw attention to the existence of approved or even obligatory methods.[1] Such publications will be mentioned as appropriate throughout this book. If the analyst has a free hand, he will base his decision on a number of criteria, several of them related to performance of possible alternative methods. Before going further, then, it will be helpful to say a little about statistical testing of results and performance of methods.

2.2 A statistical view of analytical procedures

Statistics may be described loosely as the science of extrapolating from the practicable to the impracticable: on the basis of a finite and usually rather small number of observations or measurements one attempts to draw conclusions relevant to a much larger bulk of material or number of objects. It is important to distinguish between a *population* (which refers to the bulk system under investigation, whether it comprises individual entities such as people or articles or is simply a large mass of material) and a *sample* (which refers to that part of the population which is taken for study or measurement).

It is common experience that if one takes a few portions of something thought to be quite uniform and homogeneous (e.g. a dilute aqueous solution) and carries out an analytical determination on each of these portions (the samples) the results will not be in perfect agreement. Two problems arise: one is to explain why the results differ as much as they do, and the other is to quote a figure for the composition of the bulk of the solution (the population). The first of these might not be too difficult, but the second may be far from easy.

2.2.1 Standard deviation

Let us assume that we make a number of replicate determinations on portions of some homogeneous material, obtaining values $x_1, x_2, \ldots x_i, \ldots x_n$ for the n portions taken. We can calculate the *mean* value of x for the material from

$$\bar{x} = \frac{x_1 + x_2 + \ldots + x_i + \ldots + x_n}{n}. \tag{2.1}$$

For each determination there will be a deviation from the mean equal to $(\bar{x} - x_i)$, some positive and some negative. If we make a very large number of determinations and construct a plot of the number of times any particular value of x is obtained, as a function of the value of x, we should obtain a symmetrical curve called a Gaussian distribution, described by

$$\frac{dN}{N} = \frac{1}{\sigma\sqrt{2\pi}} \cdot e^{-(\bar{x} - x_i)^2/2\sigma^2} \cdot dx. \tag{2.2}$$

Here dN/N is the fraction of the total number of results which lie in the range x to $(x + dx)$ and is a probability function. The constant σ (that is, constant for a particular set of results) describes the relative width and sharpness of the peaked distribution curve illustrated in Fig. 2.1 and will be expressed in the same units as x or as a fraction of $\bar{x}$. It is termed the *standard deviation* for the set of values of x. The area under a part of the curve gives the fraction of all results occurring within a particular range of values of x. Thus, about 68.3% of the values lie in the range $(\bar{x} \pm \sigma)$, i.e. about two results out of three, while 95.5% of them lie in the range $(\bar{x} \pm 2\sigma)$, i.e. about nineteen results out of twenty. Since one result in every three being wrong would not be considered very satisfactory performance, but one failure in twenty would be satisfactory for most purposes, the range $(\bar{x} \pm 2\sigma)$ is taken as a good guide to the spread of results from a method under investigation.

It is of course not practicable to examine the whole of a population to obtain a value for σ, so we denote the experimentally determined standard deviation by s. There are two convenient ways of estimating this for a set of

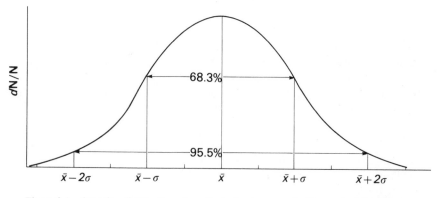

Figure 2.1   Gaussian distribution of results $\bar{x}_i$ about a mean $\bar{x}$ with standard deviation σ.

results, the simpler and rather approximate way being based on the *range* of the values, R, being the difference between the highest and the lowest values of x. For small numbers of results, say n between 4 and 6, s is given by

$$s = R \cdot k \tag{2.3}$$

where the appropriate value of k is taken from Table 2.1.

Table 2.1   Values of k for calculating standard deviation by the range method

n	3	4	5	6	7
k	0.59	0.49	0.43	0.39	0.37

If more results are available—about 10 would be suitable—it is worth calculating s from the relationship

$$s = \left(\frac{\sum\limits_{i=1}^{i=n} (\bar{x} - x_i)^2}{(n-1)} \right)^{\frac{1}{2}} \tag{2.4}$$

which shows that s is in fact the root-mean-square deviation for the set of results. The sum of the squared deviations is divided by $(n-1)$ rather than by n because one degree of freedom has already been used in calculating $\bar{x}$ from the individual values.

When the number of determinations is very large, now denoted by N, the value of s for the set of samples approaches the true value σ for the population. In this case we can write

$$\sigma = \left(\frac{\sum\limits_{i=1}^{i=n} (\mu - x_i)^2}{N} \right)^{\frac{1}{2}} \tag{2.5}$$

where μ is the average value of x for the whole population.

These formulae are easily handled on pocket calculators (indeed many calculators offer this as a built-in program) but students should avoid using an alternative formula mentioned in some books, which involves taking the difference between (x_i^2) and $(\sum x_i)^2/n$ since many smaller calculators do not handle enough significant figures for this difference to be determined reliably and will therefore give wrong values for s.

We have so far assumed that if n is sufficiently large, s will approach σ and $\bar{x}$ will approach μ, the true average value for the population. The former assumption is true but the latter is not necessarily valid, and we must now consider a classification of errors.

2.2.2   Errors

Random errors are those we have considered in the argument so far, where the deviation on any one result is as likely to be positive as negative. The error will be a matter of chance only, and if a sufficient number of samples are taken, the mean value $\bar{x}$ will be a good approximation to the true value for the population μ. Such errors, which Eckschlager[2] calls errors of measurement, arise when an operator fills a pipette or flask to the mark, reads a burette, decides on a colour change, reads a chart recorder or a meter, and so on, and indeed, the random error for a complete procedure is accounted for in terms of these individual random errors, each of which can usually be assessed in a separate experiment such as that of calibrating the glassware. If we denote s_w as the relative standard deviation of weighing the sample, s_f that of making up to the mark in a standard flask, s_p that of taking an aliquot portion by pipette, and s_t that of determining the end-point in a titration, we may expect the overall standard deviation of the complete analytical procedure, S, to be given by

$$S^2 = (s_w^2 + s_f^2 + s_p^2 + s_t^2). \tag{2.6}$$

If this calculated value of S turns out to be significantly different from the observed value for a number of complete determinations then we must look elsewhere for other errors, such as inhomogeneity in the sample, or some changes in the laboratory conditions, the titrant solution, or the procedure.

Systematic errors (Eckschlager's errors of procedure) are those which, when present, remain constant throughout all determinations on a set of samples. A systematic error will lie in only one direction for the set of determinations, introducing a *bias*, so that the mean value $\bar{x}$ can no longer be equated with the true value μ for the population, or the bulk of the material being analysed, and will always be wrong. Such errors may arise when a standard flask or burette is wrongly calibrated, when the solution is not of the concentration stated, when an instrument has gone out of calibration, or even when the chemistry is not behaving as one would expect. Some of these errors can be checked for quite simply by calibrating each piece of apparatus individually, and it is possible to check the procedure as a whole if reliable analysed standards (such as metals and ores) are available. However, in many cases encountered in trace analysis such standard reference materials are not available and it is necessary to painstakingly check each step for quantitative transfer, separation, reaction and determination, and preferably to cross-check by analysing the samples by an entirely different procedure. Tölg[3] has amply demonstrated the effectiveness of this approach in analysing high-purity metals for various trace elements.

Gross errors are supposed to happen only to other people on unlucky days, and cover such events as dropping the sample bottle on the floor, knocking the tap out of the burette during a titration, or finding a large flake of rust fallen into a solution in which traces of iron have to be determined. However, they can happen to you too, and provided they don't happen too often, the statisticians have provided tests to allow you to reject the occasional bad result.

The simplest test is to compare the deviation of the suspect value with the mean and the average deviation of the remaining values. Since for a large normally distributed population the average deviation $\bar{d}$ is 0.8 of the standard deviation s, a deviation of $2.5d$ corresponds to $2s$ and not more than one value in twenty should fall outside this range. The so-called $2.5d$–test states that if the deviation of the suspect value exceeds $2.5\bar{d}$, the value may be rejected. This is only a rough test and may lead to rejection of a valid result, but it is still useful as a working guide.

A more reliable approach is to use the Q-test, where, if x_n is suspect

$$Q = \frac{x_n - x_{n-1}}{x_n - x_1} \tag{2.7}$$

and x_n and x_1 represent the highest and lowest of the values arranged in order. Q is calculated and compared with the values in Table 2.2. If the experimental value of Q exceeds the tabulated value for the number of determinations in the set, and for the desired degree of confidence, then the suspect result should be rejected. This test is intended for use with small numbers of determinations when the standard deviation cannot be estimated reliably.[4]

Typical sources of error in trace analysis are discussed in Section 2.4, and some examples are presented in Chapter 8.

Table 2.2   Values of Q for rejection of a grossly wrong result

	Degree of confidence		
n	90%	95%	99%
3	0.89	0.94	0.99
4	0.68	0.77	0.89
5	0.56	0.64	0.76
6	0.48	0.56	0.70
7	0.43	0.51	0.64

The *precision* of an analytical procedure is a measure of the repeatability, and is best quoted as a standard deviation, either in the same units as the value determined, or as a percentage relative to that value. As an example, one might quote the precision for a trace iron determination as $s = 0.5\,\mu g$ at the $10\,\mu g$ level, or as $s = 5\%$ at the $10\,\mu g$ level, implying that a determination on a sample containing $10\,\mu g$ will give a result nineteen times out of twenty in the range 9–$11\,\mu g$.

Good classical titrimetry can give standard deviations of 0.1–0.2%, good spectrophotometric or atomic absorption determinations around 0.5%, many instrumental methods on small samples around 1%, while at trace levels 5–10% is not uncommon.

Accuracy of an analytical result (or of the mean of several values) is a measure of its correctness—of the closeness of $\bar{x}$ to μ. It may be very difficult, particularly in extreme trace analysis, to prove or disprove that a result is accurate, and only much careful work aimed at eliminating all possible sources of error, and at showing that they have been eliminated, can give the analyst real confidence in such results. This is illustrated in the case of a trace mercury determination described by Tölg[5] (see also 8.10).

2.2.3   Limits of detection and determination
We have seen how we can measure the precision of a procedure at a specified working level, but often we have to answer the question "How little of this substance can I detect?" This can usually be answered from statistical considerations if we introduce the concept of the *blank*: the reading or value we get when no sample is taken, but only the reagents and solvents are put through the procedure. We can show this diagrammatically as a typical

calibration plot for a spectrophotometric determination in which absorbance is plotted as a function of amount of analyte present (Fig. 2.2).

The straight line intersects the absorbance axis at a value A_b which may be due to contamination from the reagents or just to the absorbance of the reagents themselves. There will be an uncertainty in this value, and if the measurement of the blank is repeated several times we can calculate the

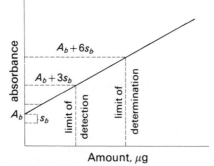

Figure 2.2 Limit of detection and limit of determination for a spectrophotometric method. A_b = absorbance of the blank; s_b = standard deviation of A_b.

standard deviation of the blank s_b. We now define the limit of detection as being that amount of substance which will give a reading of $3s_b$ above A_b, and also a limit of determination as that giving a reading of $6s_b$ above A_b. The latter is preferred by many workers because it is the lowest level at which one can begin to put a number, rather than just saying, "Yes, it is present". Both of these factors are valuable indicators of performance of a trace analytical method, and must be seen as pertaining to complete procedures, not just to individual steps.

2.2.4   Calibration graphs and regression analysis
In all instrumental methods of analysis based on comparison of some physical quantity which is known to depend on a concentration or amount of substance sought, the results are most easily handled graphically as indicated in Fig. 2.3.

The choice of scale for the two axes is important: for optimum readability the line with slope close to 45° would be chosen, but it is also advisable to equate a sensible length of axis to the unit of concentration, preferably on a 1:1 or a 5:1 ratio, but certainly avoiding 3:1 or even fractional ratios. The size of the graph should be just big enough for adequate readability, which for many purposes means a 10-cm or a 20-cm length of axis. Using a whole large sheet of graph paper is wasteful; small ones can be inserted between paragraphs of text in the final report.

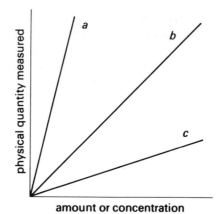

Figure 2.3   Choice of scale for a calibration graph; line *b* is to be preferred.

Regression analysis is a statistical tool useful for handling the raw data used to construct a calibration curve. Figure 2.4 shows a typical calibration for a spectrophotometric method, with a significant signal being recorded for the blank due to the colour of the reagent itself. Figure 2.4 also shows the magnitude of the standard deviation for each data point.

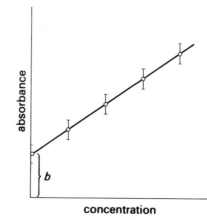
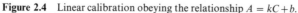

Figure 2.4   Linear calibration obeying the relationship $A = kC + b$.

The line can be described by the simple equation

$$A = kC + b \tag{2.8}$$

which is of the form

$$y = mx + c. \tag{2.9}$$

It would be quite feasible to make the five measurements shown and calculate the constants k and b for the line, and then for each sample to calculate the concentration C from the measured absorbance A. Indeed, for a straight line, theory tells us we only need two points, so it seems we could save ourselves a lot of work by following this approach. But when we remember that any single measurement is subject to experimental error, we shall not be surprised to find that each pair of points taken will give a slightly different pair of values for k and b. If we can adopt some form of averaging procedure to find the best straight line to fit all the points we shall minimize the error in the two constants, and therefore also minimize the error in any subsequent deter- mination made using the calibration. Statisticians have given us the tool of regression analysis—the so-called least-squares method of calculating the best straight line for such sets of data. However the results are handled, it is important to realize that the more calibration points one has (up to say five or six) the greater will be the confidence in the individual results obtained by using the calibration.

When is a straight line a curve? When sodium is determined by flame emission photometry the calibration is likely to appear as sketched in Fig. 2.5. Of course we can pretend that this is a straight line (especially if the

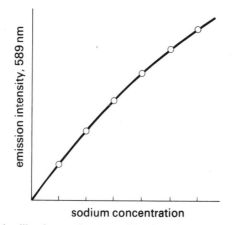

Figure 2.5 A curved calibration needs more points than a straight one—flame photometric determination of sodium.

bottom two points are omitted) and calculate the parameters accordingly, but the performance of the method will be most unsatisfactory. So we admit that the points do lie on a curve, and remember that several points will be needed to define a curve, not two, and a few more to allow for errors. If a computer is available for handling the data, regression analysis can also be applied to calibration curves as well as to straight lines and a number of manufacturers of more expensive analytical equipment with built-in mini-computers offer this method of processing as a standard feature. Some manufacturers claim that only four points are needed to establish curved calibrations in atomic absorption spectrophotometry, but the authors feel that this is being rather idealistic and that more calibration points really are necessary. If the calibration graph is a curve, make enough measurements to be sure of it!

2.2.5   Comparison of results

A question frequently asked about analytical results for different (but similar) samples is "Are the results significantly different?" The answer may be perfectly obvious in some cases, but at other times it may not, and it will be necessary to consider the difference between the means of two sets of results in terms of the standard deviations of the sets. This can be done by using Student's t-test. For the very simple case where n determinations have been carried out on each of two sets of samples, A and B, and where the standard deviations are the same for the two sets, the value of t is calculated from

$$t = \frac{\bar{x}_A - \bar{x}_B}{s} \cdot \sqrt{\frac{n}{2}} \tag{2.10}$$

and compared with the values in Table 2.3 according to the number of samples and the degree of confidence desired. If the experimental value of t

Table 2.3   Values of t for testing the significance of a difference between the means of two sets of n values. From Fisher and Yates (1974) with permission.

| n | Degree of confidence | | |
	90%	95%	99%
3	2.92	4.30	9.92
4	2.35	3.18	5.84
5	2.13	2.78	4.60
6	2.01	2.57	4.03
8	1.86	2.31	3.35
10	1.65	2.23	3.17

exceeds the tabulated value, the two means are significantly different. As a very approximate guide, the means for two sets each of 5 results may be considered significantly different if the difference exceeds twice the standard deviation. For a further discussion on statistical testing applied to chemical analysis, see Laitinen and Harris.[6]

2.3   Criteria for selecting a method

Having seen how we can compare the performance of analytical methods quite objectively, we can go on to add some rather more subjective criteria, some of which will be dependent on local circumstances.

2.3.1   *Accuracy and precision*

These have been defined in Section 2.2.2. We must now ask what degree of accuracy and precision we need to meet the requirements of the job in hand, and we should be aware that for a ten-fold increase in performance we must probably invest ten times as much time and effort and therefore also cost. We should compare the errors inherent in the proposed method with the expected variation in the results from "normal" samples. We should also remember that good precision, which is easier to attain than good accuracy, may be what is most important when we are interested in variations in the level of some component rather than in the absolute values themselves.

The distinction is sometimes made between *repeatability*, the agreement between replicate determinations in one laboratory, and *reproducibility*, the agreement between results obtained for the same material analysed in different laboratories. Clearly, reproducibility is a more severe test than repeatability, but it is also a more realistic one.

2.3.2   *Sensitivity*

This will give us some idea of how little material must be present before we are able to put a figure to the amount. It is properly considered as a proportionality constant relating the measured parameter (depth of colour, meter reading, volume of reagent etc.) to the amount of analyte present in the sample. While it may help to compare, say two different chromogenic reagents for one particular metal at trace levels, this concept of sensitivity can be very misleading, as the real indicator of performance, the limit of detection, is affected by several other factors as well, notably contamination and variation in the blank values. However, a good starting point is to ask what the usual working range is, for example in $\mu g\,g^{-1}$ or $mg\,l^{-1}$ of the sample material.

2.3.3   *Selectivity*

Separation is an essential step in all methods of analysis. It may be real, in which case two components of a sample are presented for determination in two different phases (as in a solvent extraction procedure) or at two different times (as in gas chromatographic analysis), or it may be apparent, as when one selected spectral line or band is monitored in the hope that any change in signal is caused only by the species being determined and by no other. Very often a procedure may be reasonably selective, such as one using an electrode which gives a predictable change in potential when the concentration of one particular ion changes, but may also give a small change in potential when other ions are added to the system. It is then necessary to know at what levels the other species present cause a sufficient change in potential for the error to be significant, i.e. at what levels they begin to interfere.

2.3.4 *Interferences*

Different substances may cause interferences in a proposed method at widely differing levels, but generally for one of two reasons:

   (i) the interfering species also gives rise to a response from the measuring system, e.g. also gives a colour with the reagent, a potential change at the electrode, or emission in the same part of the spectrum, or
   (ii) the interfering species removes the analyte from effective participation in the measuring process, a phenomenon called masking, e.g. calcium atoms bound as phosphate compounds in a flame, or fluoride bound as the FeF_6^{3-} complex which is not detected by the fluoride electrode.

The first class of interference may be observed for widely differing concentrations of interfering species, being serious sometimes at very low levels, and sometimes only at high levels. The second class, however, will need at least comparable amounts of both species before any significant effect will be seen.

The likelihood of interferences arising in any procedure adopted makes it all the more important that as much information as possible about the sample be collected before the analysis is planned in detail.

2.3.5 *Speed*

The legendary cartoon depicting an excited young man rushing into the laboratory with a bottle in his hand, asking for the results "by yesterday afternoon, please!" is regrettably not far from reality. However, let us accept that the analysis must be completed as quickly as possible: this is particularly critical in the case of biological samples where microbial degradation will certainly alter the composition in a matter of a few hours, but it is also surprisingly important in inorganic systems such as formation water (concentrated brines from oil wells) where barium sulphate, previously kept in solution by the high pressure at great depth, will slowly crystallize out of solution at normal atmospheric pressure. It may be desirable to "freeze" the sample, either literally, in refrigerant, or metaphorically, by adding some chemical inhibitor, if there is to be an unavoidable delay in processing the sample.

Another aspect of analysis which is often overlooked is the distinction between the time required for a determination as compared to the time for a complete analysis. Thus, in the determination of protein-nitrogen, the colorimetric estimation may be carried out on a Technicon "Autoanalyser" at a rate of 120 samples per hour, but the rate-determining step is the Kjeldahl decomposition which may typically take $2\frac{1}{2}$ hours per sample. Similar comparisons could be made of the times for determination of a trace metal by atomic absorption spectroscopy, and the time taken to ash some plant material and dissolve the residue so as to provide a solution for the final determination.

A third aspect of the speed of an analysis is that of the setting-up time for a one-off analysis. Preparation of standards, together with checking the procedures for performance and possible interferences, takes hours if not days: considerably longer than the seconds or minutes needed for an individual determination. Straightforward chemical methods are often to be preferred over instrumental procedures for such non-routine one-off samples.

2.3.6 Cost and facilities

It is convenient to consider these two very much interdependent factors together. Equipment for mechanized laboratories is expensive, but if a sufficient number of samples can be run, the unit cost becomes quite low. At the same time, a technician must be paid his normal salary irrespective of the cost of the equipment, and also of the work load. We have attempted, with the help of some colleagues, to cost some typical analyses and to make comparisons for manual operation with fairly basic equipment, against automated procedures for handling large numbers of samples. The figures shown in Table 2.4 (1981 prices) also give some idea of how a method can be costed: salaries, chemicals and gases, depreciation of equipment, (10% per year usually, but 30% per year if it is mainly glass!), services (electricity, gas, heating, workshops, maintenance) and overheads (secretaries, library, computer, transport etc.). While the final unit prices look impressively low for the automated rock analysis, one should perhaps stop to consider how many geologists would be needed in the field to keep up such a supply of samples! In the end it is still more meaningful to cost the provision of a service rather than the individual analysis. This is particularly so in environmental analysis where large numbers of samples will have to be analysed in order to build up the detailed picture and to help establish trends, causes and effects.

2.3.7 Operator skills

An interesting report[7] of an interlaboratory comparison on the determination of ethanol in medicinal products (using distillation followed by measurement of specific gravity, or using gas chromatography as an alternative technique, see Section 8.9) revealed that each laboratory obtained better results when using the method to which its staff were accustomed. It was therefore rather difficult to say which technique was actually better, but it seems fair to conclude that when a method has to be chosen from the literature, it is

Table 2.4 Costing analysis of some analytical services. (Thanks are due to Prof. P. Brown, Dr. R. A. Chalmers, Dr. J. Davidson and Prof. S. Frazer for assistance in compiling this table: figures in £ at 1981 prices.)

Type of analysis	Depreciation (10% of capital)	Chemicals	Salaries (staff)	Overheads + services	Total cost	Sample throughput per day	per year	Cost per analysis	per determination
Classical C/H (organic)									
manual	200	200	4400	2000	6800	12	2880	2.36	1.18
automated combustion	1500	500	4400	2000	8400	30	7200	1.16	58p
Nitrogen in biological samples:									
manual NH$_3$ determination	(30%) 360	1500	4400	2000	8260	40	9600	1.90	⎰0.86
Kjeldahl decomposition	500	600	4400	2000	7500	30	7200	—	⎱1.04
Autoanalyser NH$_3$ determination	(10%) 360	1240	4400	2000	8000	160	38 600	1.25	0.21
Ten-element rock analysis micro, rapid manual methods	1000	1000	4400	2000	8400	12/week	576	14.60	1.46
automated X-ray fluorescence	10 000	1800	13 200 (3)	5000	30 000	40	9600	3.12	31p
Large hospital laboratory analysis of blood and urine etc.	(14%) 60 000	16 000	275 000 (33)	60 000	411 000	500	150 000	2.74	(av.) 27p

preferable to select one using a technique with which one is familiar. Research students are often dismayed to discover how hard it is to get some published methods to work in their own laboratories. This may be due to lack of experience and attention to detail on their part, but it is often because the author has not given adequately detailed instructions, or has simply not tested the method on a range of "real" samples, but has only analysed synthetic mixtures instead.

2.3.8 Scale of working

Two factors are of prime importance here: the sensitivity of the determination step, and the amount of material available for what will usually be a destructive analysis.

An example of the former is the determination of tin in foodstuffs. A paper published in 1917 described the wet-acid decomposition of 75 g of tinned rhubarb in 150 ml of concentrated acids, followed by a gravimetric determination of the tin as the oxide. The procedure consumes large quantities of reagents, produces huge volumes of waste gases and acid fumes and takes several hours to complete.[8] In contrast, a report published in 1973 described two modern methods for this analysis, starting with 10 g of food, dissolving it in 10 ml of acid and determining the tin in the 10–100 μg range photometrically:[9] very much faster and cheaper than the older method.

An extreme example of the second limitation is the analysis of coins in a museum collection. It has been found possible to rub off a minute amount of the metal on to a piece of roughened fused silica (of high purity) and to determine the copper, silver and gold on the silica by neutron activation analysis. The amount of metal rubbed off amounts typically to a few micrograms:[10] it is not weighed as such, but the analysis gives the proportions of the elements present.

A fascinating example of very small-scale destructive analysis is the determination of heavy metals in human hair by carbon-rod atomic absorption spectroscopy: a piece of hair 1 cm long (weighing about 50 μg) is adequate for a single determination of say cadmium, or lead or arsenic. The variation along the hair can be reconstructed as a diary of exposure to the toxic element over a period of some weeks.[11]

Sometimes the size of the sample is dictated by neither of these factors, but by the problem of homogeneity. Thus, it has been shown[12] that high failure rates in tungsten lamp filaments can sometimes be attributed to minute particles of iron oxide in the tungstic oxide taken as the starting product for the powder metallurgical processing. Such a particle of rust results in a high local concentration of iron at one point in the tungsten wire, and at this point the wire will break when heated to normal working temperature. The chances of such a rust particle getting in are very small, so that for control purposes a large sample—preferably of 50 g—should be taken for analysis. The problems of lack of homogeneity are discussed again later under Sampling (Section 2.5).

2.4   Sources of error in trace analysis

Most analytical methods can be broken down into a number of recognizable steps, and these few steps can be seen, perhaps modified, perhaps repeated or extended, in the majority of methods. Sometimes it is possible to "lose" one of the steps by effectively combining two in one, but the processes are usually still there. The four recognizable steps are sampling, dissolution, separation and determination. We shall examine some of the general problems found in each of these stages, paying particular attention to the errors which can creep in at each stage, but further details relevant to specific materials, such as gases, waters, soils and so on will be dealt with in the appropriate chapters later on. However, some very important sources of error involving contamination or loss are common to all stages of a method, and these will be discussed first.

2.4.1   *The laboratory environment*

It has been said that a chemical laboratory is the worst possible place in which to do trace analysis, since so many elements and compounds are to be found in the laboratory air at concentrations greatly exceeding those found elsewhere. All too frequently we make matters worse by working in a fume cupboard: it does improve the comfort of the analyst, and may even prolong his useful working life, but the substantial flow of laboratory air into the working space and over the samples brings with it a considerable load of dust and volatile materials which may constitute a serious problem of contamination. The list of elements likely to be encountered at troublesome levels in a laboratory includes Si, Al, Fe, Ca, Na, K, Mg, C, Ti, P, S and Hg, along with Pb, V, Br, Zn, Ni, Cu and Cl in urban areas.

Handling samples and reagents in a simple glove-box filled with carefully filtered air is a step in the right direction, but working at a "clean bench" with a vertical laminar flow of air which has been passed through a high-efficiency particulate air filter (Fig. 2.6) is a much better solution. Boutron[13] has quoted results for the determination of some common elements at the $10 \mu g \, l^{-1}$ level in water following evaporation to low bulk in the open laboratory and in a "clean work station" which clearly illustrate the magnitude of the problem (Table 2.5). The ultimate in this direction is the use of a suite of "clean rooms" in which particulate contamination can be kept to very low levels indeed. Tölg[3] has shown that the common elements can be successfully determined in very high-purity metals only by working in such rooms with highly purified reagents and specially cleaned fused-silica glassware.

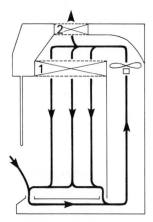

Figure 2.6 Clean work station with high-efficiency particulate air filters (1 and 2). 90% of extracted air is recycled, 10% goes through filter 2 to waste. (By courtesy of Microflow Pathfinder Ltd, Fleet, Hampshire—model 11120).

Table 2.5 Contamination of very dilute solutions by laboratory air

Element determined	Na	Mg	K	Ca	Fe
Found, open bench	13.2	12.4	13.7	9.1	20.6
Found, "clean bench"	10.2	10.0	10.5	9.1	9.3

Concentrations in $\mu g\,l^{-1}$. Each element added at $10\,\mu g\,l^{-1}$. Data taken from Boutron (1972) *Anal. Chim. Acta* **61**, 140, by permission.

2.4.2   *Containers*

As few materials used in the manufacture of containers are even tolerably inert towards a wide range of liquids and chemicals in solution, we must give consideration to the choice of container material for any particular type of sample or reagent which we wish to handle. Even weak attractive forces between surfaces and solute species give rise to losses from solution by *adsorption*, and for ionic species and inorganic surfaces we may have *ion-exchange* phenomena as well. The effects become serious when the concentrations of solutes go below 10^{-3} M (say at the $\mu g\ ml^{-1}$ level), but vary widely from one material to the next and also between solutes. It is safe to say that one cannot reliably predict the behaviour of one system from a knowledge of another: the possibility must be tested for experimentally in each case.

Evidence for adsorption of ions on to surfaces has been collected by Tölg and co-workers[14] amongst others, using radioisotopes of different elements and measuring the activity picked up by discs of the different materials suspended in test solutions. Adsorption is frequently rapid over the first hour or so, but continues to increase slowly thereafter.

Losses may be seen when a series of solutions of widely varying concentrations are analysed with a view to preparing a calibration curve. Figure 2.7 shows results for the gas chromatographic determination (see Section 3.10) of acrylic acid, $CH_2{=}CH{\cdot}COOH$, and butyric acid, $C_3H_7{\cdot}COOH$, in

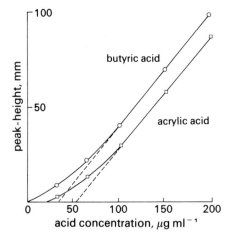

Figure 2.7   Calibrations for gas-chromatographic determination of two acids showing losses by adsorption from acetone/water. Author's results.

aqueous acetone solutions in soda-glass standard flasks. The similarity of the slopes of the linear parts of the calibrations suggests that the sensitivity of the chromatograph detector is the same for the two compounds, but the displacement of the two lines suggests that quite a lot of acrylic acid is being lost from the solutions (in fact equivalent here to $25\,\mu g\,ml^{-1}$).

The curvature at low levels is typical of many such calibrations, even for what should be a more favourable solvent, such as diethyl ether. Figure 2.8 shows calibrations for acrylic acid in several containers. We should note

  (i) the very substantial loss on to polypropylene
 (ii) the significant loss on to soda-glass
(iii) the better performance with Teflon (polytetrafluoroethylene), although we are dealing with an organic solute, and
 (iv) the almost ideal performance with fused silica if the solution is acidified.

We should remember that acrylic acid is a weak acid ($pK = 4.2$) but will nevertheless dissociate to a reasonable extent in very dilute aqueous solution (i.e. about 18% at the $10^{-3}\,M$ level $= 48\,\mu g\,ml^{-1}$) and also to some lesser extent in ether. As the acidity is increased by addition of hydrochloric acid, the dissociation is suppressed: it would seem that the undissociated acid is not adsorbed on to silica surfaces, whereas the anion of the dissociated acid is. This problem has been discussed in detail so as to emphasize a number of points connected with the loss of solutes by adsorption on to container surfaces. To sum up:

(i) the losses are more serious at lower concentrations
(ii) the magnitude of the loss depends on the container and the solvent, and
(iii) other properties of the solvent, e.g. pH also matter.

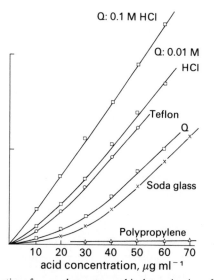

Figure 2.8   Calibrations for gas-chromatographic determination of acrylic acid kept in different vessels and at different acidities, in ether. Q = fused silica (quartz).

Inorganic materials used for the fabrication of containers include a variety of glasses of varying composition, all with more or less silica. Table 2.6 gives the compositions and some physical properties of some commonly-used glasses. Those with lower thermal coefficients of expansion have better resistance to sudden changes in temperature. These glasses consist of a three-dimensional silicate network with other ions bound less strongly, and therefore susceptible to leaching. This has important consequences in trace analysis, since it results in contamination of solutions (particularly by sodium and calcium but also by potassium, magnesium, iron, aluminium and silicon) and since leaching produces a much enlarged surface area it also increases the probability of loss from solution by adsorption or by ion-exchange. While serious attack sufficient to cause a visible change in the surface is only likely to be caused by contact with hydrofluoric or phosphoric acid, or with concentrated alkaline solutions, simply boiling water in a glass vessel will leach small amounts of sodium and silicon from the surface.

Table 2.6 Composition of glasses for laboratory ware

Type	Softening pt.	Coeff. of expansion	SiO_2	Na_2O	CaO	Al_2O_3	B_2O_3	Li_2O
Soda-lime	710°	92×10^{-7}	72	15	11	2	—	—
Borosilicate "Pyrex"*	820°	33×10^{-7}	80	4	—	2	13	—
"Jena G20"	—	—	76	6.5	0.4	4.5	8	—
High silica "Vycor"*	1530°	8×10^{-7}	96	—	—	—	3	—
Fused silica	1590°	5.5×10^{-7}	100	—	—	—	—	—
Chemically strengthened "Corex"*	910°	44×10^{-7}	66	9	—	20	—	5

* Trade names of Corning Ltd.

Fused silica is now quite widely employed for laboratory glassware for trace analysis as it suffers much less from problems of adsorption, leaching and chemical attack, and is not so much more expensive than borosilicate glass.

Cleaning of glassware poses some problems: there is no single recommended procedure since the reagents used will depend on what "dirt" has to be removed, and on what species in particular should not be present on the "clean" surface. However, the traditional sulphuric acid–potassium dichromate mixture at room temperature is still to be recommended for general use on glass and silica, provided that the articles are then washed many times with distilled water to remove adsorbed chromium species. As chromium compounds are considered to present a health hazard, and as the mixture is in any case extremely corrosive, special care should be exercised when it is being handled, particularly when water is first run into the vessels to rinse them. As an alternative, mixed nitric and sulphuric acids are also quite effective, and for fused silica just hot concentrated hydrochloric acid will often prove satisfactory. Most organic detergents scarcely attack glass, but they may be difficult to remove, even with copious washing. Steaming out is helpful for removing both ions and molecules adsorbed on surfaces. Adams, and Hetherington and Bell[15] have written good accounts of glass and silica containers and their care.

Organic materials used for laboratory containers come from a wide range of synthetic polymers. Bottles, standard flasks, measuring cylinders and many other items are now available in one or more different plastics. The properties differ not only from one type of polymer to the next, but even between chemically similar polymers made by different processes. The attractive features are cheapness, toughness (they bounce!) and inertness towards many inorganic chemicals. The disadvantages are the low softening points and the low resistance to attack by organic solvents. Table 2.7 lists some of the commonly used plastics encountered in the laboratory.

Table 2.7 Characteristics of some common plastics for laboratory ware

| | | | Chemical resistance | |
| | *Max. temperature* | | | |
Polymer	*continuous use*	*Transparency*	*acids and alkalis*	*organic solvents*
Polyethylene (low density)	80°	poor	good	—
Polyethylene (high density)	100°	opaque	good	—
Polypropylene	120°	fair	good	—
Poly(vinyl chloride)	65°	good	good	poor
Polyacrylate	80°	v. good	good	poor
Polycarbonate	125°	good	attacked by alkali	poor
Poly(methylpentene)	180°	good	good	—
Poly(tetrafluoroethylene)	260°	opaque	excellent	excellent

Relative performance of container materials is not always easy to assess since it depends so much on what is being put in them, but attempts have been made to indicate which materials should be avoided for certain purposes. Thus, for inorganic cations in acidic solution, Tölg[14] rates the following materials in increasing order of performance: borosilicate glass, soda glass, platinum, fused silica, polyethylene, polypropylene, and best, polytetrafluoroethylene (Teflon). He does stress, however, that simply changing the pH of the solution may reverse the order of some of the materials. Experience has shown that lead at low levels in drinking water is slowly picked up by polyethylene surfaces, but not by Teflon.

General precautions can be recommended for handling samples for trace analysis: samples of water to be analysed for trace metals should be acidified to prevent both ion-exchange and precipitation of hydroxides, and should be stored in plastic (polyethylene, or Teflon). Samples to be analysed for trace organics should be collected in fused silica bottles. Bock[16] has given a lengthy survey of the literature on the adsorption of inorganic species, and Robertson[17] has summarized the problems in collecting samples of sea water for analysis.

2.4.3 *Volatilization*

It is perhaps stating the obvious to say that volatile constituents of a sample will tend to be lost to the atmosphere unless precautions are taken to prevent this happening. Thus, it can be difficult to distinguish between diesel oil, paraffin or petrol as contaminants in surface waters after they have been exposed to the weather for some time. But there are also many cases in inorganic analysis where losses through volatilization may occur at some stage in a procedure. Mercury in the presence of reducing agents presents a special problem even at room temperature, but at elevated temperatures (in boiling acid, for example) Hg^{2+}, Sb^{3+}, Sn^{4+}, As^{3+}, Se(IV), Ru, Os, and B can all be lost through volatilization of molecular halides or oxides. A further instance of this problem is the loss of volatile organometallic compounds under conditions where inorganic species would present no problem. From the point of view of environmental studies, the organometallic compounds are often much more hazardous than the inorganic ones, and such losses therefore become even more serious.

2.4.4   *Reagents*

Any chemical processing of samples inevitably makes use of greater quantities of reagents than of sample: solvents, acids, fused salts, pH buffers and so on may be required in amounts ten to one hundred times that of the sample, as a result of which even very low levels of contamination can lead to serious errors in trace analysis. Consider a sample with a given element present at $1 \mu g\,g^{-1}$ (1 ppm w/w): if a ten-fold amount of reagent is taken and the blank value should not exceed 10% of what is being determined, then the reagent must not contain more than $0.01 \mu g\,g^{-1}$ of that trace element. The obvious question then arises as to which reagents can be easily purified, and while many salts may be recrystallized (with some degree of loss), it is distillation which is likely to prove most effective. The volatile acids (hydrochloric, nitric, hydrofluoric, and acetic) along with ammonia and hydrogen peroxide, can be purified in this manner and are available commercially in a very high state of purity, as are some organic solvents. Sub-boiling distillation has been shown to be a particularly effective method for purifying volatile aqueous acids as it avoids carry-over of spray, but even simpler for the very volatile reagents (in particular for hydrochloric acid and ammonia) is isothermal distillation at room temperature, in which an open dish of concentrated reagent and another of very pure water are positioned close to each other in a closed atmosphere (Fig. 2.9). After a few hours or so the water will have become a very pure solution of the reagent, at half the original concentration.

Grades of reagents with varying degrees of purity are available from manufacturers to suit different purposes. The labelling on the bottles is often quite detailed, but is also often misinterpreted by users. Figure 2.10 shows the label for a high grade reagent chemical: "AnalaR" is a trade name, but indicates that the chemical meets the specification laid down in a published compilation, and that specification is reproduced on the label, representing maximum levels of certain impurities which are tested for before the batch of chemical is packaged. The actual levels present may well be lower than the limits stated (if higher, the batch will be further purified or sold as a lower grade reagent).

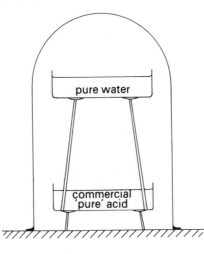

Figure 2.9 Apparatus for isothermal distillation to purify volatile reagents such as ammonia and hydrochloric acid.

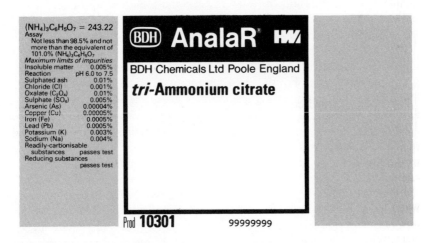

Figure 2.10 Label of an AnalaR grade chemical (reproduced by courtesy of BDH Ltd).

While one or more of the main constituents may be determined prior to packaging, there is no guarantee that the figure quoted will still hold for a sample which has been on the laboratory shelf for some months or years after being opened. Thus, hydrated salts such as $MgSO_4 \cdot 7H_2O$ may have the expected composition when prepared, but may either lose or gain water on exposure to the atmosphere, depending on the relative humidity. An old sample may still have a satisfactorily low calcium value, for example, but yet be quite unsuitable for the preparation of standard magnesium solutions for atomic absorption determinations by simply weighing out and making up to known volume. Water is by far the most common "contaminant" in laboratory chemicals, followed by carbon dioxide for any alkaline materials.

It is apparent that "purity" is a concept of somewhat complex significance. A "pure" chemical may be one with exactly the theoretical composition—ideal for preparation of standards for instrumental methods of analysis—or it may be one which is understood to be free from contamination to any measurable extent by one or more specific impurities. Indeed, whether a reagent is considered to be "pure" or not will depend on the use to which it is put and on the methods used to test it. Some of the reagents now available (e.g. Merck Suprapur, BDH Aristar, J. T. Baker Ultrex) are of a very high quality, but the practising analyst should always be aware of the possibility of contamination from his reagents. Perrin et al. have written a monograph[18] on methods for the purification of reagents.

Water is by far the most important solvent in the laboratory and deserves to have a little more said about it and the methods for purifying it. Traditionally distillation has always been the preferred approach, and we tend to take it for granted that distilled water is available in all analytical laboratories. Tinned copper pipes were formerly used to distribute distilled water, but plastic pipes are now the norm. Double distillation in quartz apparatus is an attractive route for producing high-quality water at a rate of a litre or so per hour, but this does not remove volatile organic compounds. To achieve this a multi-stage clean-up is necessary. The water should be acidified with phosphoric acid, boiled and purged with a stream of nitrogen, then distilled. Potassium hydroxide and potassium permanganate are added to the distillate which is again boiled and purged and finally distilled once again. Full details of this and similar procedures are given by Smith.[19]

Filter methods are becoming increasingly widely used for purification of water in the laboratory: they are simple and avoid the use of heating, though one has to reckon with the cost of occasional replacement of the filter elements. As an example, the Millipore Reagent Grade Water system makes use of a series of filters to purify water taken straight from the tap, removing both inorganic and organic impurities.

Gases should not be forgotten as possible useful reagents in the laboratory. A wide range of gases is available in cylinders of varying size and at different grades of purity, and of these, oxygen, nitrogen, air, hydrogen, argon and helium are probably the most important for the analytical chemist. Gases are relatively easy to purify further if need be, and are used in many procedures for opening out (breaking down) insoluble materials, especially because the degree of contamination is so very low (see Section 2.6.3).

2.5 Sampling

So many of the problems of sampling are peculiar to the particular aspect of the environment being studied that only a few general points can be made at this stage.

2.5.1 *Heterogeneity*

Many, if not most, "real" samples for analysis are likely to be heterogeneous, i.e. the composition of any one small portion will not correspond to the average composition of the whole sample or the whole bulk of material under investigation. The entomologist attempting to make a count of an insect population in a cultivated field, and the botanist surveying the frequency of occurrence of a plant on a hillside, for example, are well aware of the difficulties of dealing with large objects or areas and will be familiar with the use of grids and systematic sampling procedures whereby observations are made at regular distances across a large area. If the soil is to be analysed, samples would also be taken at many points on a grid, and probably at different depths as well. Rivers and lakes should be sampled at different depths, particularly if the dissolved oxygen levels are of interest. Air samples required for a study of the dispersion of some pollutant from a factory stack will also be taken over a large area and different distances and directions from the stack. The locations of the sampling points will become significant when the strength and direction of the prevailing winds are taken into account: this will serve as a reminder that establishing correlations between different sets of observations is often very important in environmental studies.

2.5.2 *The time factor*

The importance of this factor in sampling programmes is demonstrated by the data depicted in Fig. 2.11 showing variations in the level of carbon dioxide in the atmosphere over a period of several years. When the measurements are made with good precision, small variations become evident: monthly means are plotted here and show a clear cyclic variation throughout the year with a maximum in spring due to combustion of fossil fuels in winter, and a minimum in autumn, due to increased photosynthesis by plants during the summer. One can also see a clear trend over the years which many workers would like to be able to extrapolate into the future. That is not so easy, as the rate of increase is not constant. We can learn a great deal from a consideration of this figure.

(i) One-off measurements of the carbon dioxide level will tell us very little, except that the value is "about normal".

(ii) Samples taken at different months in succeeding years (e.g. as part of different student practical classes) could even indicate a downward trend, though it is more likely that the scatter on students results would mask any trend, whatever the direction.

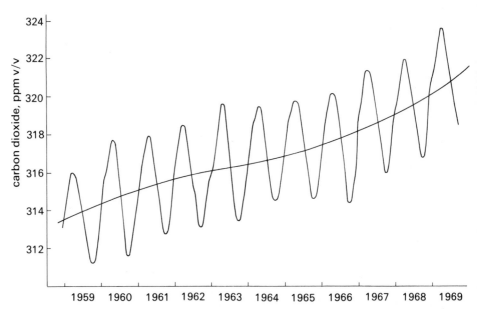

Figure 2.11   Variation in level of atmospheric carbon dioxide over several years (values are monthly means). Reproduced by courtesy of *Scientific American* from Bolin, 1970[20].

(iii) A small change in procedure could introduce a correspondingly small change in a systematic error sufficient to obscure the natural variations.

(iv) If samples are collected in a forest, there will even be hour-by-hour variations which may make comparison of results difficult.

(v) The value of a large number of results collected over a period of years is particularly high when it enables us to establish baseline trends (say before a factory or town is built) or to predict likely values in the future. This is of great concern to workers in the field of environmental health and medicine.

(vi) Any sampling programme for environmental studies must take into account cycles of activity (natural or man-made) in order to identify periodic variations and to establish differences between maximum values and mean values.

2.5.3   *Errors arising during sampling*

There are many possible sources of error connected with sampling in addition to the problems of time and place just discussed. Some, such as contamination or loss on to containers, are fairly obvious, but nevertheless common. Mitchell[21] has described the incidence of high boron contamination in soil samples in paper bags brought in for analysis by farmers: boron continued to transfer from the paper to the soil over a period of days giving values several times what they should have been. Glass or plastic bottles intended for foodstuffs are often used for liquid samples, sometimes without any cleaning, and are often inappropriately chosen. The danger of incurring serious errors by wrong sampling can always be used as an excuse for visiting the site, when the customer does not wish to have intruders on the premises: if the customer is uncooperative it is more than likely that some important information is being withheld, and under these circumstances it is better not to analyse any samples at all. One of the worst examples of this kind in the authors' experience was a bottle of black estuary sediment and some water, stinking of hydrogen sulphide, with the request to "prove that this river is toxic to fish". The reader may care to draft an appropriate reply to this customer!

2.5.4 Storage and preparation of samples

The interaction between sample and container has already been dealt with (Section 2.4.2). A rather more subtle problem which is not always so obvious is the variation in the composition of the sample over the period of storage and preparation. Sometimes one only discovers this accidentally. Some cases which illustrate this are worth quoting.

(i) A tap-water sample to be analysed for lead was submitted in a polyethylene bottle. Because it was felt desirable to repeat the determination three days later after an aspect of technique had been improved (a new electrode had been made for the anodic stripping voltammetric determination, (Section 4.22.3) a significant drop in the lead level was discovered, due to slow adsorption on to the bottle.

(ii) A steel gas cylinder containing a mixture of helium and oxygen was reported to have a smell rather like that of bleach. Due to pressure of other work, this sample was not examined till three days later, by when the smell had disappeared completely.

(iii) A sample of oil-well formation water was brought in for a fairly complete analysis. particularly of alkaline earth metals and of sulphate. As each of the mutual interferences was investigated the sample was re-analysed, and it became clear that the barium level was decreasing day by day as barium sulphate crystallized out of solution.

It is, of course, not surprising that samples of food, animal tissue, plants, blood etc. will change quite quickly. The best way to keep such samples is frozen in liquid nitrogen, in which state they can also be ground up in a silica mortar.

2.6 Dissolution and decomposition of samples

These procedures—often referred to as "opening-out"—are an important preliminary step to any subsequent analysis of solid materials. Although a small number of principles is involved, a wealth of accumulated detailed knowledge and practical tricks may make the difference between success and failure of a projected analysis. Bock[16] has given an excellent and comprehensive account of the current state of the art, while the earlier monographs by Gorsuch[22] and by Doležal et al.[23] are restricted to organic and inorganic substances respectively. We may summarize the approaches briefly under three headings: those involving oxidation, those involving reduction, and those involving neither of these processes.

2.6.1 *Dissolution*

In the simplest processes the solvation energy exceeds the crystal lattice energy and the solid dissolves, possibly assisted by gentle heating. Water is best for ionic solids; organic solvents including dichloromethane, chloroform, toluene, butanone and hexane may be tried for organic substances.

Acids (and occasionally alkalis) may be added to the water for dissolution of carbonates and oxides (or acids). The anion may be important as a complexing ligand to help keep metal ions in solution (e.g. chloride, fluoride).

Concentrated acids, often used hot, may be effective in dissolving some minerals. Hot concentrated sulphuric acid also dehydrates and chars organic matter, but for such materials it is more helpful to add an oxidizing agent such as nitric or perchloric acid, or hydrogen peroxide. Fairly inert plastics such as poly(vinyl chloride) can be attacked by boiling in concentrated sulphuric acid into which is dropped 50% hydrogen peroxide (care!).

Borosilicate glass or fused silica beakers are suitable for most of these reagents, but platinum or Teflon must be used if hydrofluoric acid is called for. Teflon-lined stainless steel bombs are available which make it possible to carry out decompositions at slightly higher temperatures and under pressure without losing volatile substances such as mercury or organo-metallic compounds.

2.6.2 *Fusion in melts*

Molten salts have very different solvating powers to water, and also allow much higher temperatures to be used to help break down minerals. Some are acidic (potassium bisulphate, $KHSO_4$, m.p. 219°) while others are basic (borax, $Na_2B_4O_7$, m.p. 878°, potassium hydroxide, KOH, m.p. 404°, or sodium carbonate, Na_2CO_3, m.p. 853°). When a strongly oxidizing mixture is required, potassium nitrate (KNO_3, m.p. 339°) may be used, alone, or mixed with potassium hydroxide ($KNO_3 . 2 KOH$ eutectic, m.p. 230°).

Platinum crucibles may be used for all of these melts, though there is some attack when nitrate melts are involved. Silver crucibles are also useful for low-temperature hydroxide melts. The crucibles may be heated directly over a gas burner, or inside an electric muffle furnace, but heating should not be continued for more than 10 minutes or so in most cases since the melts change in composition and need higher temperatures to stay molten (e.g. $KHSO_4 \rightarrow K_2SO_4$, m.p. 1074°; $KOH \rightarrow K_2CO_3$, m.p. 903°). Once the melt has been cooled and has solidified, it is dissolved in dilute acid. The crucible should always be examined for the presence of any remaining undissolved material.

2.6.3 *Heating in a gas stream*

The high purity of some commercially available gases has already been referred to in connection with contamination of samples. The most common choices are the following:

(i) *Helium,* in which organic materials, particularly high polymers, are pyrolysed and the fragments examined by gas chromatography or mass spectrometry.

(ii) *Air* or *oxygen,* in which organic matter is burned off and metals are converted to oxides or carbonates to be subsequently dissolved in acid. Combustion in the oxygen flask (see Section 6.11.1) in an enclosed volume of oxygen with a small volume of suitable absorption solution is a useful opening-out for determination of halogens and sulphur.

(ii) *Hydrogen,* in which organic compounds undergo pyrolytic reduction giving volatile hydrides such as CH_4, NH_3, H_2S etc.

(iv) *Moist oxygen,* in which inorganic materials are heated, usually intimately mixed with an acidic oxide such as V_2O_5, to release fluoride as HF and boron as $B(OH)_3$. This is called pyrohydrolysis, and can break down some very resistant solids.[24]

(v) *Vacuum,* being the absence of a gas, still has to be handled in a system of glass (or fused silica) tubing, and is particularly useful for the determination of dissolved gases in metals, with a finish by gas chromatography.[25]

Of these possibilities, heating in the open air, known as ashing when there is organic matter present, is very widely used. Care should be paid to the choice of crucible and often to lining it with freshly ignited magnesium oxide to prevent the sample ash from coming into contact with the silica or porcelain crucible and fusing to it. Choice of temperature and additional ashing aids can affect the success of the operation. Bock has discussed these problems in detail.[16]

2.7 Separation

The third stage in the typical analytical method involves the separation of the species sought from the bulk of the sample material, often called the *matrix.* The process of separating one specific component (or group of them) from a mixture is referred to as the *clean-up* stage, and is often as important as, if not more so than the subsequent determination step in guaranteeing the success-ful outcome of the complete analysis. Examples will be given as appropriate throughout the text in later chapters, but the general principles will be dealt with here. Dean[26] and Berg[27] have written books on the subject of chemical separation methods.

2.7.1 *Separation by phase-change*

A two-phase system is produced from the original sample material whether it be a crude heterogeneous mixture or a simple solution. The phases are then separated physically and retained separately for further treatment. The simple physical processes are best indicated diagrammatically for the case of a single substance (e.g. ice–water–steam) as in Fig. 2.12.

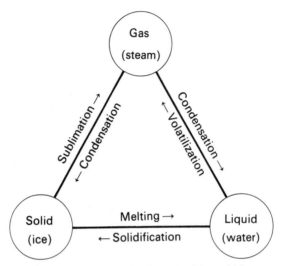

Figure 2.12   The main phases of H_2O and the phase transitions which can occur.

It is often possible to make use of one of these phase changes to separate one component from a mixture: in the example, we can separate water from many solid substances by evaporation (provided they are finely divided). The weight-loss arising is then taken as representing the water content of the sample. However, other components of the mixture might also be volatile and therefore be lost on heating. It would therefore be preferable to condense the water and collect it by adsorption on a selective adsorbent (a drying agent such as magnesium perchlorate) and then determine it by the gain in weight. We are then using a second phase transition involving adsorption from the gas phase on to the solid to achieve an improvement in the selectivity of the process and hopefully also to improve the reliability of the whole procedure. A clean-up procedure may thus incorporate several two-phase separations so as to recover one component in a reasonably high state of purity.

2.7.2   *Partition between two liquid phases*
While it is possible to achieve separation when dealing with a single component on its own (e.g. evaporation of a solvent in a vacuum line with subsequent condensation in a cold trap) it is usually easier to work with two bulk phases in the form of two reagents, solvents, liquids, or gases. The

component of interest is then partitioned between the two phases, each of which is taken by the analyst in amounts which are easy to handle. Achieving the physical separation, e.g. filtering a solid phase from a suspension or drawing off one liquid phase from another in a separating funnel, is then mechanically much simpler than when the amount of one phase is so small that it can hardly be seen.

There is another advantage in using two-phase reagent systems: the degree of separation achieved in one step may not be very high, but if the process is repeated several times, each time with a fresh portion of second phase, then quantitative recovery becomes possible. This is such an important concept that it is worth exploring in a little more detail.

If we have two liquid phases—which we shall assume for convenience are water and an immiscible organic solvent such as benzene which is lighter than water—and a compound which dissolves to some extent in both liquids (see Fig. 2.13) then the Nernst distribution law tells us that

$$\frac{C_o}{C_w} = P = \text{partition (or distribution) coefficient} \qquad (2.11)$$

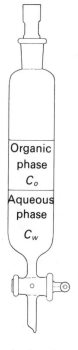

Figure 2.13 Solvent-extraction in a separating funnel.

where C_0 and C_w are the concentrations of the same species of the solute in the organic solvent and the water respectively. This expression is not of much practical help if the volumes of the two phases are different because we are concerned more with total amounts than with concentrations. However, as $C_0 = m_o/V_o$ (the amount of solute divided by the volume of solvent) we can rewrite equation (11) as

$$\frac{m_o}{V_o} \times \frac{V_w}{m_w} = P. \tag{2.12}$$

Finally, we let f be the fraction of the solute extracted into the benzene layer, and deduce that

$$f = \frac{m_o}{m_w + m_o} = \frac{P \cdot V_o}{V_w + P \cdot V_o}. \tag{2.13}$$

Let us now put some numbers into these equations and follow the course of a separation process. We can start with 100 mg of solute A with a partition coefficient of 9 so that with 10 ml of solvent and also of water we shall find 90 mg of solute in the organic phase: $f = 0.9$, or, recovery $= 90\%$. How can we improve the recovery?

The first way is to take more solvent (or less water). If we take 100 ml of solvent and 10 ml of water, then $f = 9 \times 100/910 = 0.99$, or, recovery $= 99\%$. The disadvantage is that the solute is now diluted ten-fold.

The second and more elegant way is to perform two extractions, each with 10 ml of solvent. The first extraction recovers 90% as before and the second recovers 90% of what is left behind, i.e. 9% of the original 100 mg. Combining the two extracts gives us a recovery of 99% and a dilution by a factor of only two. Clearly, a third extraction would give 99.9% recovery with dilution of three times.

It is now instructive to work out what happens to a second solute B which is more soluble in water. Let us assume that the partition coefficient this time is $\frac{1}{9}$. Then one extraction will remove 10% and a second 9% of the original total (each time into 10 ml portions of benzene from the same original aqueous solution). A third extraction will make a total recovery of 27% in the organic phase, which is not a very good separation if we are trying to obtain pure samples of A and of B. But there is another trick, the back-wash. In this procedure the combined organic phase (of 20 or 30 ml) is washed once with 10 ml of water. We apply the same equation to calculate the overall recovery, remembering that the volume of the organic phase is two or three times that of the aqueous phase. The results are summarized in Table 2.8. To sum up: procedure (4) will give the highest recovery of solute A, but procedure (3) will give a reasonable recovery of A with minimum contamination by B, so the clean-up is more efficient. Of course, if the two partition

Table 2.8   Solvent-extraction recoveries with and without back-wash

Steps	% of solutes in water		% of solutes in solvent		Volume of solvent, ml
	A	B	A	B	
1 1 extraction	10	90	90	10	10
2 2 extractions	1	81	99	19	20
3 2 extractions + back-wash	6	96.5	94	3.5	20
4 3 extractions	0.1	73	99.9	27	30
5 3 extractions + back-wash	3.7	93.3	96.3	6.7	30

coefficients are any closer we would be well advised to look for an alternative solvent.

There is yet another approach, which is useful if we can change the nature of the species in the aqueous solution, e.g. by protonation (of an amine), dissociation (of a carboxylic acid) or complexation (of a metal). In such cases pH control is the key to efficient separation. We can illustrate this by considering benzoic acid:

$$(C_6H_5 \cdot COOH)_{org} \overset{P}{\rightleftharpoons} (C_6H_5 \cdot COOH)_{aq} \overset{K_a}{\rightleftharpoons} (C_6H_5 \cdot COO^-)_{aq}.$$

The second component is common to both equilibria, so we can combine the equations to give the relationship between concentrations:

$$\frac{[C_6H_5 \cdot COOH]_{org}}{P} = [C_6H_5 \cdot COOH]_{aq} = \frac{[H^+] \cdot [C_6H_5 \cdot COO^-]_{aq}}{K_a}.$$

At high pH's the anion predominates, so the *Distribution Ratio* is given by

$$D = \frac{[C_6H_5 \cdot COOH]_{org}}{[C_6H_5 \cdot COOH]_{aq} + [C_6H_5 \cdot COO^-]_{aq}}$$

which approximates to

$$D = \frac{[C_6H_5 \cdot COOH]_{org}}{[C_6H_5 \cdot COO^-]_{aq}} = \frac{P \cdot [H^+]}{K_a} \tag{2.14}$$

or

$$\log D = \log P + pK_a - pH. \tag{2.15}$$

Thus, by changing the pH we can control the recovery of any solute showing acid-base properties, and often find conditions for separating pairs of solutes. This is made use of, for example, in the survey methods for the analysis of priority pollutants (see Section 4.28).

This topic has been discussed in detail because liquid–liquid extraction is so important in analytical chemistry, and because the concept of repeated extraction and back-wash helps us to achieve the quantitative separations we need. The principle of repeated extraction with fresh portions of clean solvent is also applicable to other systems, such as volatilization into a moving gas phase, or dissolution of a solid by a moving liquid phase. The reader may care to apply these principles to the culinary problem of how to prepare the best coffee (taking steam-distillation into account as well) and then to read the fascinating paper on the subject written in 1812 by Count Rumford.[28]

2.7.3 *Practical separation techniques*
The most commonly used separation techniques making use of two-phase systems are summarized in Fig. 2.14.

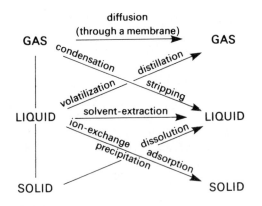

Figure 2.14 Diagrammatic summary of the possible combinations allowing separation by partition between two phases.

Diffusion makes use of three phases: two similar ones isolated by a third quite different one. Gases can diffuse through membranes such as thin polymer films, the rate depending on the size and molecular weight. This makes it possible to transfer a dissolved gas from one solution to another leaving possible interfering substances behind (see, e.g. the oxygen cell, Section 4.13.3) or, by taking advantage of the differences in diffusion rates, to separate isotopes (e.g. uranium isotopes as volatile UF_6). Temperature control is important in these processes.

Condensation can be a means of trapping less volatile impurities in a stream of gas or air as it passes through a vessel held at low temperature. Liquid nitrogen should not be used as coolant, as oxygen will collect (as liquid) when air is passed through the trap and present an explosion hazard when it warms up. Liquid oxygen itself can be used as a coolant ($-183°$); carbon dioxide in propan-2-ol ($-78.5°$) and iced water are two other possibilities.

Stripping of dissolved volatiles from solution (usually aqueous) is achieved by bubbling a stream of nitrogen gas through the solution and then scrubbing the nitrogen to recover the volatiles. Traces of halocarbon solvents in waters are best determined this way, with final analysis by gas chromatography. The scrubbing may be effected by a solid adsorbent, or by a solution of a selective reagent which will trap the species sought, e.g. zinc acetate to trap hydrogen sulphide (see Section 3.11).

Volatilization of gases or vapours in solution may be used to assist their determination in the presence of non-volatile fats and oils in foods for example. A sample of food is equilibrated with the air space over it in a sealed bottle at an elevated temperature. After some time a portion of the air over the sample is analysed by gas chromatography. This is known as head-space analysis (see Section 7.7). Volatilization coupled with determination of weight-loss is useful for the determination of solvents or water.

When solvents driven off by heating are collected by condensation, the process becomes *distillation*. A good example of this technique is the determination of ethanol in alcoholic beverages and pharmaceutical preparations. The ethanol and some of the water is distilled, thus separating it from sugars, fats etc., and diluted to the original volume. The actual determination is by way of specific gravity, and can be done with excellent accuracy if temperature is carefully controlled. The technique can also be used for compounds not normally considered to be very volatile at 100°, provided that they are steam-volatile, such as 2-nitroxylenol in the determination of nitrate (see Section 4.16.3) or some organophosphorus pesticides (see Section 7.8.2). Many essential oils contributing to the flavour of foods are also separable by steam-distillation.

Solvent extraction (liquid–liquid extraction) in which a solute is transferred from one liquid to another by shaking the two together, is very widely used in trace analysis. It is only important that the two phases have rather low mutual solubilities in each other. The technique is an obvious approach for the determination of trace organics (phenols, hydrocarbons etc.) in waters, but is also useful for the determination of metal ions (as organic chelates) or inorganic anions (as ion-pairs with quaternary amines). Choice of solvent and control of pH are important aspects of this technique which allows sequential separation of several components of a mixture. Efficient use of the separating funnel demands a vigorous and fast wrist action, easily acquired with a little practice; the procedure is then fast and simple. Details of many practical applications are described in the literature.[29]

Adsorption and desorption on to solids (usually characterized by their high specific area) are effective for removing traces of sparingly soluble solutes from solution, particularly trace organics from water (e.g. on to porous polymers such as Porapak or Tenax). Adsorption from the gas phase on to charcoal, molecular sieves, silica gel etc., is efficient for many organic vapours. The process is usually reversed at higher temperatures, which allows the vapours to be released for determination. In some cases (e.g. the determination of benzene vapour in air) charcoal can be washed with a solvent such as carbon disulphide and a portion of the extract injected on to the gas chromatograph column (see Section 3.10). Contact time, particle size, packing of the tubes, loading levels of the trace on the solid, and number of washes with solvent, are all important parameters.

Ion-exchange techniques represent one special class of liquid–solid (or liquid–liquid) separation, where the ionic species are held on a substrate which has ionic groups bonded to it (e.g. a sulphonated polystyrene resin). Poly(acrylic acid), for example, can exchange its hydrogen ions for metal ions in solution, and the process can be reversed if the resin beads are then washed with an aqueous acid. Resins having bonded amine groups can be used to retain anions, and are also used for column liquid chromatography for the analysis of mixtures of anions (see Section 4.21). Liquid ion-exchangers, based on long-chain organic amines dissolved as ion-pairs in a suitable solvent, can be used to exchange metals as anionic complexes (e.g. $FeCl_4^-$).

Precipitation of relatively insoluble ionic solids from aqueous solution has long been used as a basis for quantitative separations in gravimetric analysis, for amounts ranging from 1 mg to 1 g, but for smaller amounts it is less useful because

   (i) the solubility of the precipitate becomes significant,
   (ii) a tiny amount of precipitate is difficult to handle, much being lost on the walls of the container, and
   (iii) at low concentrations the precipitates àre slow to form.

However, we can use a precipitate of another compound to collect traces of species in which we are interested, making use of *co-precipitation*: iron(III) hydroxide and silicic acid are good carriers of other ionic solids, and find application in the separation of traces of radioactive isotopes following neutron activation analysis.

Dissolution would be an obvious choice if we had a mixture of salt and sand to analyse: the salt dissolves in water, the sand is filtered off and weighed after drying. However, sometimes we can find a selective reagent which will attack certain minerals in rock samples, leaving others untouched: boiling concentrated phosphoric acid will dissolve many silicate minerals such as feldspars, but will leave crystalline quartz which may then be filtered off and weighed (or, better, determined by weight loss after treatment with sulphuric and hydrofluoric acids). Particulate solids collected on filters through which large volumes of air have been pumped are often examined by selective dissolution with a range of organic solvents.

2.7.4 *General problems associated with separation techniques*

When a new method involving a separation procedure is tried, a number of important experimental variables should be carefully considered, and their effect on the completeness of recovery should also be investigated before the method is adopted. These include time for equilibration to be reached, temperature, upper and lower limits for quantitative separation, reagent concentrations, pH, and compatibility of the separation step with the subsequent determination step.

In some cases separation may accompany opening-out in one step; examples are the phase analysis procedures mentioned above, or heating in a gas stream when a trace element is separated by volatilization. The advantage in such cases is the reduction of handling steps in the procedure, and therefore the decreased possibility of introducing errors. Tölg[3] has described a good example of such a unified procedure for the determination of boron in high-purity metals. The sample is dissolved in hydrofluoric acid in a stream of nitrogen which sweeps out boron as BF_3. This is trapped in a solution of sodium fluoride to form the fluoroborate BF_4^-, and is then determined photometrically as an ion-pair with methylene blue, after extraction into trichloroethane.

2.7.5 *Apparent separations*

It is often possible using instrumental methods—particularly the spectroscopic ones—to make a specific determination of one compound or element in the presence of many others. In atomic spectroscopy (e.g. flame emission or absorption) this is achieved by selecting one particular wavelength with a spectrometer; in molecular spectroscopy (e.g. in the determination of gaseous pollutants in the atmosphere) it is achieved by measuring the absorption of infrared radiation at a narrow band of wavelengths in the spectrum. In both cases interferences are possible, and must be checked for, but in favourable cases such spectroscopic methods can be used on samples after only a simple preliminary treatment, thus saving time and money.

Another branch of spectroscopy offering good resolution for elemental analysis is γ-spectroscopy in combination with neutron activation. In activation methods (where samples are irradiated with neutrons, usually in a nuclear reactor, giving rise to radioactive isotopes of most of the elements present in the sample) separation is the key to successful analysis. The separation may be a specific chemical one (e.g. sequences of solvent-extraction procedures) followed by counting of the radioactivity using very simple apparatus, or it may be apparent: all the γ-emission lines are detected simultaneously by a high-resolution Ge(Li) detector crystal and analysed in a multi-channel γ-spectrometer. This requires a much greater cash investment in equipment, which is justified by the increased speed and numbers of elements which can be determined in a single sample. Given time, however, most of the analyses could be performed on much simpler equipment, though probably at greater cost because of the need for more irradiations in the reactor and for considerably more operator time in processing the sample by chemical treatment.

2.8 Determination

Details of the principles and practice of most of the commonly used analytical techniques will be presented in subsequent chapters, but it may be worthwhile to discuss here a few general points to conclude our survey of the steps in a "typical" analytical method. It is customary to make the distinction between classical and instrumental methods. While the distinction may be valid for the different techniques used for the determination step, it is not at all helpful when complete analytical procedures are being discussed, since in most cases a complete procedure will include both chemical steps (e.g. for separation or dissolution) and physical steps (e.g. for instrumental measurement). Table 2.9 gives a very simple classification of determination techniques.

Table 2.9 Classification of analytical determination techniques, according to parameter measured

Technique	Parameter measured
Gravimetric	weight
Titrimetric	volume (of liquid)
Volumetric	volume (of gas)
Spectroscopic	absorption
	emission
	fluorescence
Electrochemical	potential
	current
	charge
	resistance
Miscellaneous	heat
	radioactivity

2.8.1 *Errors in determination*

Readability is one of the simplest parameters to investigate for all these methods, being taken as the smallest change in the measured value which can be observed with confidence. The analytical balance is a truly impressive piece of engineering, enabling a 0.1 mg change in the weight of a 10 g sample to be detected easily, representing a precision of one part in 10^5. On the other hand, a moving-coil meter (as used in a pH meter for example) has a readability of about 0.5 % of full scale reading, and a 10″ chart recorder about 0.25 %. Most currently available analytical measuring instruments are fitted with electronic digital read-out, which has a number of advantages over the older analogue presentation: it is cheaper, has better readability, is less tiring to read, and does not suffer from non-linearity. Users are, however, often misled into thinking that because a read-out is given to, say, four figures, the result is both accurate and precise to this extent. The linearity and freedom from interference of the sensor element and indeed of the whole measuring system must be taken into account and checked before an estimate can be made of the performance of the system.

2.8.2 *Speed of response*
Most of the outputs produced by analytical instrumentation consist of a signal, more or less steady or varying from one sample to the next, and conveying information about the sample, superimposed on some *noise*, a short-term variable quantity which tends to obscure the signal. If we damp the response of the measuring system we effectively average the noise level and get a steadier reading, but in so doing we slow down the response of the system to changes in which we are interested. This will in turn affect the rate at which different samples can be put through the system and hence the overall speed of determination.

2.9 The complete analytical procedure—a survey of the sources of error
To round off this chapter on the structure of analytical methods it will be helpful to reproduce a summary of the steps and the associated sources of error, illustrated by the results of a thorough investigation into the gas chromatographic determination of traces of beryllium, as described by Tölg.[3]

Recoveries of beryllium at each step of the method (decomposition, solvent-extraction, back-washing to remove excess of reagent, transfer of solution, evaporation to low bulk etc.) were checked by using the radioactive tracer ^{7}Be which was detected by its γ-emission at 0.4 MeV. It was observed that the complex chosen for extraction (with trifluoroacetylacetone) formed much more slowly at very low levels than when microgram amounts of beryllium were taken, and also that the complex was adsorbed from benzene solution on to glass, but not on to fused silica.

One lesson from such studies is that the less we handle the sample and the fewer stages we introduce into a procedure, the more likely we are to succeed with a near-quantitative recovery of the species in question. It may be possible for instance to combine decomposition with separation, releasing the trace element as a gas, and it may then be possible to examine the gas stream directly, say by passing it into an argon plasma for measurement by plasma emission spectroscopy, thus cutting down the handling to the absolute mimimum. This approach has been recommended[3] for the determination of traces of boron and of mercury down to the nanogram level.

Table 2.10   Sources of error in a complete analysis

Procedural step	Contamination	Loss	Other
Sampling and storage	containers operator	containers	inhomogeneity
Weighing			balance and weights
Decomposition	container reagents air	container air	
Separation	solvent	container	
Preconcentration	reagent solvent	air	calibrated glassware
Determination			measuring equipment

Table 2.11   Systematic errors in the determination of beryllium. From Tölg, G. (1974) *Talanta*, **21**, 327. Reproduced with permission.

Procedural step	Losses (%)
Decomposition with excited oxygen	< 1
Decomposition with HNO_3 under pressure	$\leqslant 2$
Elimination of interferences	< 1
Formation of the Be–TFA complex	$0.5–1$
Removal of excess of TFA	$\leqslant 2$
Stripping of alkali from the benzene	~ 1
Transfer of benzene phase for concentration	$\leqslant 2$
Concentration step	$\leqslant 2$
Injection on to the column	~ 1

The golden rule for success in trace analysis is to consider all the sources of error and the interferences, to check the method for all likely combinations of elements in the sample and for performance characteristics, and only then to attack the sample itself. It is regrettable that few workers take the time to follow this approach, and it is perhaps therefore not surprising that when results from different laboratories are compared for the analyses of portions of the same sample, the discrepancies may be quite alarming. We shall return to this theme in the last chapter of this book.

References

1 Hanson, N. W. (1973) *Official Standardised and Recommended Methods.* Society for Analytical Chemistry, London.
2 Eckschlager, K. (1961) *Errors, Measurements and Results in Chemical Analysis,* Van Nostrand, London.
3 Tölg, G. (1974) *Talanta,* **21**, 327.
4 Dean, R. B. and Dixon, W. J. (1951) *Anal. Chem.,* **23**, 636.
5 Tölg, G. (1977) *Z. Anal. Chem.,* **283**, 257.
6 Laitinen, H. A. and Harris, W. E. (1975) *Chemical Analysis,* 2nd edn., ch. 26, McGraw-Hill, New York.
7 Islam, A. (1975) *Proc. Anal. Div. Chem. Soc.,* **12**, 266.
8 Goss, R. C. (1917) *J. Ind. Eng. Chem.,* **9**, 144.
9 Engberg, Å (1973) *Analyst,* **98**, 137.
10 Gordus, A. A. and Gordus, J. P. (1974) in *Archaeological Chemistry,* ch. 8, Beck, C. W. (ed.): *Advances in Chemistry,* vol. 138, American Chemical Society, Washington.
11 Renshaw, G. D., Pounds, C. A. and Pearson, E. F. (1972) *Nature,* **238**, 162.
12 Lassner, E., Ortner, H. M., Schedle, H., Kantusek, E. and Klupacek, U. (1974) *Mikrochim. Acta,* p. 483.
13 Boutron, C. (1972) *Anal. Chim. Acta,* **61**, 140.
14 Tölg, G. (1972) *Talanta,* **19**, 1489.
15 Adams, P. B. (1972) "Glass containers for ultrapure solutions"; Hetherington, G. and Bell, L. W., "Vitreous silica", in *Ultrapurity,* Zief, M. and Speights, R. (eds.), Marcel Dekker, New York, (chs. 14 and 15).
16 Bock, R. and Marr, I. L. (1979) *Decomposition Methods in Analytical Chemistry,* International Textbook Co., London, p. 17.
17 Robertson, D. E. (1968) *Anal. Chem.,* **40**, 1067.
18 Perrin, D. D., Armarego, W. L. F. and Perrin, D. R. (1966) *Purification of Laboratory Chemicals,* Pergamon, Oxford.
19 Smith, V. C. (1972) Ref. 15, ch. 10.
20 Bolin, B. (1970) *Sci. Am.,* Sept 1970, 128.
21 Mitchell, R. L. (1963) in *Analytical Chemistry, 1962*: Proc. Fritz Feigl Symposium, Birmingham. West, P. W., Macdonald, A. M. G. and West, T. S. (eds.), Elsevier, Amsterdam, p. 314.
22 Gorsuch, T. T. (1970) *The Destruction of Organic Matter,* Pergamon, Oxford.
23 Doležal, J., Povondra, P. and Šulcek, Z. (1968) *Decomposition Techniques in Inorganic Analysis,* Iliffe, London.
24 Berns, E. G. and van der Zwaan, P. W. (1972) *Anal. Chim. Acta,* **59**, 293.
25 Elwell, W. T. and Wood, D. F. (1975) "Determination of gases in metals by fusion methods", in *Comprehensive Analytical Chemistry,* vol. III. Svehla, G. (ed.), Elsevier, Amsterdam, ch. 4.
26 Dean, J. (1969) *Chemical Separation Methods,* Van Nostrand, New York.
27 Berg, E. W. (1963) *Physical and Chemical Methods of Separation,* McGraw-Hill, New York.
28 Rumford, B. (1813) *Of Coffee and the Art of Preparing it*: abstract in *Phil. Mag.,* **41**, 108.
29 Morrison, G. H. and Freiser, H. (1957) *Solvent Extraction in Analytical Chemistry,* John Wiley, New York.

3 The atmosphere

3.1 Composition of the atmosphere

In spite of the great interest attached to the investigation of atmospheres around other planets and their moons we take for granted the availability of an atmosphere all around us. However, that interest serves to remind us that life as we know it is finely adjusted to an atmosphere of one particular composition, both in quality and in quantity. Indeed, even the modest decrease in the oxygen pressure to three-quarters of its normal value, which is experienced by someone climbing to 2500 m above sea level, can have marked physiological effects if a person is not accustomed to these altitudes.

As the water vapour level in air can vary considerably over the range 0–5%, it is customary to quote the composition of dry air, as shown in Table 3.1. Many other gases can be found in "clean" air at very low levels, e.g. it is

Table 3.1   Composition of dry air, by volume

Nitrogen	78.09%	Neon	18.2 ppm
Oxygen	20.95%	Helium	5.2 ppm
Argon	0.93%	Methane	1.2–1.5 ppm
Carbon dioxide	0.032%	Nitrous oxide	0.2–0.6 ppm

thought that the natural level of H_2S in air is about 0.0001 ppm, but these very low levels are difficult to establish, partly because of the difficulty in making the determinations and partly because it is impossible to define precisely what is meant by the "natural" level.

3.2 Common air pollutants and their sources

An air pollutant may be defined as something present in the atmosphere (such as dust, fumes, gas, mist, odour, smoke or vapour) at levels injurious to human, plant or animal life or property, or which interfere unreasonably with the comfortable enjoyment of life and property. This definition is adapted from the American Engineers' Joint Council definition of air pollution (see Ledbetter[1]). A pollutant can be of natural or of man-made origin, and for this reason any assessment of the level of a particular pollutant species in a given area should always take into consideration the natural levels of the species, and also the mass balance of the world ecosystem with respect to that

50

pollutant. The sulphur cycle (see Fig. 3.1) serves as a good example for this discussion.[2]

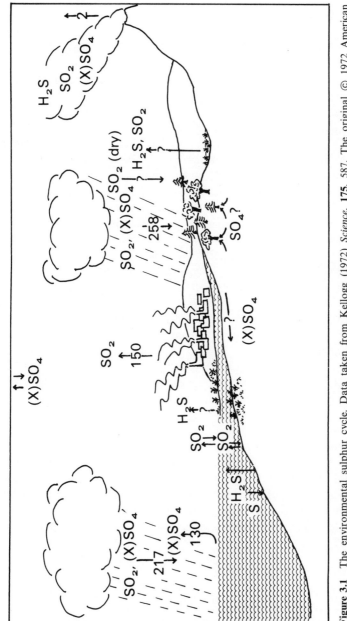

Figure 3.1 The environmental sulphur cycle. Data taken from Kellogg (1972) *Science*, **175**, 587. The original © 1972 American Association for the Advancement of Science. This version reproduced by permission.

It is interesting to consider how some of the values in the figure can be arrived at. For example, very careful analyses[3] of air samples over an American Atlantic salt-water marsh have shown H_2S to be present at levels ranging from 0.15 ppb to over 10 ppb (parts per 10^9, v/v). These compare well with values found over an estuary in Scotland at low tide: 1–10 ppb when the gas is detectable by smell (author's own results). The averaged emission rate was estimated, on a July evening, to be around 10 g of sulphur per square metre per year: this multiplies up to 10 tons per year per km^2, but is a long way short of the 10^8 tons per year for the earth's whole land surface. One of the problems with the figures for H_2S is that they are obtained by difference from the figures for other sulphur species.

One might feel inclined to ask whether it is valid to average such figures for the entire global surface. The answer must be a qualified yes—qualified because a weighted average might be more appropriate, but yes because nature does manage to distribute materials thrown into the atmosphere over a very wide area. Much interest now centres on the analysis of ice samples from the polar ice caps. Analysis of samples from different depths allows reconstruction of a diary for the averaged levels of various minor components in the atmosphere over long periods of time. For carbon dioxide there are indications that the atmospheric concentration 10 000 years ago was only half what it now is.[4] Gases are well mixed and it is reasonable therefore to assume that these conclusions, based on occluded CO_2 in air in the Antarctic ice, are valid. It is, however, more surprising that solids should be transported over such enormous distances. Transport of particulate matter some 5000 km from the northern industrial nations to the Arctic in the winter and spring has been proved, confirming the belief that the marked increases reported for lead levels in Arctic ice at decreasing depths correspond to deposition since the beginning of the industrial revolution (Fig. 3.2).[5]

3.3   Gases, vapours and particles

The distinction has already been made between gaseous (e.g. CO_2) and particulate (e.g. dust containing lead) components in the atmosphere. This distinction is important for two main reasons: the sampling and analytical techniques for the two classes are very different, and some aspects of legislation are concerned specifically with solids released to the atmosphere and not with gases. Pollutants may be classified according to particle size.

Visible smoke:	particles of 0.1–10 μm diameter
Dust:	particles of 10–100 μm
Grit:	particles of $> 100 \mu$m
Vapour:	gas-phase of a substance normally liquid at the temperatures concerned
Mist (fog):	tiny droplets of liquid small enough to remain suspended in air
Aerosol:	suspension of particles or droplets in air (or other gas)
Gases:	in the vapour phase because the temperature is above their boiling points.

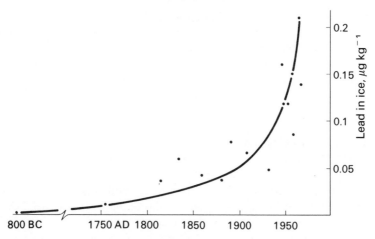

Figure 3.2 Lead levels in Arctic ice from different depths and hence of different ages, demonstrating the increase in levels of airborne lead. Reproduced by courtesy of *Geochim. et Cosmochim. Acta* from Murozumi *et al.* (1969).[5]

The range of fine particles known as smoke is particularly important for pollution studies since these are the particles which reach the lungs when inhaled (larger particles being held back by the fine hairs in the nasal passage). Moreover, they are capable of adsorbing substantial amounts of gases and vapours from the air and effectively transmitting these to the lungs, where efficient absorption into the body fluids is facilitated.

3.4   Odour thresholds

Students who have attended laboratory courses will have become aware of how much more or less tolerant some of their colleagues are to diverse "smells" or odours. One of the authors, for example, cannot smell hydrogen cyanide, but a friend can detect it by nose if someone takes the top off a potassium cyanide bottle at the other side of the laboratory. Perfumes intended to be attractive to the opposite sex may be perceived as unpleasant or even not detected at all. It is apparent that the sensitivity of the human nose—the olfactory organ—varies enormously from one individual to the next, and also from one chemical to the next. Attempts have been made to quantify the phenomenon by measuring the concentration of a particular compound in air which is necessary before it can be perceived (perception threshold) or identified (identification threshold). An approach to finding an order of magnitude for people in general rather than for an individual leads to the level at which 50% of a population sample can correctly identify the compound in question—the PIT_{50} (population identification threshold). Values range around 0.001 ppm for H_2S and butyric acid, through 0.1 ppm for styrene, to 10 ppm for ethanol or hydrogen chloride.[6] It is worth noting that it is sometimes associated impurities which give a characteristic odour, so that the source of the gas used for such experiments should be noted.

3.5 Air pollution and health
The World Health Organization (WHO) definition of (good) health is "a situation of complete physical, mental and social well-being". As we have seen, a component of the atmosphere becomes a pollutant when it interferes with this state of well-being. Man-made pollution has certainly been with us since the early days of the industrial revolution, and reached its peak in the middle of the twentieth century in the form of the smogs—mixtures of fogs and smokes—which reduced visibility in industrial cities to a few metres for long periods during the winter months. Just how injurious to health these smogs were become apparent after a number of particularly severe episodes in the Meuse valley in Belgium (1930), in London (1952 and again in 1962), and in New York (1966).

3.5.1 *Legislation in the UK*
The great London smog of 1952 lasted four days, and some 4000 extra deaths were recorded above the statistically predicted number, about 3000 of them in the week of the smog and most of the remainder in the week following. The peak in the death-rate occurred only two days after the onset of the smog, reaching about three times the usual mean value of 300 per day for the Greater London area.[7] This event prompted Parliament to set up the Beaver Committee which reported in 1954, as a result of which the Clean Air Act (1956) was passed to introduce some long-needed improvements. The Act deals primarily with visible pollutants—smoke in particular—since these can easily be seen and monitored. Though solids in emission gases are usually accompanied by invisible but equally unpleasant gaseous pollutants, it is feasible to remove the solids fairly effectively, but the gases themselves are more difficult to remove.

   Three sections of the Act are worthy of specific mention: it is an offence to emit dark smoke, except for brief periods as in starting up a furnace (Section 1); smoke density meters must be installed in stacks to monitor emission (Section 4); smoke-control areas will be declared in larger cities, in which only certain "clean" fuels may be sold and burned, and where grants may be made available to householders to convert fireplaces, etc. (Section 11).

3.5.2 *Monitoring the environment*

The National Survey of Air Pollution was set up in 1961 (it is now the responsibility of the Department of the Environment) with the aim of monitoring sulphur dioxide and smoke at over 1000 sites throughout the UK. Several other pollutants are routinely monitored at a small number of sites across the country.[8]

Clarenburg[9] has summarized the reasons for monitoring atmospheric composition in industrial countries.

(i) to help establish criteria for acceptable air quality, thus establishing at what level a particular component becomes a pollutant

(ii) to gather "real-time" data with the aim of safeguarding the population by taking appropriate industrial action such as shutting down factories in the event of a build-up of some pollutant

(iii) to establish long-term trends in air pollution and to measure the improvement (or otherwise) resulting from preventive action taken

(iv) to provide a basis for forecasts of possible occurrences of severe pollution made worse by adverse meteorological conditions.

Clarenburg's third point is exemplified in Fig. 3.3, which shows a summary of the data gathered by the NAPS up to 1972. The success of the Clean Air Act is seen clearly, both in the fall in the smoke and in the rise in the number of sunshine hours per winter day for London. It should be noted, however, that the reductions in SO_2 concentrations at ground level analogous to those in smoke concentrations simply reflect the fact that higher stacks are being

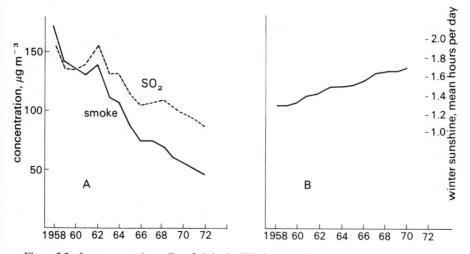

Figure 3.3 Improvement in quality of air in the UK since the Clean Air Act, 1956. *A*: decrease in concentrations of smoke and SO_2. *B*: increase in winter daily sunshine. Reproduced from Flowers (1974)[10] and Ashby (1973)[11] respectively, with permission of the Controller, Her Majesty's Stationery Office.

built. The gas is more effectively dispersed into the atmosphere, but the total emission of SO_2 remained much the same over the period 1960–1970.

3.5.3 *Working atmospheres: the Health and Safety at Work Act 1974*

This very important addition to the statute books covers, amongst many other aspects of working conditions for employees, the quality of the air both outside and inside a factory or other place of work. In part I, we find

> 5-(i) "It shall be the duty of the person having control . . . to use the best practicable means for preventing harmful emission into the atmosphere from the premises, of noxious or offensive substances . . ."

which concerns the environment, while for the air inside

> 2-(e) "It shall be the duty of every employer to ensure the provision and maintenance of a working environment for his employees that is, as far as is reasonably practicable, safe, without risks to health, and adequate as regards facilities and arrangements for their welfare at work."

The Act also allows (Section 19-(i)) that every enforcing authority may appoint inspectors with powers

> 20-(2)(g) "to take samples of any articles or substances found in any premises . . . and of the atmosphere in . . . such premises," and
> 20-(2)(i) "to examine such samples".

Coker[12] and Thain[13] have reviewed the problems and techniques for monitoring toxic gases in workplace atmospheres, and the American Conference of Governmental Hygienists has prepared an extensive list of Threshold Limit Values (TLVs), being concentrations of individual chemicals in the air to which "it is believed that nearly all workers may be repeatedly exposed day after day without adverse effect." With a few exceptions these figures are also used in the UK and form part of the criteria which are used by the Health and Safety Executive in assessing compliance with the 1974 Act.[14] A representative collection of these values is given in Appendix 1 of this book. A discussion of how toxicities can be evaluated is presented in a WHO publication.[15]

It may come as a surprise that around 600 chemicals, groups of compounds or proprietary preparations (pesticides etc.) are listed, with TLV's ranging between around 1000 ppm v/v for inflammable hydrocarbons, through 10 ppm for hydrogen cyanide, hydrogen sulphide, and benzene, 0.01 ppm for some organic isocyanates, to 0.0002 ppm for osmium tetroxide. Clearly, the industrial-hygiene analytical chemist has a difficult problem when attempting to analyse working atmospheres for so many possible contaminants and at such low levels. His methods must be both selective and sensitive. Just how these goals may be achieved will, it is hoped, be made apparent in this chapter, the remainder of which is divided into three sections to deal with solids, with direct methods for gases, and with preconcentration methods for gases. One particularly valuable compilation of methods and practical details has been published jointly by several official bodies in the USA.[16]

3.6   Sampling of airborne solids

3.6.1   *Smoke and dust*

These two physically distinct components of polluted air (or exhaust gases in a factory stack) are normally measured optically, with some mechanical design factor to differentiate the two particle-size ranges. A light beam crossing the inside of a factory stack will be absorbed (or scattered) by all particles, but only dust particles will settle out on a horizontal surface. In a dust meter developed by CERL, manufactured by Kent Instruments, dust on a horizontal window is monitored by measuring the transmission of a vertical light beam. After 15 minutes the accumulated dust is blown off the window by a jet of air and the process is repeated. A recorder trace such as that in Fig. 3.4 is obtained, giving a continuous record of the dust level.

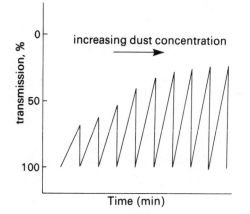

Figure 3.4   Recorder output of automatic dust-level analyser (courtesy of Kent Instruments).

The importance of particle size analysis in air pollution work has already been mentioned. One device which sorts air-borne solids into rough classes according to size is the cascade impactor,[17] in which large volumes of air are pumped through a set of nozzles of decreasing diameter, each time impinging on a receiving plate (a piece of copper foil) which collects the particles with greatest momentum (i.e. of greatest mass for a given air velocity) allowing the smaller particles to pass on to the next nozzle. A more efficient arrangement includes sets of thick stainless steel plates with many holes arranged concentrically. Each successive plate has smaller-diameter holes, giving the air stream a higher velocity, so that eventually only the very finest particles are swept away in the air stream (Fig. 3.5) The operator collects as samples a set of foils, each with a ring of little circles of air-borne dirt, but on each of the foils the particle size range is different. Each little circle of dirt may then be taken for a different analytical determination. For urban air with $300 \, \mu g \, m^{-3}$ of dust, pumping for one hour at $5 \, m^3 \, h^{-1}$ gives spots 1–10 mm in diameter, with $3-30 \, \mu g$ of dust according to particle size, enough for many analytical procedures.[18]

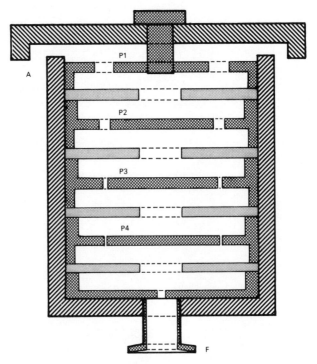

Figure 3.5   Cascade impactor—disc and plate type.

3.6.2   High-volume air samplers

High-volume air samplers are used to pump air at rates of $75 \, m^3 \, h^{-1}$ through large-diameter filters (say about 20–25 cm diameter*). The earliest models were simply domestic vacuum cleaners. The sampling time depends on how clean the air is—1 h for city air, 12 h for "clean" country air. The choice of

---

* e.g. Model GMWS 2310 from General Metal Works Inc., Village of Cleves, Ohio 45002, USA; Research Appliance Co., Cambridge, Maryland 21613, USA.

filter material depends on what is to be determined in the collected dust. The usual choices are (i) cellulose filter paper, for determination of metals and anions; (ii) glass-fibre paper, for determination of organic compounds; and (iii) silica felts, for inorganic species if levels are not too low; these are good for organic compounds.

3.6.3 Portable "personal" air samplers

From the environmental health point of view it is preferable to sample the atmospheric environment where people are working. For this purpose, several firms (e.g. Cassella*) have developed light-weight battery operated pumps which can pump air at $2 \, l \, min^{-1}$ through a 3.7-cm glass-fibre paper for up to 8 h on one charge of the batteries. The small size and reasonable price of these pumps makes them ideal for use when samples of polluted air must be gathered at several points to build up a picture of the distribution of an air pollutant.

3.6.4 Where to sample

"Sample where people are working" is not as straightforward an answer as it may seem, but we can consider three approaches to the problem:

(i) Sampling at source, so as to facilitate control procedures and comply with the Clean Air Act.

(ii) Sampling in the air, to see how much material is being carried away from a source by the movement of air, and to trace this movement—e.g., the transport of SO_2 from the UK and Germany north to Scandinavia (see Clarenburg,[9] p. 301).

(iii) Sampling on the ground, to see what is deposited at any one place and to identify the nature and possibly the source of the pollution. In practice the high-volume samplers used are positioned above ground, usually between 2 and 15 m.

3.6.5 Units for measurement of airborne dust

Total dust is measured in units of $mg \, m^{-3}$, with typical values lying around $1 \, mg \, m^{-3}$ in a good factory workshop (TLV $10 \, mg \, m^{-3}$). Individual undesirable components, such as lead, are measured in $\mu g \, m^{-3}$ (with values of 1–$10 \, \mu g \, m^{-3}$ for air in busy streets, rising to perhaps 20–$25 \, \mu g \, m^{-3}$ for air in busy road tunnels.[19]

3.6.6 General background

Lodge et al.[20] have written a detailed review on non-health effects and properties of airborne particulate matter which gives references to many specialist papers, and Malissa has written a book on analytical methodology.[21]

* Cassella Ltd., Regent House, Britannia Walk, London.

3.7 Examination of airborne solids

What is looked for in an analysis of airborne solids, as with all environmental materials, depends very much on why the sample was collected in the first place. Dust in urban air may be examined for lead or for carcinogenic organic compounds, dust in a granite yard for crystalline quartz, dust in an old factory being demolished for asbestos, and so on. But a common plan of preliminary investigation can often be adopted for all of these examples. As an illustration, the results are presented for a sample of dust and dirt gathered at the side of a busy road in Aberdeen.

3.7.1 *Total weight and particle size distribution*

The TLV gives $10\,mg\,m^{-3}$ as a working guide for dust in air, so any investigation will determine the relevant figure by weighing the filter paper before and after a known volume of air is pumped through it. A high-volume sampler $(1-2\,m^3\,min^{-1})$ is preferable, but a pumping capacity of $10-15\,l\,min^{-1}$ can still be useful.

Particles in the size range $0.5-100\,\mu m$ are likely to be encountered, and the fraction $< 10\,\mu m$ is of special interest because these small particles reach the lungs when inhaled. The cascade impactor with a pump running somewhere in the range $2-5\,m^3\,h^{-1}$ $(33-90\,l\,min^{-1})$ is most useful for sorting small particles (they are far too small to be separable by sieving). It is possible to carry out a crude separation by swirling a slurry of the collected solid in water, and decanting after waiting different lengths of time. Particle sizes can then be estimated by optical microscopy.

3.7.2 *Identification of minerals—optical microscopy*

Identifying individual minerals in a sample of airborne dust is important for two main reasons:

(i) some minerals are known to be injurious to man, such as quartz (causes silicosis of the lungs) and asbestos (causes cancer of the lungs). In the second case, one must also be able to distinguish one particular form (blue asbestos, or crocidolite) from the several other asbestos minerals.

(ii) the source of the dust may become apparent when its composition is known.

Minerals may be identified either by optical microscopy or X-ray diffraction.

Figure 3.6 shows photomicrographs of four fractions of urban airborne solids, with indications of the range of sizes. Transparent crystalline particles can be identified[22] from (i) their refractive index (observation in different liquids till the edges disappear), (ii) their ability to rotate the plane of polarization of light (observation through crossed polarizers), and (iii) crystal shape. Minerals identified optically in these particular dust samples included quartz, feldspars and mica.

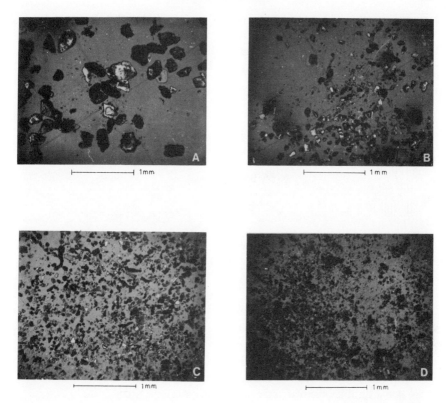

Figure 3.6 Photomicrographs of four fractions of an urban airborne solids sample (see Table 3.2). A, coarse: quartz, feldspars and mica predominate. D, very fine: mainly iron oxide, soot, and clay particles.

3.7.3 Identification of minerals—X-ray diffraction

A single crystal can act as a diffraction grating for a beam of X-rays; the spacing between the layers of atoms in the crystal is equivalent to the spacing between the lines of a ruled diffraction grating for visible light. The principle of a reflection type diffraction grating can be demonstrated by viewing the light of an electric lamp reflected at a very shallow angle off the surface of a long-playing gramophone record: coloured fringes surround the image of the lamp as the light of different wavelengths is reinforced at different angles, determined by the spacing between the grooves and the wavelength of the light. The effect is more marked if a mercury (blue) or sodium (orange) street lamp is used as the source. The fundamental equation for diffraction was worked out by Bragg in 1912. If one considers two planes of atoms in the crystal (represented as two rows of dots in Fig. 3.7) with a beam of X-rays reflected off the two planes, the two reflections will be in phase, and thus reinforce, if the path of one is an integral number of wavelengths greater than that of the other. If we denote wavelength by λ the relationship becomes

$$\sin \theta = n\lambda/2d.$$

The practical experimental arrangement is to collimate a narrow beam of X-rays of one specific wavelength on to the crystal and to record the reflections on a piece of photographic film bent into a circle with the crystal

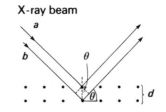

Figure 3.7 X-ray diffraction by atoms in a crystal. Condition for reinforcement is that path-length for beam b is a whole number of wavelengths greater than for beam a.

at the centre. When the film is developed, a pattern of spots is revealed, each one representing one possible reflection from a plane of atoms in the crystal. As the set of spacings between the planes of atoms is characteristic for that particular crystal, so therefore is the pattern of spots on the photograph.

When a sample of powdered crystalline material is taken instead of a single crystal, each spot becomes a circular reflection, because the powder has small, randomly oriented crystals. It is only necessary to photograph one strip of a diameter of these circles, to record the diffraction pattern (Fig. 3.8). When the

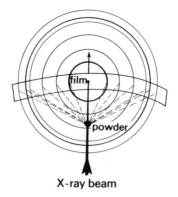

Figure 3.8 X-ray diffraction by many small crystals in a powder sample: only a narrow slice of a full circular diffraction pattern is actually recorded on the film.

dimensions of the film holder—the camera—are known, it is easy to work back from the measurements on the film to the spacing in the crystal. This is done for all the intense lines on the film, and the "fingerprint" thus obtained may be used, by comparison with data for known minerals, to identify the mineral(s) present. Diffraction patterns for three of the dust samples in Fig. 3.6 are shown in Fig. 3.9 and for comparison a pattern is included for quartz

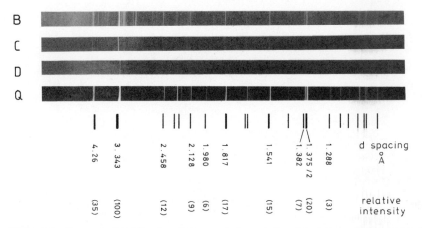

Figure 3.9 X-ray powder diffraction photographs for samples of dust shown in Figure 3.6. B, medium; C, fine; D, very fine; Q, quartz. The d-spacings should be compared with the tabulated values in Figure 3.10.

as a standard. The X-ray diffraction data for a very large number of compounds have been catalogued in the ASTM Index[23] which makes identification quite straightforward. The analyst looks up in the index the most intense line, then the three next strongest lines, and is then referred to the card in the index with all the data to complete the match for reliable identification. Figure 3.10 shows the ASTM card for quartz.

3.7.4 Quantitation by X-ray diffraction

This is much more difficult, though it is possible under favourable conditions. The intensities of the lines depend very much on the size of the crystals, and moreover, the reflected X-rays from planes further inside the crystals suffer significant absorption as they pass through the crystals. The problems are well illustrated in a report[24] on the determination of crystalline quartz in the volcanic ash from the eruption of Mt St Helens on 18th May 1980. As the volume of ash was sufficient to cover large areas of land to a depth of one metre or more, there was considerable concern about the health hazard posed by the high level of crystalline quartz.

5-0490 Minor correction

d	3.24	4.26	1.82	4.26	SiO$_2$	
I/I$_2$	100	35	17	35	silicon IV oxide	alpha quartz

			dÅ	I/I$_2$	hkl	dÅ	I/I$_2$	hkl
Rad. CuKα$_1$	λ 1.5405	**Filter** N1	4.26	35	100	1.228	2	220
Dia.		**Coll.**	3.343	100	101	1.1997	5	213
I/I$_2$ G.C. diffractometer		d corr. abs.?	2.458	12	110	1.1973	2	221
Ref. Swanson and Fuyat, NBS circular 539,			2.282	12	102	1.1838	4	114
vol. III (1953)			2.237	6	111	1.1802	4	310
Sys. Hexagonal	S.G. D$_3^4$ − P3$_1$21		2.128	9	200	1.1530	2	311
a$_0$ 4.913 b$_e$	c$_0$ 5.405	A C1.10	1.980	6	201	1.1408	1	204
α β	γ	Z 3	1.817	17	112	1.1144	1	303
Ref. *Ibid.*			1.801	1	003	1.0816	4	312
δα nωβ 1.544δ	γ 1.553	Sign +	1.672	7	202	1.0636	1	400
2V D$_X$2.647 mp	Color							
Ref. *Ibid.*			1.659	3	103	1.0477	2	105
Mineral from Lake Toxaway, N.C.			1.608	1	210	1.0437	2	401
Spect. anal.: 0.01 % Al; 0.001 % Ca, Cu,			1.541	15	211	1.0346	2	214
Fe, Mg.			1.453	3	113	1.0149	2	223
X-ray pattern at 25°C.			1.418	1	300	0.9896	2	402, 115
				7				
		3-0427, 3-0444	1.382	7	212	0.9872	2	313
Replaces 1-0649, 2-0458, 2-0459, 2-0471, 3-0419			1.375	11	203	0.9781	1	304
			1.372	9	301	0.9762	1	320
			1.288	3	104	0.9607	2	321
			1.256	4	302	0.9285	1	410

Figure 3.10 X-ray powder diffraction data for quartz. Reproduced with permission from International Centre for Diffraction Data.[23]

The workers who recorded the diffraction pattern of dust samples as received reported finding little or no pure silica: the material was mainly a mixture of aluminosilicates. But those who employed a preliminary separation involving selective dissolution of the silicates in hot concentrated phosphoric acid[25] did find crystalline silica in the residue. In fact small amounts of all three crystalline forms, crystobalite (5–10 %), quartz (1 %) and tridymite (1 %), were found, the first of which is the high-temperature form, normally produced by crystallization above 1490°C. There was yet another possible source of conflict in the reported results: some workers analysed bulk powder samples, while others investigated only the very fine material which would normally constitute an airborne hazard.

3.7.5 *Interconversion of solid species on filters*
Klockow[26] has shown that aerosols of sodium chloride, typical of seaside air, in which SO$_2$ levels are appreciable, leave a deposit of sodium sulphate on

the filter, the volatile hydrogen chloride having been driven off and the sulphur fixed by oxidation to sulphate. In this case identification of particles on the filter is quite misleading. This is another source of error which can give rise to erroneous results.

3.7.6 *Non-destructive elemental analysis—X-ray fluorescence and emission*

Energy transitions involving the innermost electrons of atoms correspond to photons of very short-wave electromagnetic radiation, falling in the range 0.1–100 Å (0.01–10 nm), which are known as X-rays. There are three ways in which these electronic transitions can be observed.

(i) *Absorption.* If the wavelength of a beam of X-rays is just a little less than that corresponding to the energy of the transition, the X-rays will be strongly absorbed. The spectrum (a plot of absorption vs. wavelength) shows a number of so-called "edges" corresponding to different transitions.

(ii) *Emission.* The excitation of an electron from a lower to a higher energy level may be brought about by bombarding the atoms with fast electrons (accelerated through say 30 kV), and the X-rays emitted as the inner electron drops back to ground state are analysed according to wavelength and intensity.

(iii) *Fluorescence.* The first two phenomena can be combined in a third: the sample is irradiated with short wavelength X-rays and the longer-wavelength emitted X-rays are then analysed according to wavelength and intensity.

The energy levels are shown diagrammatically in Fig. 3.11 with figures given for iron. The important advantage for the analytical chemist is that the wavelengths are virtually independent of oxidation state or the nature of the compound being examined. This makes identification of individual elements a fairly easy matter, especially as there are only a few intense lines for each element.

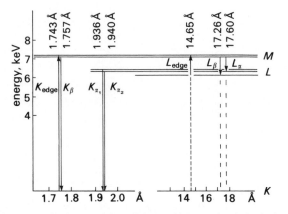

Figure 3.11 Diagrammatic representation of electronic energy levels in the iron atom, and of the associated X-ray spectral lines.

An important disadvantage is that absorption of the emitted X-rays is different for each wavelength and depends on the mean atomic mass of the sample. The corrections are difficult to calculate, so quantitative analysis is usually done by comparison with standards. Large samples (say 2–5 cm² area) are best examined by X-ray fluorescence: the paper filter is examined directly for analysis of the dust on it and can be used afterwards for other analyses. Elements from sodium onwards are determined without difficulty, but the lighter elements do present difficulties as the longer-wavelength X-rays are absorbed by nearly everything. A good introduction to X-ray analytical spectroscopy has been written by Birks.[27]

The electron microprobe. Smaller samples—down to individual particles of dust—are best examined in the scanning electron microprobe X-ray analyser, in which a finely focused beam (resolution ~1 μm) is scanned, as in a television picture, over the sample (say 0.1 mm across) and the emitted X-rays, analysed according to wavelength, are used to modulate the brilliance of a TV-type display[28] (see Fig. 3.12).

An alternative display is to use the electron current through the sample to modulate the display on the picture tube. Additionally, it is possible to examine the specimen through an optical microscope at the same time.

Figure 3.13 shows the finest fraction of the airborne dust sample, as seen on a transmission electron microscope with an X-ray analyser. Only very small particles can be examined by this technique (say ~1 μm or less), but there are two important advantages over the electron microprobe analyser. (i) As samples are very thin, errors due to variable absorption of X-rays and electrons are small, and (ii) it is also possible to record an electron diffraction pattern, as mentioned earlier. Figure 3.13 shows the electron diffraction pattern of one very thin mica crystal in the dust sample. Figure 3.13 also shows the X-ray emission spectra for several different particles: this illustrates the power of this technique for the study of solids.

3.7.7   Chemical analysis for individual elements

In urban air, lead is the element most likely to be determined, since it arises as a product of combustion of tetra-alkyl lead additives in petrol. Both inorganic and organometallic forms of lead may be determined in air, but require different sampling procedures.[29]

Procedure for lead. Treat the dust collected from a 100-l sample of air, still on the paper filter, with 2 ml of dilute nitric acid (5 ml concentrated acid diluted to 100 ml with water) at room temperature or with very gentle warmth, for 5 min. Decant, wash the filter, and determine the lead as described in Section 4.22.1. TLV is 150 μg m⁻³.

Procedure for fluoride. Treat the paper filter with 2 ml of 0.1 M sodium hydroxide (0.4 % w/v) in a plastic beaker, then determine the fluoride by the ion-selective electrode method after dilution with TISAB as described in Section 4.20.3. The TLV is 2.5 mg m⁻³.

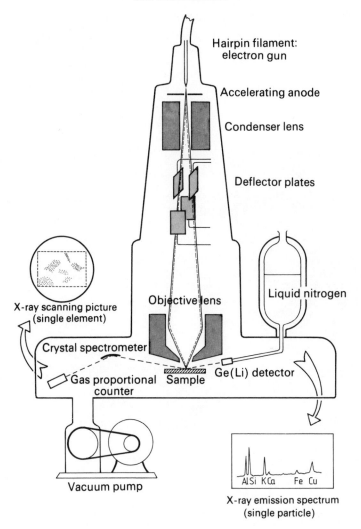

Hairpin filament: electron gun

Accelerating anode

Condenser lens

Deflector plates

Liquid nitrogen

Objective lens

X-ray scanning picture (single element)

Crystal spectrometer

Gas proportional counter

Sample

Ge(Li) detector

Vacuum pump

AlSi KCa   Fe Cu

X-ray emission spectrum (single particle)

Figure 3.12 Electron microscope microanalyser.

Procedure for iron. Treat the paper filter with 5 ml of concentrated nitric acid, heating to dryness to destroy the paper, repeating the addition and heating if necessary. Dissolve the dry residue in 5 ml concentrated hydrochloric acid and make up to 25 ml with water. To 5 ml of this solution add 5 ml of 20 % potassium thiocyanate solution and dilute to 50 ml. Measure at 475 nm and compare with standards of 10–50 μg of iron taken through the same procedure. Marczenko[30] describes a procedure based upon an extraction into two portions of methyl isobutyl ketone, followed by dilution to 50 ml, and absorbance measurement at 495 nm.

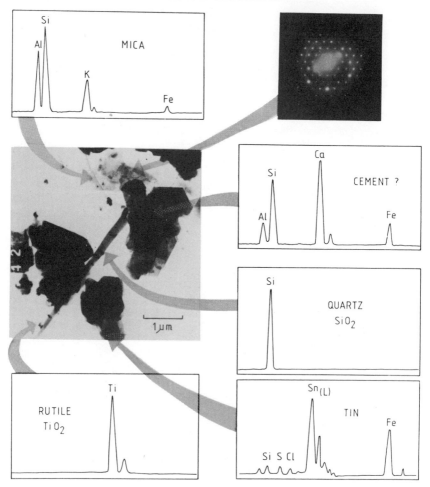

Figure 3.13 Electron micrograph of a sample of very fine airborne solids fraction (sample D, Figure 3.6) with X-ray emission spectra of several particles, and an electron-diffraction pattern of a mica platelet. The authors thank Dr. Eric Lachowski for his assistance with this sample.

3.7.8 *Toxic organic compounds*

As a first approach an organic carbon analysis can be done (combustion method), and as a second, a weight-loss on washing with an organic solvent. Small solid particles have a large specific surface area and are therefore capable of adsorbing significant amounts of even relatively volatile organic compounds from the air. Some of these may be quite harmless (unburned hydrocarbons or long-chain carboxylic acids), but others may be potentially hazardous, such as the polynuclear aromatic hydrocarbons (PAH's) of which benzo(a)pyrene is probably the commonest, and has been found at levels of 10–$100 \, \text{ng m}^{-3}$ in urban air.

Glass-fibre filter papers should be used with a high-volume air sampler, and thoroughly cleaned in pentane before use. The PAH's are dissolved from the airborne dust by refluxing in benzene. The solution is evaporated, and the residue dissolved in pentane and the compounds separated by chromatography on an alumina column. Identification is achieved by UV spectrophotometry and spectrofluorimetry. The techniques have been reviewed by Sawicki[31] and are described in this text in Section 6.9.1. Many of these compounds have quite characteristic fluorescence spectra, and so are readily identified after separation.

Mention should be made here of a group of very dangerous compounds— the polychlorinated dibenzo-p-dioxins—of which the tetrachloro- member (TCDD) gained special public notoriety as a result of the Seveso incident in July 1976 in which a 600 kg batch of process chemicals exploded.

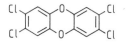

At Seveso the TCDD arose as a by-product in the manufacture of 2,4,5-trichlorophenol, used to make defoliants. The toxicity is very high: the LD (dose which will kill 50% of an animal test population) is $5 \, \mu\text{g kg}^{-1}$ body weight, which meant that dangerous levels were present in the area after the explosion but were not even identified until two weeks after the event, because they were so low. These compounds are not produced only in selected chemical processes: they have been identified as products of municipal waste incinerators, reaching levels of several $\mu\text{g g}^{-1}$ in the smallest airborne particles. They have been separated by GLC[32] (see Section 3.10) and identified by GC/MS[33] (see Sections 4.26 and 7.4.2) in the fly ash from urban refuse incinerators.

3.7.9 Radioactivity of airborne dust

During the 1950's, when the super-powers were still carrying out atmospheric test explosions of nuclear weapons, there was much concern about the levels of radioactivity in the air, and many countries initiated sampling and measurement programmes to monitor the situation. The ^{90}Sr activity, for example, was found to increase substantially after this series of tests, with an annual seasonal peak each spring arising from global patterns of air circulation.[34] Similar but more dramatic activity peaks were observed after the 1961–62 tests.

The unique properties of radioactive isotopes make the monitoring of individual isotopes relatively straightforward at astoundingly low concentrations. Thus results may often be expressed in terms of atoms cm^{-3}, a level some ten orders of magnitude (i.e. 10^{10}) lower than the typical pollutant levels we have considered so far.

It should be remembered that atmospheric activity may arise from natural origins, as well as from nuclear weapon tests. These origins include emission of natural radioactive rare gases from the earth's surface and the production of radionuclides by interactions with cosmic radiation. The latter are formed primarily in the upper atmosphere. Radionuclides that are not naturally gaseous rapidly enter into chemical compound formation and are transported with regular atmospheric aerosols.

3.7.10 Results for an urban dust sample
To illustrate the approach to the examination of airborne solids, samples were collected directly from the roadside on the ground: sedimentation was used to discard the bulk of the very coarse material. The remainder was fractionated, also by sedimentation. The analytical results are summarized in Table 3.2.

Table 3.2 Composition of an urban dust sample (see Fig. 3.6)

Fraction	Particle size range	Mass fraction, %	C, %	Pb, %	Fe, %
Coarse	$100 \mu m$	58	4.1	0.04	2.3
Medium	$30-100 \mu m$	31	4.3	0.11	3.0
Fine	$10-30 \mu m$	7.1	15	0.20	2.3
Very fine	$10 \mu m$	3.7	16	0.22	2.9

Minerals: quartz, feldspars, mica, rutile, iron oxide; soot was also present.

3.8 Direct instrumental methods for gaseous pollutants

3.8.1 Infra-red spectrophotometry
Many small molecules encountered in environmental analyses have characteristic IR absorption spectra, the wavelengths (or frequencies) of the bands corresponding to the differences in vibrational energy levels of the bands. Thus $C{=}O$ simply has a stretching frequency of $2150 cm^{-1}$, while CO_2 has both an antisymmetrical stretching and a bending frequency of $2350 cm^{-1}$ and $650 cm^{-1}$ respectively. It is apparent that IR is a valuable qualitative technique for the identification of many gases, but to understand the quantitative aspects we must consider briefly the theory of absorption photometry, which applies equally to gases, liquids and solids provided they transmit some light.

The spectrophotometer. Figure 3.14 shows the schematic layout of the essential elements of most spectrophotometers. The instrument is operated by (i) selecting the correct wavelength (by adjusting the angle of prism or grating); (ii) adjusting the light intensity via variable slits or the power supply to give a full-scale signal (I_0) on the read-out with no absorbing species in the light path; (iii) placing the absorbing sample in the light beam and reading the intensity of transmitted light, I_t.

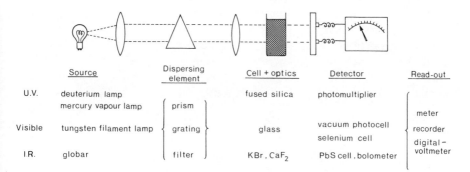

Source	Dispersing element	Cell + optics	Detector	Read-out
U.V.	deuterium lamp		fused silica	photomultiplier	
	mercury vapour lamp	prism			meter
Visible	tungsten filament lamp	grating	glass	vacuum photocell	recorder
				selenium cell	digital –
I.R.	globar	filter	KBr, CaF_2	PbS cell, bolometer	voltmeter

Figure 3.14 Schematic diagram of a spectrophotometer.

The amount of light absorbed may be expressed in terms of % transmission (% T), i.e. $I_t/I_0 \times 100$. However, this function does not vary linearly with the concentration of absorbing species. Suppose a filter in the light path absorbs a fraction f of the initial light beam: $I_t/I_0 = f$. If a second filter is inserted in the light path then

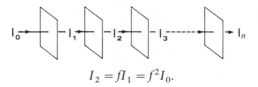

$$I_2 = fI_1 = f^2 I_0.$$

Similarly, after n filters,

$$I_n = f^n \cdot I_0$$

$$\frac{I_0}{I_n} = \frac{1}{f^n}$$

$$\log \frac{I_0}{I_n} = -n \log f.$$

Since $f < 1$, $\log f$ is negative, and is a constant for that filter (i.e. for that absorbing species) at the wavelength we are using. More important is the dependence on n, the number of absorbing bodies, which is proportional to the concentration (c) and to the path-length of cell (l). If $\log I_0/I_n$ is called the absorbance, A, then:

$$A = \log_{10} \frac{I_0}{I_n} = c \cdot l \cdot \varepsilon \qquad (3.1)$$

and the proportionality constant, ε, is called the *molar absorptivity* when c is a molarity. Equation 3.1 is known as the Lambert–Beer law. Figure 3.15 shows the variation of transmittance (I_n/I_0) and of absorbance ($\log I_0/I_n$) with number of filters (with $f = 0.5$) or with concentration (with $l = 1\ cm$) and $\varepsilon = 1$. For species in solution, ε varies from 1 for $Mn^{2+}(H_2O)_6$, 10 for $Cu^{2+}(H_2O)_4$ to 235 for benzene at 256 nm and to 7×10^4 for lead dithizonate at 520 nm, and even higher for some dyestuff ion-pairs. For gases the

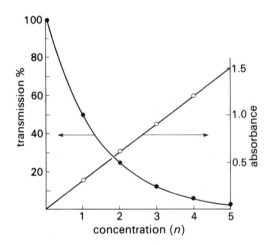

Figure 3.15   Transmittance and absorbance as a function of concentration (or number of filters, n).

absorptivities are not very high: a partial pressure of 3–5 mm of Hg of gas in a 10-cm cell is usually adequate to give a good spectrum. This means a concentration of around 0.5–1 % (in air, say). But if a longer absorption path is used, say 20 m, (by fitting several mirrors inside the gas cell) it is possible to push determination limits down to 10 ppm, and to detect even less of some gases. The absorption spectra for several common gases are shown in Fig. 3.16.

    Adsorption by water vapour in the sample may obscure the weaker peaks of the trace gases, and the apparent molar absorptivity of a gas changes as the total pressure of inert gas is increased, due to pressure broadening of the many fine absorption lines which make up the absorption band which is being measured: these two factors make quantitative work difficult.

Useful compilations of IR spectra of gases and vapours have been published by Beckman[35] and by Perkin-Elmer[36].

Gases are usually contained in cylindrical glass cells with 5-cm diameter end windows of sodium chloride (transparent down to $650\,cm^{-1}$), potassium bromide (to $400\,cm^{-1}$) or calcium fluoride (to $1250\,cm^{-1}$). The last-mentioned is much more resistant to attack by water than the other two, but is also much more easily chipped or cracked.

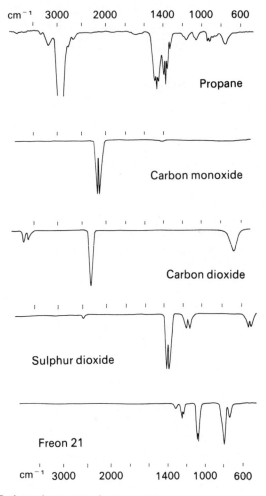

Figure 3.16 IR absorption spectra of some common gases.

3.8.2 Non-dispersive infrared analysers

A gas absorbing infrared radiation becomes heated, resulting in an increase in the pressure if the volume is kept constant. The more intense the beam of radiation, the greater the pressure change. The gas selectively absorbs at all its characteristic wavelengths, not just at one, as when monochromatic radiation is employed. This is the basis of the Luft non-dispersive detector[37] shown in Fig. 3.17. Light is split along two paths: in one is a reference cell with clean air, in the other is the sample of contaminated air. The detector consists of two sealed chambers filled with the same (pure) gas which is to be

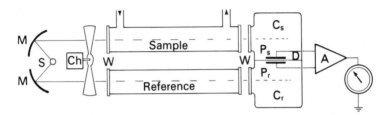

Figure 3.17 Non-dispersive infrared gas analyser of the Luft type. A, amplifier; C_s, C_r, Luft detector cells for sample and reference beams; Ch, chopper; D, thin metal diaphragm; M, mirrors, curved to focus beam from source S on to windows W of suitable IR-transparent material; P_s, P_r, fixed plates of double capacitor P_s-D-P_r.

determined in the air sample. As less radiation reaches the half C_s, the pressure increase is less than in C_r, so the flexible metal diaphragm D is bent towards the plate P_s of the differential capacitor P_r-D-P_s. The chopper then cuts off radiation from both halves and the pressure differential falls off. The output is a series of pulses, the height of which increases with increasing contamination (absorbance) of the sample gas. The detector is efficient in that it "sees" all the wavelengths of interest simultaneously. It is also selective in that interference by another gas at one particular wavelength will be minimized because it is not present at most other wavelengths. These non-dispersive gas analysers are in common use for on-stream factory analysis and for monitoring levels of carbon monoxide in road tunnels, etc.

3.8.3 Infrared emission spectroscopy

This technique is anything but routine, but has proved valuable for analysing some very special atmospheres, namely those of other planets and their satellites. A Fourier transform infrared spectrometer[38] carried by the spacecraft Voyager 1 has sent back to earth IR emission spectra indicating the presence of several gases, including CH_4, C_2H_6, C_2H_4, C_2H_2, C_3H_8 and, more surprising, methyl acetylene, C_3H_4, and diacetylene, C_4H_2, in the atmosphere of Titan, Saturn's largest moon.[39]

3.8.4 *UV laser remote sensing—LIDAR*

From the Lambert–Beer law (Equation 3.1) it is evident that path-length is the main factor limiting the sensitivity of trace gas determinations, but molar absorptivity is another. By choosing a different wavelength, particularly in the UV instead of the IR, it is possible to get a high molar absorptivity, and hence to determine lower concentrations. The problem of even longer path-lengths is that the light beam is seriously attenuated by any other gaseous components and is scattered by the airborne particulates, so that little light would reach the detector after being reflected back from (say) a mirror on a building 1 km away from the source. This is where the laser comes into its own as a source, because the beam of light is both intense and highly collimated (it diverges only slightly over a long distance but sufficiently to render the beam safe after only a few metres). Finally, it is possible to make use of airborne particulates as minute reflectors distributed all along the light path, so that light reflected back by particles at different distances from the source can be collected by a telescope for measurement (Fig. 3.18). If the light is emitted as very brief pulses by firing the laser at intervals, the time taken by the light to come back to the telescope can be measured: it is proportional to the distance travelled—the radar principle—and we can thus get a measure of the extent of absorption (and thus of the concentration of a particular trace gas) at different distances from the measuring equipment. In order to relate the intensity of light received at the telescope to the concentration of SO_2 in the atmosphere, the laser is switched between two wavelengths corresponding to a peak and a valley in the fine structure of the UV spectrum (Fig. 3.19) and

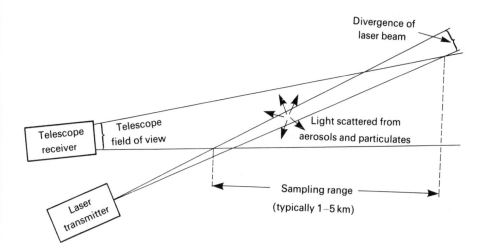

Figure 3.18 The differential absorption LIDAR technique. Courtesy of Dr. Andrew Morrison.

the difference in intensity of the back-scattered beam can be interpreted in terms of average SO_2 concentrations at the selected range. LIDAR stands for light detection and ranging. The technique is capable of producing enough information in a short time to map the SO_2 concentration over a whole town, without the operator ever leaving his measurement station where the laser transmitter and telescope are permanently mounted.

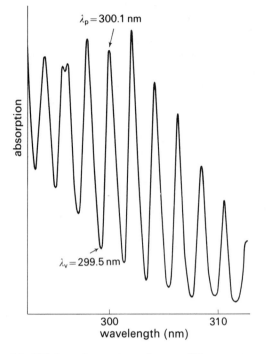

Figure 3.19   Part of the UV absorption spectrum of gaseous SO_2.

3.8.5 *Mass spectrometry*
Molecular ions formed by collision with a beam of accelerated electrons may be sorted according to the mass:charge ratio (m/e) by accelerating them through an electrical potential and deflecting them by a magnetic field, the heavy ions being deflected least (Fig. 3.20). Either the magnetic field or the accelerating potential may be scanned, and the current flowing at the ion-collector is monitored.

Mass spectrometry can be useful for isotopic analysis, e.g. to determine the isotopes of argon in air (Fig. 3.21), but as many small molecules have nearly the same molecular masses (e.g. CO, N_2 and C_2H_4 are all 28) analysis of

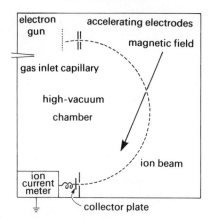

Figure 3.20 Schematic diagram of mass spectrometer.

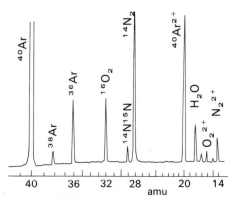

Figure 3.21 Mass spectrum of argon with some air.

mixtures is difficult unless an expensive, high-resolution instrument is available (the precise masses are $CO = 27.995$ m.u., $N_2 = 28.006$ m.u. and $C_2H_4 = 28.032$ m.u.).

The mass spectrometer is finding increasing application as a detector in gas chromatography,[41] where it enables the operator to identify each component of a complex mixture as it comes off the column (see Sections 3.10.6, 4.27 and 7.4.2).

3.8.6 Draeger detector tubes*

These allow spot checks for individual gases or vapours without taking samples back to the laboratory for analysis. A hand-operated bellows pump

---

* Draeger Safety, Draeger House, Sunnyside Road, Chesham, Bucks.

(100 ml per stroke) is used to suck air through a glass tube packed with a selective solid absorbent which gives a colour reaction with the gas in question. The more gas enters the tube, the further the coloured region extends down the packing. The tube has approximate calibration markings on it (e.g. for one or for ten strokes of the pump). Tubes are available for the detection of most common hazardous gases and vapours. The colour reactions used in these tubes are explained in an instructive book published by the makers.[42]

3.9   Sampling of gases and the atmosphere

One approach to sampling involves filling a container which is subsequently connected directly to the measuring equipment. Alternatively, a measured volume of air may be pumped through a suitable absorbent which is later treated to release the trapped trace gas.

3.9.1   *Containers*

Plastic bags are often used to collect gaseous samples: they may be of polyethylene or, better, polyester (oven roasting bags), or Mylar, or of a more inert material such as Tedlar. Ordinary roasting bags are very convenient, and are best contained inside a 1-l glass jar as in Fig. 3.22. Blowing into the

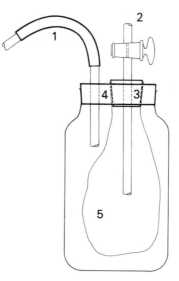

Figure 3.22   Bag in a bottle for air sampling. 1, tube with mouthpiece for emptying bottle; 2, tube for air to pass into bag; 3, smaller bung, carrying 2, cut out of 4, main bung; 5, plastic bag (see text) held between bungs 3 and 4.

space between bag and jar through tube (1) expels the contents of the bag through tap and tube (2), sucking on (1) will serve to fill the bag. If the flow of gas being sampled is fairly fast the bag fills itself.

Gases bubbling up from estuarine sediments through pools of water are best collected in an up-turned separating funnel filled with water. In the authors' laboratory the stoppered funnel can then be fitted directly to a vacuum line and analysed by gas chromatography or IR spectrophotometry. A "grab" sample can be taken by opening the top of an evacuated glass vessel, but these containers should be handled particularly carefully when empty.

If the source of gas is at a slight positive pressure it can be used to blow up a balloon-type container made of silicone rubber. It is then a simple matter to expel the gas through some measuring instrument by squeezing the balloon. These balloons should not be used to keep the air sample for any length of time, as some gases diffuse through the rubber quite fast, and others are strongly absorbed on to it.

3.9.2 Solid adsorption systems

Charcoal is an efficient adsorbent for all manner of vapours in air. A convenient design of tube is shown in Fig. 3.23. Air is pumped through the tube at a rate around $1\,l\,min^{-1}$. In the laboratory the charcoal is washed with a suitable solvent such as CS_2, and the solution is then analysed by gas chromatography[43] (see Section 3.10.10: procedure for air).

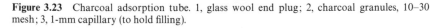

Figure 3.23 Charcoal adsorption tube. 1, glass wool end plug; 2, charcoal granules, 10–30 mesh; 3, 1-mm capillary (to hold filling).

Some porous polymers have also proved very effective adsorbents for vapours in air. (Tenax, Porapak series and Chromosorb series are typical commercial products.[44]) Usually they have to be heated to release the absorbed gases, but they can be reused many times.

3.9.3 Cold traps

Another possible approach, useful for gases as well as vapours, is cold-trapping. The authors have used a glass loop fitted to a gas sampling valve on a gas chromatograph: the loop is immersed in liquid oxygen, (*not* liquid nitrogen, even if it is more readily obtained, as its lower boiling point of $-186°C$ enables it to condense the oxygen (b.p. $\sim 183°C$) of any air sample, soon filling the trap with liquid oxygen). Simple glass traps will stand surprisingly large pressures but the experiment is better read about than repeated at the bench! A slurry of solid carbon dioxide in acetone at $-78°C$ is often quite adequate.

3.9.4 Small "personal" diffusion samplers

Where a mean 8-hour value for a vapour in a working atmosphere is required, the need for air pumps for continuous sampling is avoided by using an open-ended diffusion device.[45] One design takes the form of a lapel badge, in which a piece of charcoal-impregnated cloth is held in a plastic disc under a film of silicone rubber which is permeable to many solvent molecules in the vapour state. The rate of diffusion through the membrane is proportional to the concentration in the atmosphere and can be measured in the laboratory. At the end of the working period the badge is opened and the charcoal cloth is washed with a suitable solvent (n-heptane, for example, in the determination of halogenated solvents and styrene) which is then analysed by gas chromatography.

Another design uses a length of stainless steel tube the size of a fountain pen, worn in the top pocket. The absorbent is fitted into a carefully-measured length of tube, with a short space of the air column between it and the silicone rubber diffusion membrane (intended mainly to keep water out). In the Perkin-Elmer ATD-50 system* the tube is handled by an automatic system which thermally desorbs the trapped vapours and analyses them by gas chromatography. The absorbent is therefore never handled in the open laboratory, and can be re-used many times.

3.9.5 Liquid absorption systems

An attractive feature of this approach is the selectivity attainable by careful choice of the chemistry of the absorption reaction of the gas in contact with a suitable solution. The key is to choose an appropriate absorbent, and to effect a long contact time and efficient transfer of the trace gas from the air to the solution. Some kind of disperser is used to break the air stream into tiny bubbles, and a little surfactant such as propanol may be added to give a modest amount of foaming—all inducive to efficient gas–liquid extraction. Many designs have been suggested, three of them shown in Fig. 3.24.

3.9.6 Efficiency of absorption

It should not be assumed that any of the absorption systems described works with 100% efficiency for all gases: the performance must be checked in each case, and the following factors should be considered.

---

* Perkin-Elmer Ltd., Beaconsfield, Bucks., England.

(1) *Pumping rate.* The impinger needs to have an adequate pumping rate in order to break up the bubbles and give an adequate contact time. Slow pumping rates give low recoveries.

(2) *Concentration of trace gas.* It is not safe to assume that because the efficiency is good for high concentrations it will be so for low levels. Dissociation of complexes and solubility of precipitates can cause problems in the determination of low levels of trace gases, while break-through after the absorption capacity has been reached will give losses from higher concentrations.

(3) *Temperature and humidity.*

(4) Presence of *incompatible pairs of gases*, which apparently do not react at low concentrations simply because the rate of reaction is too slow, may react when concentrated in an absorption vessel. Thus SO_2 and O_3 or SO_2 and H_2S may give difficulty.

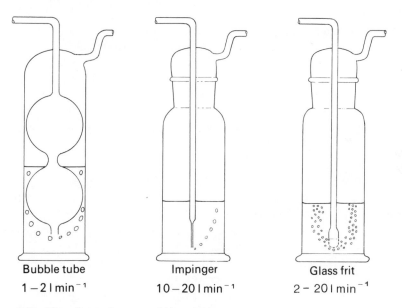

Bubble tube	Impinger	Glass frit
$1-2\,l\,min^{-1}$	$10-20\,l\,min^{-1}$	$2-20\,l\,min^{-1}$

Figure 3.24   Three designs for gas-scrubbing vessels.

It is possible to assess efficiency by pumping through two traps in series and determining the amount of gas caught in each, but a better approach is to use a standard gas mixture if one can be made or bought. The bag-in-the-bottle described earlier can be used to prepare some mixtures: e.g. 1000 ppm of methane and other light hydrocarbons in air, by filling a glass pipette with the gas and flushing it into the bag in a stream of air. Four of five components can be added to make a mixture, but it must be left to stand for at least half an hour to mix thoroughly. The preparation of gas mixtures has been reviewed by Barratt.[46]

Permeation tubes are particularly useful when reactive gases have to be handled.[47] A small amount of the gas is sealed under pressure into a plastic tube or a glass tube with a plastic stopper (usually fitted at low temperature). The gas diffuses out through the plastic at a constant rate as long as some liquid remains in the tube and the temperature remains constant. For SO_2 (3.8 atmospheres) some stiff polyethylene or Teflon tubing sealed with two ball bearings suffices. For gases with a higher vapour pressure (e.g. H_2S, ~19 atmospheres; NH_3, 10.7 atmospheres) Klockow's design, (see Fig. 3.25) based on a Teflon greaseless stopcock with a hole bored down the plug, is convenient and satisfactory.[48] These tubes are calibrated by weighing each day: losses of the order of 1 μg min^{-1} are typical.

3.10   Gas chromatography

Gas chromatography is probably the single most useful analytical technique for most analytical chemists engaged in environmental studies, particularly if these are concerned with gases or organics. The wide field of application of the technique will become evident from the number of times it is referred to in this text (see in particular Sections 4.26, 4.27 and Chapter 7). The application to gas analysis has been described in detail by Jeffery and Kipping.[49]

3.10.1   *Partition between a moving phase and a stationary phase*

In Section 2.7.2 the partition of a solute between two equilibrated liquid phases was discussed in some detail, and the discussion was expanded to show how separation of the phases, repeated extractions and stripping could be used to improve the separation of similar compounds. In chromatography, this concept is extended further, so that one phase (the mobile phase) moves continually in contact with the other (the stationary phase). In simple column liquid chromatography, the solute is present in a solution washed down a column packed with a solid absorbent, such as alumina or silica gel. The solvent is the mobile, liquid, phase, and the alumina or silica gel is the stationary, solid, phase. In gas chromatography (GC) two different modes of action are employed, namely gas–solid chromatography (GSC) and gas–liquid chromatography (GLC), but both use the same experimental arrangement. The mobile phase is always a gas, usually nitrogen or helium, but sometimes hydrogen or argon.

Solid phases include active charcoal (for separation of air, CO, CH_4, CO_2, light hydrocarbons), active alumina (for light hydrocarbons), silica gel (for CO_2, light hydrocarbons), porous polymers such as Porapak, Chromosorb, Tenax (for many polar gases), and molecular sieves such as 5A (for H_2, O_2, N_2, CH_4, CO).

Liquid phases are retained in position by coating on to solid phases such as

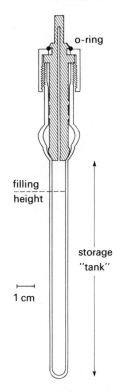

Figure 3.25 Permeation tube for H_2S by Teckentrup and Klockow (1978).[48] Reproduced by courtesy of *Analytical Chemistry*.

finely divided minerals, e.g. diatomaceous earths. The solid is slurried with a solution of the liquid phase and the solvent is evaporated, leaving a powder with a loading of 3–20 % w/w of liquid phase. The powder still feels quite dry because the specific surface area is very large. The essential properties of a liquid phase are (a) negligible vapour pressure over a range of temperatures, (b) good thermal stability, and (c) selective attraction for the compounds to be determined. There are very many liquid phases to choose from (see catalogues from chemical supply houses*), but three broad classes find very wide application. Silicone oils have relatively low polarity (depending on substituents) and are best for separating low to medium polarity compounds such as hydrocarbons, esters, and even phenols. Long-chain esters are best for polar compounds (e.g. SO_2, alcohols, esters, acids). Ethylene glycol polymers often offer good selectivity for special cases such as for aromatic hydrocarbons in the presence of aliphatic hydrocarbons.

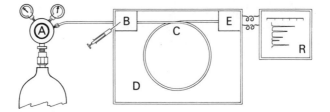

Figure 3.26 Schematic diagram of a gas chromatograph. *A*, carrier gas supply; *B*, injection port (for syringe) or gas-inlet valve; *C*, column in oven (*D*) along with detector (*E*); *R*, recorder.

3.10.2 *The gas chromatograph*
Figure 3.26 shows a basic gas chromatograph. Samples are injected into a column and vaporized, and the various components then migrate through the column at different rates: some spend more time adsorbed on the stationary phase, others less. Each component is detected when it reaches the end of the column, and the electrical signal thus generated is recorded as a function of time to give a chromatogram, such as that in Fig. 3.27 for a mixture of butanes and pentanes (Camping Gaz). Peaks can be seen for five major components. The individual components of a gas chromatograph are described briefly in Sections 3.10.3 to 3.10.6.

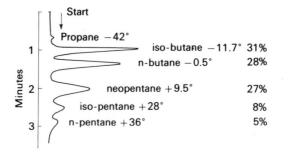

Figure 3.27 Gas-chromatographic analysis of Camping Gaz with boiling point and proportion (in % v/v) for each component.

3.10.3 *The carrier gas flow control system*
Gas is taken from a cylinder at high pressure via a two-stage regulator. The pressure applied to the column is held at 10–50 psig, (or 70–350 kN m^{-2}) or the flow-rate through the column is stabilized at 10–60 ml min^{-1}.

---

*e.g. Supelco Inc., Bellefonte, Pennsylvania 16823, USA. (Atlas-Bioscan, 7 Vikings Way, Canvey Island, Essex, UK).

3.10.4   *The sample injection system*

A silicone rubber septum through which the hypodermic needle of a microlitre syringe can be inserted is suitable for liquid samples. It is possible to inject gaseous samples directly from a 1-ml syringe (take care not to take your finger off the plunger: it can hit the ceiling when propelled by 50 psig gas pressure!), but gas-sampling valves are more satisfactory. The six-port rotary valve is in widespread use and gives excellent repeatability ($\pm < \frac{1}{2}\%$) much better than that attainable with a hand-operated syringe ($\pm 5\%$ at the 10-μl level). The valve allows a loop of stainless steel pipe to be switched first into a flow stream of the sample gas, and then straight into the carrier gas flow stream and on to the column. With care these can be used at reduced pressure, but regular cleaning and regreasing are important if leaks are to be avoided.

The injection port is usually heated to ensure rapid vaporization of sample, thus making for sharper peaks as components are eluted.

3.10.5   *The column*

Columns are typically made from 2-m lengths of glass or stainless steel tubing coiled in a circle. They are connected by compression fittings to the gas flow system. Outside diameters of 3, 4.5 or 6 mm are usual. The column is housed in an oven, the temperature of which may be kept constant (isothermal operation) or gradually increased during the run (temperature programming). When temperature programming is used, or if a thermal conductivity detector is necessary, the two columns are required, the second acting as a reference gas stream to minimize baseline drift.

3.10.6   *The detector*

The detector "sees" each component as it comes off the column. The important parameters of a detector include dynamic range, sensitivity, selectivity to certain types of compounds, speed of response, and linearity of response. These parameters are satisfied to varying degrees by different detectors and for different compounds. Table 3.3 summarizes the performances of several common detectors; these have been reviewed fully by Gough and Walker.[50]

A thermal conductivity detector measures loss of heat from a small filament or thermistor bead heated by passage of an electric current and cooled by the flow of carrier gas. When a sample component passes through the detector the change in thermal conductivity modifies the operating temperature which causes a measurable change in electrical resistance. Two detector elements (one for the sample column, one for the reference column) are connected in a balanced Wheatstone bridge circuit (Fig. 3.28) and the output is fed directly to a chart recorder (1 or 10 mV full-scale). Low temperature

Table 3.3 Detectors for gas chromatography

Type	Abbreviation	Comments	Linear dynamic range	Sensitivity
Thermal conductivity (katharometer)	TCD	Detects anything in a He carrier, especially permanent gases. Ar is used as a carrier for H_2 detection	wide	modest
Flame ionization	FID	Useful general purpose detector; does not respond to permanent gases or CS_2	very wide	good
Electron capture	ECD	Very good for halogenated organic compounds; non-linear response; also used for NO_2	restricted	very good
Argon ionization (or helium ionization)	AID	Needs a small radioactive source to produce metastable Ar atoms	wide	very good
Flame photometer	FPD	Filter transmitting at 394 nm for detection of S as S_2 or at 526 nm for detection of P as HPO; has been used for H_2S, CH_3SH and SO_2 in air	restricted	good
Infrared spectrophotometer	IR	Fast-scanning Fourier-transform instruments can give a complete spectrum for each compound to assist identification	narrow	poor
Mass spectrometer	MS	The ultimate detector for quantitation and identification if coupled directly to a computer with rapid access to stored reference spectra, programmed to make comparisons	wide	good

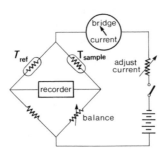

Figure 3.28 Electrical circuit for katharometer thermal-conductivity detector. T, thermistor beads in the two gas streams.

thermistors tolerate oxygen while the higher-temperature hot-wire detectors do not. The bridge current should be optimized for the carrier gas, as shown in Fig. 3.29. These detectors are essential for the determination of permanent gases, but are useful for many compounds if the amounts are not too small.

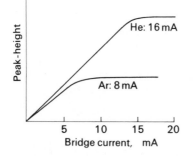

Figure 3.29 Variation of peak height with bridge current, showing the optimum values for two carrier gases with small thermistor beads.

The flame ionization detector measures the electrical conductivity of a tiny hydrogen flame into which flows the carrier gas coming off the column. The hydrogen flame itself produces virtually no ions while most organic compounds burn to produce ions and electrons. This detector exhibits a very wide linear response to nearly all organic compounds and is accordingly the most commonly employed for general purpose work. The disadvantage is the need for supplies of hydrogen and of clean air for the flame.

The electron-capture detector offers particularly high sensitivity towards compounds containing halogens and is favoured for the determination of traces of pesticides. The linearity of response is not good. *The flame photometric detector* measures molecular emission of the S_2 and HPO species at 394 nm and 526 nm respectively and offers excellent selectivity for the organophosphorus pesticides like Parathion and Dichlorvos.

3.10.7 Optimizing performance
A little time and effort spent on optimization pays high dividends when awkward samples have to be analysed. It is useful to be able to measure the efficiency in terms of the number of theoretical plates (N) in the column (i.e. the number of simple distillations which would be needed to achieve the same separation), by comparing the width of the peak (t_w) with the time it takes to come off the column, t_R (Fig. 3.30).

$$N = 16 \cdot \left(\frac{t_R}{t_w}\right)^2 \tag{3.2}$$

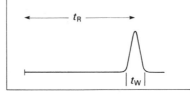

Figure 3.30   Parameters for calculation of number of theoretical plates for a column.

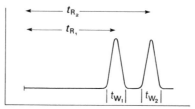

Figure 3.31   Parameters for calculation of the resolving power of a column for two specified compounds.

For 2 m columns, values of around 1000 are not uncommon, giving a height-equivalent to a theoretical plate (HETP) of 2 mm.

The resolving power (R) refers to the separation of two peaks relative to their average width and can only be quoted for a selected pair of compounds.

$$R = 2 \cdot \frac{(t_{R_2} - t_{R_1})}{(t_{w_1} - t_{w_2})} \tag{3.3}$$

Two important factors which affect performance are carrier gas flow-rate and temperature.

The effect of carrier gas flow-rate is described by the van Deemter equation, which relates the HETP to the flow-rate of the carrier gas, f:

$$\text{HETP} = A + \frac{B}{f} + Cf. \tag{3.4}$$

The shape of a typical curve (Fig. 3.32) shows that there is an optimum flow-rate to achieve the minimum HETP, i.e. the greatest efficiency.

At high flow-rates the sample molecules no longer have time to equilibrate between gas and liquid, taking a significant time to diffuse out of the liquid film, so the C-factor (resistance to mass transfer in the liquid) is significant. Thinner films (lower mass loadings of stationary phase) help here, but are more easily overloaded with sample.

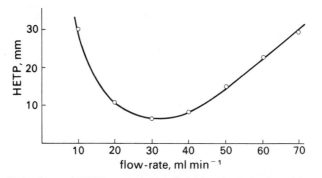
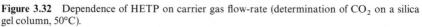

Figure 3.32 Dependence of HETP on carrier gas flow-rate (determination of CO_2 on a silica gel column, 50°C).

At low flow-rates the natural backwards diffusion of the sample molecules becomes significant, thus broadening the peaks, while the A-factor—constant at all flow-rates—represents the variation in path length as the gas stream flows round each particle down the column. Smaller particles improve efficiencies, but then a higher input pressure is needed to maintain the flow-rate.

To emphasize that these phenomena are not of purely academic interest, but can seriously affect the efficiency of analytical procedures, Fig. 3.33 shows some chromatograms run at different flow-rates (input pressure was measured) for CO_2. These chromatograms were used to calculate the points in the previous figure.

The effect of temperature is more complicated, but just as important. The columns must be held at a sufficiently high temperature to ensure a

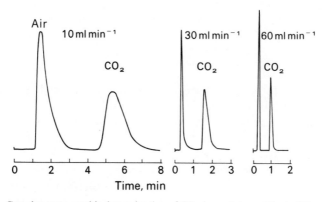

Figure 3.33 Gas-chromatographic determination of CO_2 in a mixture with air. Silica gel, 50°C, various carrier gas flow-rates.

reasonable vapour pressure of the sample molecules—it can be above or below the boiling point, but generally the performance is better at lower temperatures. It then becomes a matter for compromise, since the retention times increase at lower temperatures, and the analysis becomes slower. Chromatograms are shown in Fig. 3.34 for a mixture of light hydrocarbons run at three different temperatures: in this case cooling the column in a small refrigerator to −12°C effected a significant improvement in the resolution.

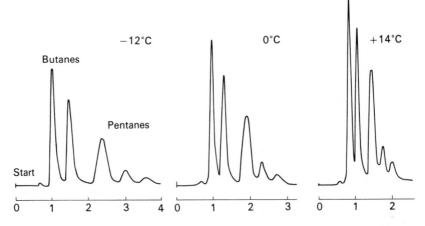

Figure 3.34 Effect of temperature in a gas-chromatographic separation: mixture of butanes and pentanes separated on a bis(methoxyethyl)adipate column. Time scale in minutes.

The boiling points range from −11.7° (isobutane) to +36° (n-pentane). Figure 3.35 shows that for the two butanes, it is the relative change in retention time which matters as this affects the resolution. The HETP for n-butane remained at 4 ± 0.5 mm for the full range of temperatures.

3.10.8   Temperature programming

When a sample contains a mixture of components with a wide range of boiling points, there is no one temperature which will give satisfactory performance for all the components. In such cases, for example hydrocarbon fuel fractions (kerosene is a 150–300° distillation cut) or methyl esters of fatty acids (C_{10}, 224°C to C_{18}, 442°), increasing the temperature of the column steadily through the analysis allows good separations to be obtained, as shown in Fig. 3.36 for a sample of kerosene. Stationary liquid phases, which tend to break down at high temperatures (a process called bleeding) give rise to an increasing background as the column heats up. Drift in the detector

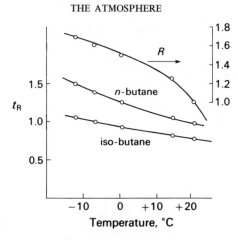

Figure 3.35 Effect of temperature in a gas-chromatographic separation: *n*- and isobutane. Retention time, t_R, and resolving power, R, as a function of temperature.

base-line can be minimized by using two columns, each with its own detector, one being used as a reference.

3.10.9 *Quantitation in gas chromatography*

The simplest approach is to measure the height of each peak, and compare samples with standards run under the same conditions. However, even if the detector exhibits a linear response to a wide range of concentrations of analyte, complications in the column leading to peak-broadening (typically

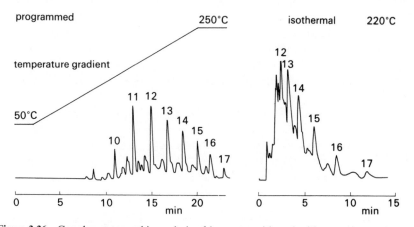

Figure 3.36 Gas-chromatographic analysis of kerosene, with and without temperature programming, on a silicone oil column.

overloading of the column or behaviour following a non-linear absorption isotherm) can result in a marked curvature of calibration graphs. In such cases it is preferable to measure peak *area*—the true total signal for each component. This can be done by triangulation (rough and not recommended), by cutting and weighing (a little tedious but reliable and with satisfactory precision), or by using a computing integrator instead of the chart recorder (more expensive but very convenient).

In gas analysis a set of loops of different volumes may be used to establish a calibration, or one loop may be filled via a vacuum line to different pressures—a very fast and convenient method as long as the valve does not leak.

For liquid samples, solutions at the 1 % or 0.1 % level may be prepared, and 5-μl or 10-μl portions injected. Many workers prefer to use the internal standard method: both sample and standard are spiked with the same concentration of some compound which is not present in the sample, and concentrations are calculated by simple proportion. For dilute solutions when an FID is used, calibrations are linear over 3–4 orders of magnitude, so this approach is satisfactory.

Grob[51] has reviewed general techniques for determining a large number of ultra-trace organics in air samples, and Grob and Grob[52] have discussed the application of capillary columns to this problem. These enable very high resolution to be obtained, and are more compatible with a mass spectrometer for identification work than are conventional columns.

3.10.10 *Determination of aromatic hydrocarbons in exhaust, in petrol and in air*
Benzene and toluene, as well as other aromatic hydrocarbons, are present in petrol (around 5 % and 10 % v/v respectively) and also appear at low levels in automobile exhaust gases along with other unburned fuel components.[53] From an environmental point of view, benzene is of interest as the TLV is only 10 ppm v/v (30 mg m^{-3}). Exhaust gases have been shown to contain a few hundred mg m^{-3} of unburned aromatics,[54] while the air beside a petrol pump in operation at a filling station can have benzene levels close to the TLV.

These levels of aromatics are easily determined by GLC with an FID and a poly(ethylene glycol) stationary phase (Carbowax 1540) run at 90°C. The standards are prepared as 0.1 % v/v solutions in carbon disulphide (work in an efficient fume-hood). Carbon disulphide is used because it gives a negligible response with the FID and there is no problem of tailing of the solvent peak.

Procedure for exhaust gas: bag-in-bottle sampling. Flush out and fill a 1-l bag-in-bottle sampler with exhaust gas through a CaCl$_2$ drying tube by placing the tap-tube inside the exhaust pipe of the vehicle. If possible, collect samples at different engine speeds.

Procedure for O_2, N_2, *CO.* Use a 1-ml loop on the sampling valve, twin 5-A molecular sieve columns at 40°C with 25 psig of helium carrier gas and a thermal conductivity detector. Cut out and weigh the peaks, using air (21 % O_2 + Ar, 79 % N_2) as standard. Use the same factor for N_2 and for CO if no pure CO is available (the error is not very big).

Determination of aromatic hydrocarbons. Use a 1-ml loop on the sampling valve, a single Carbowax 1540 column at 90°C with 10 psig of nitrogen carrier gas and a flame ionization detector. It is sufficient to measure peak-heights. Inject 10-μl portions of solutions of the individual compounds (for class work each student should prepare a different standard) and note both retention time (for identification) and peak-height (for quantitation).

Procedure for air (active-charcoal adsorption tube.) Fill a tube with freshly solvent-washed, dried, and activated (heat to 600°C in nitrogen) charcoal (as in Fig. 3.23) and close the ends with rubber plugs. At the sampling site, pump 10 l of air (at 1–2 l/min) through the tube (two large plastic aspirators, one full of water, can be used if a portable sampling pump is not available) and close the ends again. In the laboratory, wash the charcoal with 10 ml of Analar grade carbon disulphide, collecting it in a 10-ml standard flask. Make to the mark, mix, and inject 5 μl on to the column. Quantify the results by comparison with the standards (see Ref. 16, p. 894).

Procedure for petrol. Dilute 0.1 ml of petrol to 10 ml with carbon disulphide, mix well, and inject a 5-μl portion. Identify the peaks where possible, and quantify.

Calculations. Benzene is measured out by volume (a microlitre pipette): 10 μl = 8.8 mg are in the flask. By simple proportion you can find the weight of benzene in 10 l of air (and 1000 l = 1 m³) and the volume of benzene in 0.1 ml of petrol. Quote results as mg m³ for air and % v/v for petrol. Figure 3.37 shows a specimen chromatogram for petrol with some of the peaks identified.

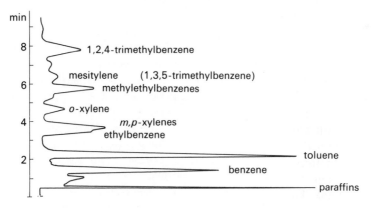

Figure 3.37 Gas chromatogram of aromatics in 5-star petrol. Carbowax 1540 column at 90°C; sample 1 % v/v in CS_2.

3.10.11 *Determination of low levels of carbon monoxide — catalytic conversion*

The permanent gases must usually be determined by thermal conductivity measurement as the FID is insensitive to them. With good modern TCD's 10 ppm of carbon monoxide can be determined (TLV = 100 ppm), but lower levels, such as those in urban air or exhaled breath, need a different approach. Use can be made of the hydrogen supply available for an FID to reduce carbon monoxide to methane over a nickel catalyst at 350°C in a small tubular reactor fitted between the column and the detector, as shown in Fig. 3.38.[55] A number of other difficult compounds can also be reduced: carbon dioxide should be reduced after the column, formaldehyde before the column.

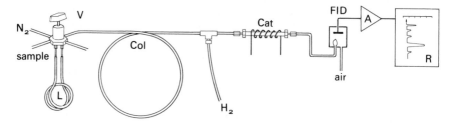

Figure 3.38 Gas-chromatographic determination of CO by catalytic reduction to CH_4. A, amplifier matching output of FID to recorder R; Cat, nickel deposited on fine brick dust in stainless steel tube heated to 350°C; Col, molecular sieve 5A at 50°C. With temperature programming to 250°C, CO_2 can also be determined. L, sample loop on six-port rotary gas-sampling valve V.

3.11   Some chemical methods for determining trace gases

The methods discussed in this section all start with pumping a measured volume of air through an appropriately chosen absorption solution at a controlled rate. Selectivity depends partly on this stage, but accuracy is very heavily reliant on the efficiency of the absorption step. Selectivity is aided by the choice of the determination step, and to get good sensitivity, this often employs a colour reaction and finishes with a photometric measurement.

Spectrophotometer cells, of 1, 2 or 4 cm path-length should be cleaned thoroughly (overnight in sulphuric acid–potassium dichromate mixture) and checked with water (or solvent) in both for identical blank absorbance. If a solvent-extraction step is included in the procedure run the solution through a plug of cotton wool to hold back droplets of water. Calibrations should involve about five different amounts (or concentrations) and also a complete reagent blank. The working range should cover absorbances between 0.2 and 0.8.

3.11.1   *Sulphur-containing gases in the atmosphere*

Two gases, H_2S and SO_2, are particularly important and present an interesting case of co-existence of two species which, from thermodynamic considerations, should react together. However, the slow rate of reaction, determined by the very low concentrations, makes it possible for these two gases to be present simultaneously. It should be remembered, though, that when pre-concentrated from an air sample the two gases may react with each other, and with ozone or oxygen.

Hydrogen sulphide is produced by reduction of sulphate and organosulphur compounds by the bacterium *Desulfovibrio desulfuricans,* and may be accompanied by methane thiol ($CH_3 \cdot SH$), dimethyl sulphide ($CH_3 \cdot S \cdot CH_3$), dimethyl disulphide ($CH_3 \cdot S \cdot S \cdot CH_3$) and carbonyl sulphide (COS). The odours of all of these species are objectionable even at very low concentrations, and the toxicity hazard of H_2S is exacerbated by the ease with which the sense of smell becomes paralysed by its presence. The TLV is 10 ppm. As H_2S is quite easily oxidized by oxygen in air, it must be trapped as an insoluble metal sulphide (CdS, ZnS, HgS or Ag_2S) in the absorption reagent.

Sulphur dioxide is released to the atmosphere in enormous quantities on combustion of fossil fuels (of the order of 10^8 tons per year over the whole world), and is responsible for injury to plants (trees in particular) and damage to building stone (particularly carbonates such as dolomite, limestone and marble). It is detectable by smell at levels above 1 ppm (TLV is 2 ppm) and causes severe irritation of the nose and throat. The gas may be selectively absorbed from a stream of air by bubbling through a solution of tetra-chloromercurate ion as the sulphitochloromercurate complex $(HgCl_2 \cdot SO_3)^{2-}$.

3.11.2   *Determination of H_2S*

Pump 100–500 l of air at 10–15 l min^{-1} through 100 ml of absorption solution in a standard gas wash bottle with fritted glass disperser. The preferred absorbent is a suspension of cadmium hydroxide: transfer to the wash bottle 50 ml of a 1 % solution of 3 $CdSO_4 \cdot 8H_2O$ and add 50 ml of 0.1 M sodium hydroxide solution. The pH remains fairly neutral (pH 7). An alternative absorbent, which has much better long-term stability, is 0.25 % w/v zinc acetate solution.

To ensure that no sulphide is lost as particles adsorbed on to the glass, the reagents for the colour reaction must be added to the wash bottle after pumping has stopped. The usual procedure for determination is the methylene blue method, which is simple, fast, sensitive and selective. Unfortunately, both the reagent and the coloured product are unstable. The ethylene blue variation, however, does not suffer from these drawbacks.[56] The reaction is an oxidative coupling of two aromatic rings:

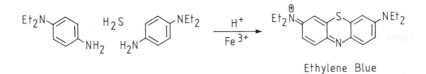

Ethylene Blue

The ion-pair with perchlorate is readily extracted into chloroform, which can be used to improve the sensitivity and reduce interferences from other coloured compounds (e.g. in the analysis of waters or sediments).

Procedure. Add to the 100 ml of absorbent in the wash bottle 2 ml of 1 M sodium perchlorate, 1 ml of 2 % w/v *N,N*-diethyl-*p*-phenylenediamine in 50 % w/v sulphuric acid, and 1 ml of a filtered 10 % w/v solution of iron(III) ammonium sulphate dissolved in 1 M sulphuric acid. After 10 min, transfer the solution to a separating funnel, extract twice with 10 ml of chloroform, then combine the extracts and make up to 25 ml. Measure the absorbance in 10-mm or 40-mm cells at 670 nm. Calibration, using a stock solution of sodium sulphide prepared by weighing out crystals washed in ethanol and dried on filter paper, is over the range 1–10 μg of sulphide.

A gas-phase *UV molecular absorption* method has been shown to offer quite good sensitivity for the determination of H_2S after collection in zinc acetate and also of sulphide in estuarine sediments.[57] The sample is acidified with hydrochloric acid and the liberated gas is swept in a stream of nitrogen down a 20-cm path-length optical cell, positioned where the flame would normally be in an atomic absorption spectrophotometer. The absorbance is recorded continuously: each sample gives a narrow pulse as its sulphide is liberated and carried through the cell. A magnesium hollow-cathode lamp may be used with the spectrometer tuned to the 202-nm line. Operation is similar to that for the determination of mercury (see Section 6.15.1). Figure 3.39 shows a typical set of calibration peaks for this determination, which is simple, fast, and tolerates most other species likely to be present in estuarine sediments.

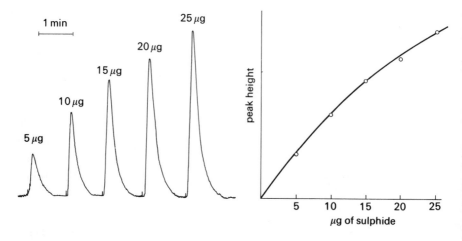

Figure 3.39   UV molecular absorption determination of sulphide at 202 nm.

3.11.3   *Determination of SO$_2$*

A useful method for the determination of SO_2 is based on the formation of an aminomethane sulphonic acid of a triphenylmethane dye, the West and Gaeke method.[58] The reagent itself becomes colourless when protonated, while the Schiff base, being the salt of a strong acid, is not protonated and remains coloured. The reaction, which involves coupling with formaldehyde, is specific for sulphur dioxide.

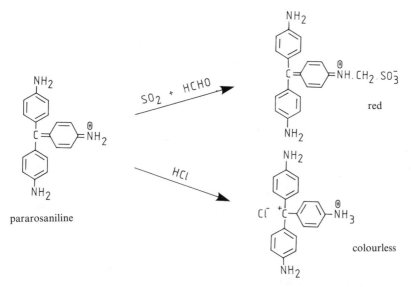

Procedure. Pump 30–60 l of air through 10 ml absorption solution (13.6 g HgCl$_2$ and 7.5 g KCl in 1 l water) in a small impinger at 1–2 l min^{-1}. Then add 1 ml of dilute pararosaniline reagent solution (4 ml of a 1 % aqueous solution acidified with 6 ml of concentrated hydrochloric acid and diluted to 100 ml with water) and 1 ml of 0.2 % formaldehyde solution (5 ml of commercial 40 % solution diluted to 1 l with water). After 20–30 min measure the absorbance at 560 nm. A dilute sodium sulphite solution checked iodometrically is used as the standard.[59]

While the pararosaniline method offers good sensitivity and selectivity and is widely used for air quality monitoring, problems can arise if a good grade of reagent is not used. An alternative method is advocated by the British Standards Institute[60] for 24-h average samples. Air is pumped at 1–2 l min^{-1} through 0.3 % hydrogen peroxide solution (10 ml of commercial 30 % hydrogen peroxide) diluted to 1 l, pretitrated to pH 4.5, and then the solution is titrated again, with 0.005 M sodium carbonate, to the same end point: 1 ml of 0.005 M titrant = 320 μg of sulphur dioxide. The method assumes that other acidic gases in the atmosphere will be present at much lower levels than SO$_2$ and will therefore not interfere. Because very large volumes are sampled (2–4 m^3) the sensitivity is adequate for routine atmospheric monitoring.

3.11.4 *Oxides of nitrogen in the atmosphere*

Three compounds are of interest here: N$_2$O, NO and NO$_2$, and all three can be found in the atmosphere at low concentrations. Because they have different toxicological properties, it is important to be able to distinguish between them. One method which can do this is IR spectrophotometry with a long-path cell. Figure 3.40 shows the IR spectrum of a mixture of oxides of nitrogen.

Dinitrogen oxide, N_2O (commonly called laughing gas, or nitrous oxide), occurs in clean air at around 0.3 ppm, as the breakdown product of nitrogenous compounds, from microbial dinitrification of nitrate in anaerobic

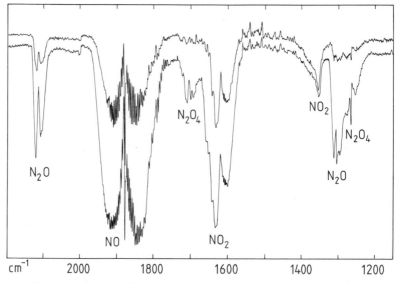

Figure 3.40   IR spectrum of oxides of nitrogen.

zones of soils, and also arising from combustion of explosives. It is a stable gas, shows no harmful effects at low levels, and is detectable by smell only at high concentrations. Determination in air by long-path IR, and at higher concentrations by GC (Chromosorb 101 at room temperature with TCD) is recommended.

Nitric oxide, NO, should, from thermodynamic considerations, react with oxygen to give nitrogen dioxide, but as the reaction is very slow at low concentrations, the gas does occur in air and should be determined as such. At high temperatures (e.g. 2000°C in a natural gas–air flame) the reaction $N_2 + O_2 \rightarrow 2NO$ reaches an equilibrium, with about 1 % conversion. If the reaction products are cooled rapidly (as when flame gases are mixed with ambient air) the equilibrium is frozen. Significantly more NO has been found in the air near a domestic gas cooker after conversion from town gas $(H_2 + CO)$ to natural gas (CH_4). Petrol and diesel engines, and gas turbine engines, produce considerable quantities of NO as a byproduct (several thousand ppm in exhaust gas), which subsequently is oxidized to nitrogen dioxide. It is difficult to say whether nitric oxide itself represents a serious danger to health, though it is known to combine with haemoglobin in the blood, because at higher concentrations in air it is always accompanied by the dioxide, which is a known hazard. The TLV is 2 ppm.

Nitrogen dioxide, NO_2, is the brown gas seen in the waste gases from sulphuric acid plants working on the lead-chamber process. It is in equilibrium with a dimer, particularly at lower temperatures, which is colourless.

$$N_2O_4 \underset{\text{cold}}{\overset{\text{hot}}{\rightleftharpoons}} 2NO_2.$$

It is detectable by its smell at 0.1 ppm (TLV 3 ppm), but on prolonged exposure one ceases to be aware of it, and may then inhale dangerous concentrations, even sufficient to cause death some time after exposure.

3.11.5 *Determination of NO_x*

Use may be made of triethanolamine to selectively absorb NO_2 from an airstream, to effect separation. The NO is then oxidized by chromium trioxide to NO_2, and each gas can be determined separately by the Salzmann method, which involves diazotization of N(1-naphthyl)-ethylene diamine and coupling to sulphanilic acid, followed by a spectrophotometric measurement (see Section 4.16.2). Alternatively one sample of air can be pumped directly through the Salzmann absorption solution for determination of NO_2, and a second via an oxidizing tube for determination of $NO + NO_2$.

The *oxidizing reagent* is prepared by soaking ground-up fire-brick in 17% w/v CrO_3 in water (*care!*) for 30 min. The granules are dried at 110°C then conditioned overnight in air at 70% relative humidity (a tray of the granules over a dish of a saturated solution of sodium acetate in a closed container).

The *absorbing reagent* is made by dissolving 5 g of anhydrous sulphanilic acid in 800 ml of water and 140 ml of glacial acetic acid, with gentle warming if necessary. Cool the solution, add 20 ml of 0.1% N-(1-naphthyl)-ethylenediamine dihydrochloride in water and dilute to 1 l. This solution will keep several months in a refrigerator.

Procedure. Pump 1.0 l of air (or enough to give a colour) through 10 ml of this solution in a small impinger at 0.05 l min^{-1} (this low flow rate is necessary to allow efficient oxidation by the solid granules), or at 0.4 l min^{-1} if only NO_2 is being determined. Wait 15 min and measure the absorbance at 550 nm. One ml of a 0.0203 g/l solution of sodium nitrite is equivalent to 10 μl of NO or NO_2 and gives a measurable absorbance (see Ref. 16, pp. 818 and 822).

Automatic analysers for NO_x make use of the chemiluminescent reaction between NO and O_3, measuring the red light emitted

$$NO + O_3 \rightarrow NO_2 + O_2 + h\nu.$$

The operating pressure is rather critical, but the method is sufficiently sensitive to allow ambient concentrations to be detected. Higher levels, as in vehicle exhaust gases, present no difficulty.

3.11.6 *Oxides of carbon in the atmosphere*

The seasonal variation of the atmospheric level of *carbon dioxide* has been referred to earlier[61] (Section 2.5.2). The annual addition to the atmosphere of carbon dioxide from burning of fossil fuels is of the order of 10^{10} tons, but most of this is assimilated by plants (photosynthesis) or by the oceans (dissolution). Exhaled breath typically contains 4–5% CO_2, automobile exhaust 7–13% CO_2, while fermentation processes produce an atmosphere in the vats of close to 100% CO_2, so that in any enclosed space where these sources are present, significantly, if not dangerously high CO_2 levels may be present. The TLV is 5000 ppm, (0.5% v/v) and levels over 5% can be lethal.

Plants, however, not only tolerate but actually respond favourably to enriched CO_2 levels: concentrations of up to 0.1% CO_2 in air give usefully increased fruit yields (e.g. from tomatoes) and may be encountered in large glass-houses (particularly if there is a brewery nearby as a source of cheap CO_2).

Carbon dioxide may be determined by IR spectrophotometry, by gas chromatography, (silica gel column at 50°C) or by a wet-chemistry titration method (see below).

Carbon monoxide is produced by incomplete combustion of carbonaceous fuels, particularly in the internal combustion engine, where it may constitute 1–4% v/v of the exhaust gas (reaching higher values when the engine is running at high speed with less efficient combustion). Cigarette smoke also contains carbon monoxide—up to 2%. Carbon monoxide is toxic to man: 0.1% v/v of CO in the air will block half of the haemoglobin in the blood of a man breathing that air, and 100 ppm of CO will, over a period of time, give a noticeable feeling of drowsiness. The cure is fresh air (or extra oxygen) as the combination with haemoglobin is reversible. The TLV is 50 ppm. Carbon monoxide may be determined by IR spectrophotometry, by gas chromatography (molecular sieve, 5 A at 50°C) or by colour reaction in a selective gas-detector tube (Draeger Ltd.).

3.11.7   *Determination of CO_2*

A very old method based on absorption in a solution of barium hydroxide (giving a precipitate of barium carbonate) with back-titration of the excess of barium hydroxide, is still widely used. There is, however, a surprising problem: though CO_2 should dissolve completely in the strongly alkaline solution (typically pH 12), in practice it does so slowly, so that care must be taken to ensure that small bubbles of air are produced, and that these have a long contact time with the absorbing solution. Addition of a few drops of propan-1-ol will lower the surface tension and cause mild foaming, particularly if a glass frit disperser (coarse porosity) is used in a 100-ml gas wash bottle, sufficient to give an acceptable recovery. Two simple procedures are available.

Procedure 1—pumping method. Pipette 50 ml of approximately 0.01 M $Ba(OH)_2$ solution (prepared in advance, decanted after standing and standardized against 0.01 M hydrochloric acid) into a 100-ml gas wash bottle, add a few drops of propan-1-ol, pump 10 l of air through it via a coarse glass frit at 1 l min^{-1}. Add a few drops of phenolphthalein indicator solution and titrate with the standard 0.01 M hydrochloric acid until the pink colour just disappears, taking care not to mix in any more air (put a plug of cotton wool round the burette tip, or keep a stream of nitrogen gas flowing over the barium hydroxide solution).

Procedure 2—Wagner's bottle method.[62] Pipette 15 ml of approximately 0.01 M $Ba(OH)_2$ solution into a 2.5-l bottle of air (filled by emptying water out of the bottle at the sampling site), add a few drops of propan-1-ol, stopper and shake well for 10 min. Add a few drops of phenolphthalein indicator solution and back-titrate with standard 0.01 M hydrochloric acid. Do a similar titration on 15 ml of barium hydroxide solution without letting it come into contact with air.

3.12   Some case studies of air pollution

The compositions of the exhaust gases of various types of engines running on liquid hydrocarbon fuels have received quite a lot of attention. Unburned hydrocarbons are of course present, but the ratio of toluene to benzene is usually higher in petrols than in the exhaust gas of internal combustion engines, suggesting that some benzene is being synthesized in the engine.[63] Studies on diesel engines aimed at establishing the source of odour in the exhaust gases have yielded some interesting results.[64] While acrolein and formaldehyde are known to be present at levels of 5–15 ppm in exhaust gases, dilution of the exhaust gases to the odour thresholds of a test panel suggested that these compounds certainly could not be responsible for the odour, but that nitrogen dioxide, (at 40–400 ppm depending on engine speed) with some contribution from hydrocarbons (at around 50 ppm) was the most likely cause for complaint.

Formaldehyde is also encountered in the exhaust gases from jet engines, detectable as much by irritation of the eyes as of the nose. But the gases which have to be monitored during testing of engines, according to Environmental Protection Agency rules, are CO_2, CO and NO (by non-dispersive IR analysis), NO_2 (by UV) and total hydrocarbons (by flame ionization detector)[65]. The same gases have also been determined in some surveys of modern airports, often a target for the environmental lobby. The results from these surveys indicate that at London's third airport, Stansted, the smallest of the nearby towns (with a population of 1500) produced more atmospheric pollution (other than hydrocarbons) than the airport.[66] A similar survey for London Heathrow[67] indicated that the levels of oxides of nitrogen never reached the maximum levels found in the city centre, and that a large contribution to the pollution came from the heating plant and the motor vehicles. It was pointed out that while the exhaust plume from an aircraft taking off was quite noticeable to the general public, it in fact represented only a small fraction of the polluting waste gases, most of which were emitted during taxiing from the terminals to the runways. The levels of hydrocarbons averaged 1 ppm, not a cause for concern, but in the case of carbon monoxide (emitted by taxiing aircraft and motor traffic) levels averaged 8.5 ppm, except in the road tunnel where they were higher. The author of a report on air pollution at Los Angeles airport concluded: "Concentrations of pollutants at airports are not observed to exceed current standards . . . the pollutant of greatest concern is carbon monoxide . . . and the highest concentrations are observed inside terminal buildings."[68] Problems of air pollution associated with airports therefore seem the province of building engineers, and no longer that of the analytical chemist.

References

1 Ledbetter, J. O. (1972) *Air Pollution: Part A, Analysis*. Marcel Dekker, New York, p. 5.
2 Kellogg, W. W., Cadie, R. D., Allen, E. R., Lazarns, A. L. and Martell, E. A. (1972) *Science*, **175**, 587.
3 Goldberg, A. B., Maroulis, P. J., Wilner, L. A. and Bandy, A. R. (1981) *Atmospheric Environment*, **15**, 11.
4 Kerr, R. A. (1981) *Science*, **212**, 1013.
5 Murozumi, M., Chow, T. J. and Patterson, C. C. (1969) *Geochim. et Cosmochim. Acta*, **33**, 1247.
6 Leonardos, G. (1969) *J. Air Pollution Control Assoc.*, **19**, 91.
7 Logan, W. P. D. (1953) *Lancet*, **1**, 336.
8 *Monitoring of the Environment in the U.K.*: Pollution Paper No. 1 (1974). HMSO, London.
9 Clarenburg, L. A. (1973) *Z. Anal Chem.*, **263**, 298.
10 Flowers, B. (1974) *Royal Commission on Environmental Pollution, 4th Report*, p. 12. HMSO, London.
11 Ashby, E. (1973) *Royal Commission on Environmental Pollution, 1st Report*, p. 19. HMSO, London.
12 Coker, D. T. (1981) *Analyst*, **106**, 1036.
13 Thain, W. (1980) *Monitoring Toxic Gases in the Atmosphere for Hygiene and Pollution Control*. Pergamon, Oxford.
14 *Threshold Limit Values*. (1980) Guidance Note EH 15/80, Health and Safety Executive. HMSO, London.
15 *Principles and Methods for Evaluating the Toxicity of Chemicals* (1978) Environmental Health Criteria. WHO, Geneva.
16 Katz, M. (ed.) (1977) *Methods of Air Sampling and Analysis*, 2nd edn., American Public Health Association, Washington DC.
17 May, K. R. (1945) *J. Sci. Inst.*, **22**, 187.
18 Grasserbauer, M., Puxbaum, H. and Weiss, O. (1978) *Z. Anal. Chem.*, **291**, 354.
19 *Lead in the Environment and its Significance to Man* (1974) Pollution Paper No. 2. HMSO, London.
20 Lodge, J. P., Waggoner, A. P., Klodt, D. T. and Grains, C. N. (1981) *Atmospheric Environment*, **15**, 431.
21 Malissa, H. (1978) *Analysis of Airborne Particulates by Physical Methods*. Chemical Rubber Co., Boca Raton, Florida.
22 Taylor, H. F. W. (1964) *Optical Microscopy*, in *The Chemistry of Cements*, Taylor, H. F. W. (ed.), Academic Press, London, p. 223.
23 *Powder Diffraction File* (1979) International Centre for Diffraction Data (including ASTM). Swarthmore, Pennsylvania 19081, USA.
24 Anon (1980) *Anal. Chem.*, **52**, 1136A.
25 Talvitie, N. A. (1951) *Anal. Chem.*, **23**, 623.
26 Klockow, D., Jablonski, B. and Nießner, R. (1979) *Atmospheric Environment*, **13**, 1665.
27 Birks, L. S. (1971) *Electron Probe Microanalysis*, 2nd edn., Wiley International, New York.
28 Birks, L. S. (1969) *X-ray Spectrochemical Analysis*, 2nd edn., Wiley Interscience, New York.
29 de Jonghe, W. and Adams, F. (1979) *Anal. Chim. Acta*, **108**, 21.
30 Marczenko, Z. (1976) *Spectrophotometric Determination of the Elements*. Ellis Horwood, Chichester, p. 307.
31 Sawicki, E. (1969) *Talanta*, **16**, 1231.
32 Baker, P. G. (1981) *Anal. Proc.*, **11**, 478.

33 Eiceman, G. A., Viau, A. C. and Karasek, E. W. (1980) *Anal. Chem.*, **52**, 1492.
34 Israel, H. and Israel, G. W. (1974) *Trace Elements in the Atmosphere*, Ann Arbor, Michigan.
35 Thompson, B. C. and Keller, C. W. (1973) *Infrared Spectra of Hazardous Gases and Vapours*. Industrial Technical Report TR-590. Beckman Instruments Inc., Fullerton, California.
36 Zeller, M. V. (1976) *Infrared Methods in Air Analysis*. Part No. 993-9236. Perkin-Elmer Corporation, Norwalk, Connecticut.
37 Lehrer, E. and Luft, K. (1937) German patent 730 478.
38 Hanel, R., Conrath, B., Flasar, F. M., Kunde, V., Maguire, W. C., Pearl, J., Pirraglia, J., Samuelson, R., Herath, L., Allison, M., Cruickshank, D., Gantier, D., Gierasch, P., Horn, L., Koppany, R. and Ponnamperuma, C. (1981) *Science*, **212**, 192.
39 Kunde, V. G., Aikin, A. C., Hanel, R. A., Jennings, D. E., Maguire, W. C., Samuelson, R. E. (1981) *Nature*, **292**, 686.
40 Sharp, B. L. (1981) *Chem. Brit.*, in press.
41 McFadden, W. H. (1967) "Mass spectrometric analysis of gas-chromatographic eluents", in *Advances in Chromatography*, Vol. 4, Giddings, J. C. and Keller, R. A. (eds.). Marcel Dekker, New York, p. 265.
42 Leichnitz, K. (1976) *Detector Tube Handbook*, (3rd edn.), Draegerwerk, A.G., Lübeck, West Germany.
43 Fraust, C. L. and Hermann, E. R. (1966) *J. Amer. Indust. Hygiene Assoc.*, **27**, 68.
44 Leinster, P., Perry, R. and Young, R. J. (1977) *Talanta*, **24**, 205.
45 Bailey, A. and Hollingdale-Smith, P. A. (1977) *Ann. Occup. Hygiene*, **20**, 345.
46 Barratt, R. S. (1981) *Analyst*, **106**, 817.
47 *Generation of Test Atmospheres of Organic Vapours*: Leaflet 17 DHS 4 (1981). Health and Safety Executive, London.
48 Teckentrup, A. and Klockow, D. (1978) *Anal. Chem.*, **50**, 1728.
49 Jeffery, P. G. and Kipping, P. J. (1972) *Gas Analysis by Gas Chromatography*. Pergamon, Oxford.
50 Gough, T. A. and Walker, E. A. (1970) *Analyst*, **95**, 1.
51 Grob, R. L. (1977) "Environmental studies of the atmosphere with gas chromatography", in *Contemporary Topics in Analytical and Clinical Chemistry*, Vol. 1, Hercules, D. M. (ed.). Plenum Press, New York.
52 Grob, K. and Grob, G. (1971) *J. Chromatog.*, **62**, 1.
53 Dimitriades, B., Ellis, C. F. and Seizinger, D. E. (1969) "Gas chromatographic analysis of vehicular exhaust emissions", in *Advances in Chromatography*, Vol. 8, Giddings, J. C. and Keller, R. A. (eds.), Marcel Dekker, New York, p. 327.
54 Häsänen, E., Karlsson, V., Leppämaki, E. and Juhala, M. (1981) *Atmospheric Environment*, **15**, 1755.
55 Porter, K. and Volman, D. H. (1962) *Anal. Chem.*, **34**, 748.
56 Rees, T. D., Gyllenspetz, A. B.and Docherty, A. C. (1971) *Analyst*, **96**, 201.
57 Cresser, M. S. (1978) *Lab. Practice*, **27**, 639.
58 West, P. W. and Gaeke, G. C. (1956) *Anal. Chem.*, **28**, 1816.
59 King, H. G. C. and Pruden, G. (1969) *Analyst*, **94**, 43.
60 British Standard no. 1747, III (1963).
61 Bolin, C. (1970) *Scientific American*, **223**, September, p. 125.
62 Leithe, W. (1968) *Die Analyse der Luft und ihrer Verunreinigungen*, Wissenschaftliche Verlagsgesellschaft GmbH, Stuttgart, p. 192.
63 Altshuller, A. P. and Clemons, C. A. (1962) *Anal. Chem.*, **34**, 466.
64 Linnell, R. H. and Scott, W. E. (1962) *J. Air Pollut. Control Assoc.*, **12**, 510.
65 *EPA Emission Standards and Test Procedures for Aircraft*. (1973) *U.S. Federal Register*, July 17th.
66 Keddie, A. W. C., Parker, J. and Roberts, G. H. (1973) *Relative Air Pollution Emissions from an Airport in the U.K. and Neighbouring Urban Areas*. AGARD Conference Proceedings, No. 125.
67 Parker, J. (1971) *Air Pollution at Heathrow Airport, London. SAE Transactions*, 80, Paper 710324.
68 Bastress, E. K. (1973) *Envir. Sci. Techn.*, **7**, 811.

4 The hydrosphere

The availability of an adequate supply of water of suitable purity is undoubtedly essential to any civilized community. We drink it, bathe in it, swim in it, wash clothes in it, sail ships on it, catch fish in it, irrigate with it and use it in chemical process control to heat things up, cool things down and to move waste products. This simple chemical also plays a vital role in all ecological systems, both in the mobilization and transport of nutrients, and also in the photosynthetic production of dry matter by plant species. It is, without question, man's most precious resource. It is important therefore that as far as possible deliberate or accidental actions of man which adversely affect the best use of water for whatever purpose should be avoided, and the analyst makes a major contribution towards the provision of adequate water supplies in every sphere of water use.

4.1 The hydrological cycle and pollution

Even in the absence of man's intervention water is subjected to a complex series of physical and chemical processes on all scales from the micro to the global. It is worth studying briefly the natural cycling of water, the so-called "hydrological cycle", because this gives a clearer picture of the ways in which human activity may adversely influence water quality. A typical schematic representation of the natural cycle is shown in Fig. 4.1.

Rainwater contains significant quantities of dissolved species, regardless of pollution attributable to human activity. Much of the dissolved material originates from the oceans, although its relative composition may differ appreciably from that of typical sea water. This happens because selective enrichment can occur during the processes of aerosol formation by air bubbles bursting at wave surfaces. Much of the dissolved salt is transported through the atmosphere after evaporation of the water as dry aerosol particles, which are subsequently redissolved in rain. Wind-blown dust, which may on occasion travel thousands of miles through the atmosphere (see Chapter 3) may also make a significant contribution, as may dissolved naturally-occurring gases, such as carbon dioxide, ammonia and oxides of nitrogen. However, rain may also dissolve gases produced by combustion of fossil fuels, particularly sulphur dioxide, and gaseous emissions from the chemical industry including organics. It is interesting that one of the effects of control of SO_2 emission from domestic and industrial sources has been to decrease the input of sulphate into the soil from rain. As a result, where much sulphate is being taken up from soils by crops, sulphur deficiency may become a problem unless supplies of the element are replenished by sulphate-containing fertilizers. At one time in industrialized nations there was usually sufficient SO_2 pollution for sulphur deficiency problems in crops to be very scarce. The problem has become aggravated by the development of high-yielding crops and the application of large amounts of the other elements, particularly N, P and K, essential to plant growth.

Some rain returns directly to rivers, lakes and the oceans, but much of it falls on to the soil, either directly or through a canopy of vegetation. The composition of the dissolved material may change very considerably when rainwater passes through vegetation, either through foliage or down the bark of trees. Some species may be selectively absorbed, while others may be introduced. As the water flows through the soil its composition may again be significantly altered. The final composition depends upon the nature of the soil, its mineral types and concentrations, the size of the soil particles, its acidity, its organic matter content and its drainage characteristics. It depends too upon the recent climatic history, which influences both the path the water follows through the soil, and thus its residence time in the soil, and the microbial activity, which controls the degradation of organic matter. Temperature too may be important, especially because of its effect upon microbial activity. Water cannot flow through frozen soil, and therefore it may run over the soil surface as thaws occur. It may also run off the surface if the intensity of rainfall is too high for normal drainage.

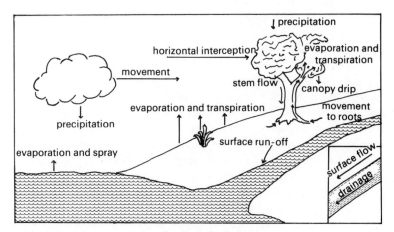

Figure 4.1   Schematic representation of the hydrological cycle.

Eventually, except in arid climates, the water enters streams, rivers, lakes or drainage ditches. However, the water entering such watercourses when a rainstorm commences may be totally different from that falling as rain, since the new water entering a catchment must first displace water already present in the soil. Rainwater passing through soil may pick up contamination from fertilizers, particularly nitrate, which is scarcely retained at all by the soil. It may also become contaminated from soluble species present in manures, sludges or industrial wastes which have been disposed of by spreading on the land. Phosphate is held quite firmly by most soils, and is therefore relatively immobile.

Stream or lake water may also pick up contamination directly from soluble industrial or domestic waste disposal, or from the slow dissolution of suspended particulate matter being transported by the water. The water chemistry may be modified by a number of precipitation, decomposition, oxidation or reduction reactions, especially in river estuaries where fresh and saline waters meet. Eventually however much of the river-borne pollution reaches the oceans. These in turn may receive further contamination directly from waste disposal from land and ships, from cargo vessel hold-cleaning, accidental oil spillage and so on, as well as from wind-blown particulate and gaseous contamination.

4.2   The oxygen balance in natural waters

Water in the environment is not only a solvent and vehicle for transport, it is also a life-supporting medium for fish and for a host of smaller organisms right down to bacteria. Most of these organisms require oxygen, which they can extract from the water. Water in equilibrium with air dissolves a small amount of oxygen. The amount decreases as the temperature increases, from around $14 \, mg \, l^{-1}$ at freezing point to half that value at 30°C. (Water equilibrated with pure oxygen does of course dissolve much more than this). This variation is rather unfortunate, since both fish and lower organisms need more oxygen at the higher temperatures where the solubility is lower. Fish of the salmonid family are very sensitive to the dissolved oxygen level (DO): Mellanby[1] has said that if trout are happy in a river, its water will be fit for almost any purpose. Coarse fish are more tolerant, and eels remarkably so.

Just as demanding as the fish are the bacteria, particularly those which we depend upon to break down the organic waste in our rivers—both sewage effluent and natural run-off from the land. As the bacteria digest the organic matter, so they consume the oxygen, and eventually, if the supply of oxygen is not adequate, as in still lake waters just a few metres below the surface, the water becomes *anaerobic*. The consequence of this is that a quite different bacterial fauna takes over, with reducing bacteria converting the elements of organic compounds to their hydrides, CH_4, NH_3, and H_2S, instead of to oxidized products like CO_2, NO_3^-, and SO_4^{2-}. Marsh gas was often produced in the stagnant canals of 19th century England in such quantities that it would burn visibly on the surface. Gas from anaerobic river sediments, collected by one of the authors, was found to contain about 30% each of methane, carbon dioxide and nitrogen, and 2% of hydrogen sulphide— genuine natural pollution!

The amount of organic waste which a river can effectively handle is determined by the level of dissolved oxygen and the volume of water passing down the river. It is possible to measure the oxygen demand of a sample of water or effluent directly in terms of the consumption of oxygen from an initially air-saturated solution maintained at 20°C over a 5-day period. This is called the Biochemical Oxygen Demand (BOD), and is quoted in mg l^{-1} of DO. There are strong arguments against this approach: five days is a very long time to wait before getting an answer; the reproducibility is not very good, and while 20°C may be warm by British standards it is cold compared to the 30°C or so of tropical lakes. Nevertheless, it does represent a fairly realistic value for what one is trying to determine. An alternative approach is to measure the Chemical Oxygen Demand (COD) by boiling a sample of water with some acidified permanganate or dichromate under carefully controlled conditions. The consumption of permanganate or of dichromate is then equated to an amount of oxygen. While the calculation is simple, and the method is fast, there is no guarantee that the bacteria will treat the organic matter in the same way as the strong inorganic oxidants.

4.3 River quality

A product of one of the early Royal Commissions on Sewage Disposal was a report of 1912 in which an attempt was made to classify stretches of river water into one of five categories varying from "very clean" to "bad". This classification system remained in widespread use in Britain until quite recently when the UK Department of the Environment defined four categories on the basis of the BOD and the DO values. They are:

Class I   Unpolluted and/or recovered from pollution.
          BOD < 3 mg l^{-1}, well oxygenated, containing no toxic discharge.
Class II Of doubtful quality, needing improvement.
          Not in Class I on the basis of BOD value; DO values significantly less than saturated.
Class III Poor quality, requiring improvement as a matter of some urgency.
          Not in Class IV on the basis of BOD value; DO values < 50% saturation for considerable periods.
Class IV Grossly polluted.
          All rivers with BOD > 12 mg l^{-1} under average conditions.

One important aspect of this classification is that it applies not to a river as a whole, but only to separate stretches of a river. It is not only possible, but to be hoped for, that river quality may *improve* on going downstream, and not necessarily only get worse, as the natural systems in the river deal with the burden of effluent discharged into it upstream. Rivers can and do effectively deal with large volumes of non-toxic waste such as treated sewage, and the working guidelines are that the waste should have a BOD level not exceeding $20\,\mathrm{mg}\,\mathrm{l}^{-1}$, and that it should not constitute more than $12\frac{1}{2}\%$ of total flow once mixed with the river.

One of the results of tightened control on discharge of waste into British rivers since the 1951 Act, which is discussed later, has been the marked improvement in the quality of the rivers and the substantial decrease in the fraction of the total mileage falling into classes III and IV, though the improvement is perhaps more obvious in the rivers than in the estuaries. The improvement in river quality has also been appreciated by fish: in 1978 it was reported that some 96 species of fish had been observed in the Thames—and even a seal! However, some of the other major British rivers are still not so clean.

An interesting indication of what can be done—by man and by Nature together—to keep a river clean is given by the River Lea in London. It is estimated that the water in this river is used three times before it reaches the Thames. Certainly the river takes the treated waste from a large populated area and yet can be used as a supply source downstream for another part of London.[2]

4.4   Legal aspects of water pollution in the UK

There are reports of the House of Commons in the mid-nineteenth century having to adjourn its business on occasions when the stench from the River Thames became unbearable. The outcome was the Rivers Pollution Prevention Act, 1876, after which a Royal Commission was set up to look into the matter. It is interesting to note that the recommendation to treat sewage and then dilute it adequately, based on the biological oxygen demand, still forms the basis of present-day approaches, though it was many years before any significant action was to be taken. Modern legislation starts with the 1951 Act, and the effectiveness of the action taken is now evident from the surveys of water and river quality carried out from time to time. The relevant Acts may be summarized briefly:

Rivers (Prevention of Pollution) Act 1951: required the setting up of river boards with the job of preventing pollution and monitoring the quality of the major rivers of the country. Permission had to be granted by the appropriate board before any new discharge of waste effluent into a river.
Clean Rivers (Estuaries and Tidal Waters) Act 1960: this extended control by the river boards to estuaries and tidal waters, which previously had probably carried more waste than the rivers themselves.

Rivers (Prevention of Pollution) Act 1961, (and 1965 for Scotland): this extended control over all discharges, including those in operation prior to 1951, thus completing the coverage.

Water Resources Act 1963: this replaced earlier river boards by a number of river authorities in England and Wales (in Scotland the boards remained). It also extended control to disposal of waste into underground strata, particularly down old mine shafts or bore-holes of old wells.

Oil in Navigable Waters Acts 1955–71: these forbade the discharge of any oily waste on any waters, rivers, estuaries or sea up to 50 miles from the coast, and permit the discharge only of waste with less than $100 \mu g \, ml^{-1}$ of hydrocarbons on the high seas. These Acts were passed following ratification of an international treaty in London in 1954. Similar legislation has been passed by many other countries.

Control of Pollution Act 1974: this dealt with all aspects of pollution, and part 2 applies to waters. Largely on account of the cost of implementing much of this legislation it is only slowly becoming effective (1981).

4.5 The need for legislation on water quality

Much of the legislation passed by Parliament takes the form of *enabling legislation*, stating what may and may not be done. Putting it into practice usually means fitting numbers to statements to make the distinction between what is polluted and what is not, between what may be permitted and what may not.

Most people would concede that the quality of water to be used for human consumption or in food preparation is of paramount importance, and in most developed countries quite extensive legislation has evolved which governs drinking water composition. Maximum admissible concentrations (MAC) are specified for a wide range of species, although often different countries differ over the precise value they put upon a particular MAC. Indeed often there may be quite wide discrepancies as to the level at which it is considered that a particular ion or substance presents a possible health hazard and becomes undesirable. Sometimes these stem from genuinely inadequate knowledge of the short term and long term physiological effects of pollutants at different levels. Sometimes they arise from economic considerations, since it is futile to produce legislation which, in its enforcement, would make prohibitively expensive demands upon national resources, and compromise levels may thus have to be adopted. Sometimes the differences may even arise from limitations of facilities or methodology for analysis, since there is little point in specifying that the concentration of a particular species should be below a given level unless it may be determined at that level by available methods. Therefore there may be considerable divergence between specified and ideal MAC values for many species.

The significance of these observations may be seen in the 1980 European Economic Community Directive (80/778) on the Quality of Water for Human Consumption (see Appendix 2). Although this specifies some 62 parameters which should be monitored, and specifies MAC values or guide levels for each, in fact individual member states are left to fix their own levels provided these do not exceed the Directive MAC levels. For softened and desalinated waters, minimum required concentrations for selected species are specified.

4.6 Programmes for monitoring water quality

Although the range of determinations carried out to monitor drinking water quality may be very extensive, in fact only relatively few determinations are completed very frequently, most being made at relatively wide sampling intervals. "Minimum monitoring", which, as its name implies, involves the bare minimum of determinations, typically covers only conductivity, residual chlorine (in treated water) and some microbial parameters. On a water supply of any size such minimum monitoring would usually be done daily. "Current monitoring" involves in addition pH, temperature, nitrate, nitrite and ammonia, and would typically be completed every three days or so. Additional "periodic monitoring" of any species which a water authority considers might affect water quality would be conducted as deemed necessary. "Occasional monitoring" of a wide range of species would be completed at relatively wide intervals to provide an overview of the water quality and check for the presence at undesirable levels of unexpected contaminants. A table of MAC values for drinking water based on the EEC 1980 directive is included for completeness in Appendix 2. These serve only as a guide to current views on water quality. The fact that the European values rather than say corresponding USA values, are quoted is not really significant in the present context, because the values are in any case not static, and within Europe individual Member States fix their own, often significantly lower values.

Ideally drinking water should be sampled at the point at which it is actually used by the consumer, in other words the kitchen tap in most instances. Because lead levels tend to build up when water is static in lead piping, for this determination the analysis is carried out on running water, and if the connection from the water main to the household supply is through lead piping, as it still is in some older houses in the UK for example, then the water is run to waste for a prescribed period prior to sampling, since the first run-off in the morning will contain a significantly higher lead level. Unfortunately many households do not always exercise such caution and occasional cases of clinical lead poisoning still occur.

In very densely populated areas where water is taken from a major river and purified by appropriate chemical treatment before incorporation into domestic supplies, the water may be recirculated many times during a relatively short time. Clearly reliable routine monitoring is essential to avoid possible serious health risks.

Aside from the need for the control of drinking water quality, water for fish and shellfish growth, for agricultural purposes and for industrial use also needs to be of adequate purity. We can show the relative purity required of water for various purposes in simplified general terms, as in Table 4.1. Quite apart from the risks of damage to the fish population or to crops there is a risk of introduction of toxic substances to the human food chain. The quality

Table 4.1 Quality requirements of water for various purposes

Quality Source	1	2	3	4	5
Rain	plants				
Streams	plants	drinking			
Rivers ⎫ Lakes ⎭		drinking	cooling	industry	waste disposal
Estuaries			cooling		waste disposal
Ocean					waste disposal

of river water is therefore carefully controlled, even when the water is not used for domestic consumption. For example, river boards in Scotland have responsibility for making sure that legislation concerning the prevention of pollution is adequately enforced. In the USA, the United States Environmental Protection Agency (EPA) requires industries to monitor and control contaminants present in their waste water. More than a hundred toxic chemicals need to be monitored and the EPA specifies certain approved methods by which the determinations should be carried out, based upon existing knowledge and available instrumentation.

Problems in water quality detected by routine analysis are traced back to their original source wherever possible, and the process causing the problem is either modified or stopped. Often substantial reductions of pollutant levels may take a considerable time to achieve. Proposed solutions to pollution problems must be economically viable and it should be possible to carry them out without plant closure and consequent unemployment.

4.7 Observations on sampling

Sampling of natural waters requires some additional comments to what has already been said in Chapter 2. It is easy to tacitly assume that because a body of water looks uniform it is homogenous, but this may be far from the truth in practice. Still water in reservoirs and lakes may well exhibit a considerable degree of thermal stratification, and the layers of water at different temperatures may have widely differing chemical compositions. Suspended solids content tends to increase with depth, whereas certain organic detritis and immiscible organic pollutants of low density may be more concentrated nearer to the surface. Even in flowing water streams (unless they are very turbulent), mixing may be incomplete and edge effects may be found near the banks or river bottom. If homogeneity is in any doubt, then samples should be taken at various points under various flow conditions to investigate the degree of variation.

Where a tributary or waste outlet pipe enters a water course, there may be incomplete mixing with the main water flow over a very considerable distance downstream from the point of entry. If this is not recognized, the "tailing" effect may cause a serious systematic over- or under-estimate of a pollutant concentration, depending upon the sampling point.

Sampling water at different depths is not as difficult as might at first be expected, since sampling bottles which may be opened and closed remotely at the required depth are readily available. In remote areas, water samples may be collected by automatic samplers, which simply use a battery-driven pump to collect the appropriate amount of sample from the water source at preset time intervals. Each sample is pumped into a separate bottle. If it is desired to follow changes in water composition through a storm event, for example, it is relatively simple to trigger the sampler to start as soon as the water level in the stream reaches a certain point, provided a stilling well is available to smooth out the surface fluctuations caused by waves.

Rainwater presents interesting sampling problems to the analyst. Rain must normally be collected over a fairly long time period, so that integrated rather than instantaneous concentrations are determined. Its composition (see Table 4.2 for some examples) may vary considerably over quite small

Table 4.2 Data for analyses of rain water (concentrations in $mg\,l^{-1}$)

Ion	Scottish highlands*	Dutch coast†	Black Forest‡	Dortmund city‡
H^+	0.058	0.06	0.06	0.07
Na^+	1.83	2.6	0.43	0.35
K^+	0.18	0.2	0.27	0.21
Ca^{2+}	0.47	0.40	0.28	0.69
Mg^{2+}	0.22	0.36	0.03	0.15
NH_4^+	0.20	1.1	0.30	1.47
Cl^-	2.9	5.0	0.67	1.85
NO_3^-	4.0	3.2	1.12	3.05
SO_4^{2-}	4.7	5.2	3.20	6.36
HCO_3^-	0.1	—	—	—

* Author's results, 1977–8.
† By courtesy of Dr. J. Slanina, Netherlands Energy Research Foundation, Petten, Netherlands (1978).
‡ By courtesy of Prof. D. Klockow, University of Dortmund, West Germany (1975, 1980).

distances, an observation which often surprises newcomers to the field. It is not sterile, and if left in a rain gauge, its composition, particularly pH, nitrate and ammonium, may change with time. Dust should preferably be excluded by fitting automatic lids to collectors which will open only while rain is falling. Rain gauges seem to attract small flies and insects, and these may cause contamination problems unless excluded by fine netting; contamination may also be caused by birds using the rain gauge as a perch. Perching may be prevented by a series of rather anti-social spikes around the funnel rim. The topic of sampling of natural and waste waters has been discussed in detail by King[3] and Wilson.[4]

4.8 Storage of samples and prevention of contamination

Often the sample collection is beyond the control of the analyst. Sometimes the person collecting the sample has no knowledge of what determinations are to be completed on the sample, and even if he does know, he may be unfamiliar with possible sources of contamination. For example, on one occasion some river water samples were received in the authors' laboratory which were found to contain apparently excessive quantities of zinc. However, when 5 ml of deionized water was poured into one of the sample bottle caps, and swirled for just two minutes, its zinc level rose to a level where the solution gave an off-scale reading when nebulized into the flame of an atomic absorption spectrometer. The zinc came from the bottle cap liner, and this of course made the analysis useless. This example serves to illustrate how important it is that a standardized sampling procedure, which is known not to introduce sample contamination, is adopted and rigorously adhered to.

For water samples, sample stability must also be carefully considered. This depends upon the nature of the sample, the determinand, the nature of the sample bottle and the addition of preserving reagents. Experimental studies of sample stability for particular analytes and sample types are invaluable, but should if at all possible be commenced immediately after sampling. Polyethylene containers are best suited to storage before most trace element or inorganic ion determinations, once it has been established that they do not present possible contamination problems. They are also more robust, an important consideration if samples are to be transported over rough terrain. However, samples must be stored in glass bottles before determination of traces of organic species.

It is generally accepted that acidification of water samples to pH 1 prevents possible losses of most trace metals by adsorption into the walls of the sample bottles. However, suspended matter must be removed first by filtration to avoid its partial further dissolution under the more acid conditions. Biocidal reagents such as toluene or chloroform, or mercury(II) chloride are often used to restrict the effects of microbial activity on the redistribution of carbon, nitrogen and phosphorus between various chemical species. Much has been written on sample conservation, and it is not therefore discussed at length here. Interested readers should refer to Wilson's monograph, *The Chemical Analysis of Water—General Principles and Techniques*, for a useful concise discussion of this topic.[4]

After reading this brief survey the reader might well assume that problems associated with water supply and water pollution belong only to recent times. That this is not so may be seen from the account[5] of Frontinus, around 100 AD, of the water supplies to the city of Rome. While his main concern was with the upkeep of the walls and aqueducts, and the illicit sale or use of the water, he also felt it necessary to legislate against pollution: "No one shall with malice pollute the waters where they issue publicly. Should anyone pollute them, his fine shall be ten thousand sestertii."

4.9   The analysis of water—what is required?

It should now be obvious that many determinands are of interest in water analysis. The discussion in the remainder of this chapter concentrates upon procedures which are of particular interest in the water industry, and which, it is hoped, will serve to give some insight into the type of approach currently being used by analysts in water quality control laboratories. Atomic absorption spectroscopy, which is much used for trace metal determinations in water, and particularly recent hydride generation and carbon rod or furnace techniques, are discussed at length in Chapters 5 and 6, and need not be considered further here, since the methodology is essentially the same. The range of monitoring programmes which may be adopted has already been mentioned. It is convenient to summarize the commonly determined parameters under seven headings.

1. *Subjective impression* is difficult to quantify, but is still important for a commodity which is supplied to the general public. This includes colour, turbidity, taste, and smell.
2. *General indicators*: pH, electrical conductivity, and temperature (the last of these must be determined at the time the sample is collected).
3. *Oxygen balance*: an important guide to the level of pollution in a water supply, reflecting the ability of the water to deal with its burden. Dissolved oxygen (DO), chemical oxygen demand (COD), biochemical oxygen demand (BOD) and total organic carbon (TOC) fall into this category.
4. *Anions*: those most often determined include chloride (for salinity), nitrate (from fertilizers), nitrite (evidence of bacteriological action), phosphate (fertilizers and detergents), sulphite (industrial sources), sulphide (anaerobic bacteriological action) and cyanide (industrial wastes).
5. *Cations*: again the choice is very wide, but may include sodium (salinity), calcium and magnesium (water hardness), ammonium (bacteriological action, fertilizers) and heavy metals, particularly lead, cadmium and mercury (dissolution of pipes, toxic wastes).
6. *Organic substances*: determination of TOC has been mentioned already but although it is a useful indicator, it is non-specific and includes both naturally-occurring substances (soil

organic matter extracts) and man-made contamination (mineral oils, pesticides, etc.). Apart from specific compounds related to processes in particular factories, hydrocarbons (fuel spillages), phenols (traces affect the taste of water), pesticides and carboxylic acids, and surfactants (detergents) can be looked for.

7. *Bacteriological examination*: particularly important where the water is intended for human consumption. The presence of coliform bacteria (those which produce gas when fermented with a lactose broth at 44.5°C) is taken as indicative of pollution by waste effluent and renders the water "potentially unsatisfactory and of unsafe sanitary quality".[6]

4.10 Selected analytical methods for water quality control

The remainder of this chapter is devoted to discussion of a selection of the analytical techniques which are widely employed in the water industry. Where appropriate, specific determinations are discussed in detail. As mentioned earlier, atomic absorption spectroscopy is not considered here, although widely used, because it is covered in later chapters.

4.11 pH measurement—the glass electrode

The pH glass electrode is a device which generates a potential varying linearly with the pH of the solution in which it is immersed. It is a Nernstian concentration cell with potential controlled by the activities of the hydrogen ion on either side of a very thin glass membrane. The latter is in the form of a bulb at the end of a glass tube containing a reference solution of fixed hydrogen ion activity (Fig. 4.2). For simplicity of use a calomel or silver/silver

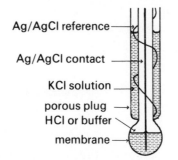

Figure 4.2 A combined glass/silver—silver chloride electrode.

chloride/potassium chloride reference electrode is usually located around the glass electrode stem, as shown.

$$E = \text{constant} + \frac{RT}{nF} \ln \frac{a_{H^+} \text{ (sample)}}{a_{H^+} \text{ (standard)}}$$

$$E = \text{constant}' + 0.058 \, pH \text{ at } 20°C.$$

To find the value of the constant, i.e. to calibrate the complete measuring system of the electrode pair and pH meter, standard buffer solutions having known pH values must be used. The combined electrode is dipped into a standard buffer and the meter adjusted (thus allowing for variation of the constant) to read the correct pH. It is desirable to check the electrode in a second buffer to show that the Nernstian factor is indeed 58 mV per pH unit: if it is too far out, the electrode is probably cracked and certainly not reliable. If the error is small, one of the buffers may have the wrong pH, usually the high pH one which picks up carbon dioxide from the air.

Procedure. Prepare freshly two of the following buffer solutions.

0.05 M	potassium hydrogen phthalate	$10.2\,g\,l^{-1}$	pH 4.00	20°
⎰0.025 M	disodium hydrogen orthophosphate .12 H_2O	$8.95\,g\,l^{-1}$⎱	pH 6.88	20°
⎱0.025 M	potassium dihydrogen phosphate	$3.40\,g\,l^{-1}$⎰		
0.05 M	sodium tetraborate	$19.1\,g\,l^{-1}$	pH 9.2	20°

Calibrate the electrode/meter pair using the two solutions, rinsing the electrode thoroughly each time with water and carefully wiping it with a tissue. Then dip it into the sample solution, swirl the solution, and wait up to a minute for a steady reading. A pH meter with a readability of ± 0.1 pH unit will be adequate for this work.

4.12 Conductivity

A simple portable conductivity meter with dip-type cell is quite adequate. The units nowadays accepted are $\mu S\,cm^{-1}$ (microsiemens per cm), the term "siemen" replacing the older term "mho" with units ohm^{-1}. A 0.005 M potassium chloride solution ($0.373\,g\,l^{-1}$) has a conductivity of $654\,\mu S\,cm^{-1}$ at 20°, and can be used to check the instrument and cell.

4.13 Dissolved oxygen

Two basic approaches are widely used, chemical (titrimetric) and electro-chemical (amperometric).

4.13.1 *Winkler method*

Dissolved oxygen is allowed to oxidize added iodide to iodine, which is in turn titrated with thiosulphate. The problem is to ensure fast, quantitative reaction of the oxygen, and to eliminate interferences from other reduced species which might be present, such as nitrite and sulphite. The first problem is solved by using manganese salts as intermediates, in a strongly alkaline medium:

$$4Mn(OH)_2 + O_2 + 2H_2O \rightarrow 4Mn(OH)_3.$$

On acidification, the Mn(III) hydroxide dissolves and oxidizes iodide to iodine:

$$Mn(OH)_3 + I^- + 3H^+ \rightarrow Mn^{2+} + \tfrac{1}{2}I_2 + 3H_2O.$$

The iodine is then reduced by thiosulphate:

$$I_2 + 2S_2O_3^{2-} \rightarrow 2I^- + S_4O_6^{2-}.$$

The stoichiometry is then four moles of thiosulphate equivalent to one mole (32 g) of DO. For convenience, 0.025 M thiosulphate solution (6.02 g $Na_3S_2O_3 \cdot 5H_2O$ in 1 l boiled-out, distilled water) may be used, in which case 1 ml is equivalent to 0.2 mg DO. If a sample volume of 200 ml is used, the relationship becomes 1 ml thiosulphate $\equiv$ 1 mg l^{-1} DO.

The second problem, of interference from nitrite (the most likely interference in waters containing sewage effluent) is overcome by adding sodium azide to the alkaline iodide solution. On acidification the nitrite is destroyed:

$$N_3H + HNO_2 \rightarrow N_2 + N_2O + H_2O.$$

Procedure. Fill a 200-ml bottle to the brim with sample, taking care to minimize contact with air. The volume of the bottle should be checked beforehand. Add from pipettes to the bottom of the bottle 1 ml of manganese(II) sulphate solution (500 g l^{-1} of tetrahydrate) and 1 ml of alkali-iodide-azide solution (400 g NaOH, 200 g KI and 5 g NaN$_3$ in 1 l), stopper and shake well. When the precipitate has settled, decant most of the clear liquid, add 2 ml concentrated phosphoric acid and some water to dissolve the precipitate, and titrate the released iodine with 0.025 M thiosulphate. Report DO in mg l^{-1}, and compare with the figure for air-saturated water at the temperature of the sample as collected.

4.13.2 *Electrochemical method—polarography*

Oxygen can be reduced at various electrodes in aqueous solutions if a small negative voltage is applied. The magnitude of the current which flows is determined by the rate at which oxygen can diffuse to the electrode, i.e., the system is *diffusion-controlled*. The diffusion may be only through the solution, or it may be through a thin plastic membrane separating the sample solution from a specially chosen electrolyte in which are immersed two electrodes, forming an electrochemical cell. This is the basis of the polarographic determination of oxygen.

The *dropping mercury electrode* possesses a number of advantages over most other electrodes for analytical electrochemistry:

1. It is being continuously renewed and therefore always has a clean surface relatively free from reaction products.
2. Hydrogen ions are not reduced at the theoretical potential, but only at much more negative values, and so do not interfere.
3. Many metals, produced by electrochemical reduction of their ions, are readily soluble in mercury.
4. Oxygen is reduced quite easily, in two stages, at the mercury electrode.

$$O_2 \xrightarrow{+2H^+ + 2e^-} H_2O_2 \xrightarrow{+2H^+ + 2e^-} 2H_2O.$$

A sketch of the apparatus required is shown in Fig. 4.3. The electrode should have a drop-time in the range 4–6 sec, and the galvanometer should be able to measure currents of 10–20 μA. Care must be taken to rinse and wipe clean the electrode capillary, and not to lift it above the reservoir because then the mercury will run back, pulling dirt into the narrow capillary.

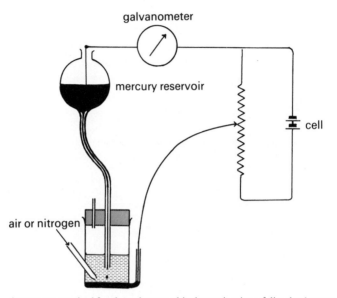

Figure 4.3   Apparatus required for the polarographic determination of dissolved oxygen.

Procedure.   Transfer 10 ml of sample to the cell, add 0.1 ml of 1 M potassium chloride (to render the sample electrically conducting), and a little mercury (to act as a pool counter-electrode). Insert the DME, with a head of 50 cm of mercury, and take readings of current at potentials increasing from -0.1 to -1.5 V. Fig. 4.4 shows the type of plot to be expected. The height of the wave, i_s for the sample, is proportional to the level of DO.

Now bubble out the solution with air for 5 min, note the temperature, and plot a second polarogram. The height of the wave will probably be less than before, because the laboratory is warmer than the river and the oxygen is less soluble at higher temperatures. Fig. 4.5 shows the solubility as a function of temperature. From this we can read off the level of DO corresponding to i_{cal}, and by simple proportion find the level of DO in the sample giving a wave-height i_s. This can finally be expressed as % saturation when referred to the level of DO in air-saturated water at the temperature of the sample as collected. For more accurate results, i_{cal} and i_s should be measured relative to a blank plot obtained by outgassing the sample with oxygen-free nitrogen.

4.13.3   *The Mackereth oxygen cell*

This device is again based upon the principle of diffusion, and the same method of calibration is applicable as for the polarographic method, but this cell offers advantages in convenience for handling, and can be plugged into a

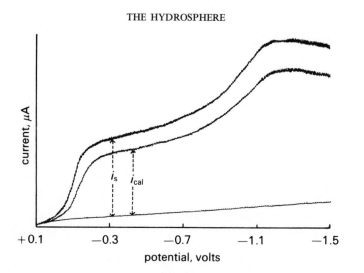

Figure 4.4 Polarographic waves for dissolved oxygen in a sample (upper wave), the aerated sample (middle wave) and a blank (deoxygenated with nitrogen).

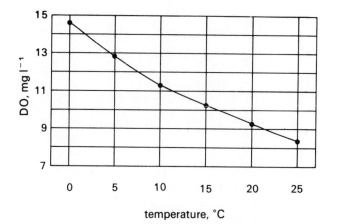

Figure 4.5 Variation in the solubility of oxygen in water with temperature.

pH meter to give a direct reading of DO in $mg\,l^{-1}$ (the scale of 0–$14\,pH$ becomes 0–$14\,mg\,l^{-1}$ DO). Two metal electrodes, one of silver and one of lead, are immersed in a saturated potassium hydrogen carbonate solution separated from the sample solution by a polyethylene membrane around $0.06\,mm$ thick.[7] This is a galvanic cell, i.e. no external potential need be applied, and the current is simply measured for the sample, for a standard (sample after air-saturation) and for a blank (sample after treatment with a little sodium sulphite to remove oxygen). The reactions are, at the silver electrode

$$O_2 + 2H_2O + 4e^- \rightarrow 4OH^-$$

and at the lead electrode

$$Pb + 4OH^- \rightarrow PbO_2 + 2H_2O + 4e^-$$

or

$$2Pb + 4OH^- \rightarrow 2Pb(OH)_2 + 4e^-.$$

The rate of diffusion of oxygen through the membrane is usually dependent on the temperature: the error can be compensated by including a thermistor in the measuring circuit and placing it near to the electrodes.

Oxygen determination has been discussed at some length, partly because it is important, and partly because the different approaches illustrate different

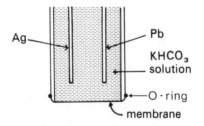

Figure 4.6 Schematic representation of the Mackereth oxygen cell.

ways in which problems have been overcome. The galvanic cell method is to be preferred for polluted waters, for continuous measurement, and for recording profiles of DO levels at various depths in, say, a lake or a river. Two practical tips are worth remembering: take care never to let the membrane and/or cell dry out, and, if it is to be left in a stream or river for any length of time, inspect it regularly for the presence of slimes covering the membrane which may cause low readings.

A recent inter-laboratory investigation has shown that both the titrimetric and electrochemical methods tended to give results on the high side, but this was ascribed to lack of care in handling the samples, thus permitting some contamination from laboratory air.[8] The errors were more serious for samples with low DO levels (around $1 \, \text{mg} \, l^{-1}$), than for fully-saturated waters.

4.14   Biochemical oxygen demand

Despite the doubts expressed concerning the reproducibility of this determination and even about the validity of the results as a measure of the real oxygen demand, it continues to be widely used. Because of the time factor—a waiting period of 5 days—it may not be convenient to incorporate it into a student's practical course.

Procedure.   Thoroughly aerate a sample of the water, make a measured dilution with distilled water if the BOD is likely to be greater than the DO level, seed with a little diluted domestic waste water (1–2 ml per litre), and carry out a DO determination on a suitable portion. Fill a screw-topped incubation bottle to the brim with the remainder of the diluted sample, seal the bottle, and incubate in the dark for 5 days at 20°C. Carry out a DO determination on a suitable portion of this incubated sample, and, allowing for dilution of the sample, find the BOD from the difference in the two DO levels.

Various stages of pre-treatment are required if waste-waters or sewage effluents are to be analysed for BOD. These are discussed in detail in the appropriate literature (see for example Refs. 6 and 9).

4.15   Chemical oxygen demand

Two chemical oxidants are used: permanganate offers the advantage of an easy-to-locate titration end-point, but is unstable on boiling in acidified aqueous solution, while dichromate, the officially preferred reagent, is stable on boiling and gives more reproducible results. Rodier[9] describes the permanganate method: the dichromate method can be found in all reference handbooks. The important point to watch in all variations is that the times of heating and boiling *must* be strictly adhered to, as some materials are oxidized only slowly and will consume more oxidant if boiled for a longer time. Interference from chloride is avoided by adding silver sulphate in the acid, and the oxidation process is aided by the presence of mercury sulphate as a catalyst.

Procedure.   Take 50 ml of sample in a 250-ml conical flask with a ground glass joint, add 10.0 ml of 0.00833 M (0.05 N) potassium dichromate solution (2.45 g l^{-1}), 1 g of mercury(II) sulphate, 80 ml of acid (concentrated sulphuric acid containing 10 g l^{-1} of silver sulphate) and a few glass beads. Fit a reflux condenser (no grease!), heat gently to boiling, and boil for exactly 10 min. Leave a minute or so to cool, rinse the condenser with 50 ml of distilled water, and cool the flask under a running tap. Add two drops of ferroin indicator solution (M/40) and titrate with 0.025 M ammonium iron(II) sulphate solution (9.80 g with 5 ml concentrated sulphuric acid diluted to 1 l) till the colour changes from blue–green to red–brown. Do a blank determination as above, on 50 ml of distilled water, and check the molarity of the titrant against the standard dichromate solution. Then 1 ml of difference in the titration volumes with 0.025 M iron(II) solution is equivalent to 0.2 mg oxygen demand, or 4.0 mg l^{-1} oxygen demand if a 50 ml sample is taken.[10]

4.16 Methods for the determination of inorganic nitrogen

As mentioned in Section 4.9, ammonia, nitrate and nitrite are usually monitored regularly in water supplies which are to be judged fit for human consumption, because all are deemed potentially hazardous to health if present above the MAC levels (500, 50 and $0.1\,\mu g\,ml^{-1}$ for the three ions respectively). Nitrate is known to be particularly dangerous to infants less than six months old. Sometimes these levels may be exceeded for brief periods, if for example a surge of microbial activity due to warm, wet weather after a prolonged dry period causes greater than normal mineralization and nitrification of nitrogen and higher levels of the ions then flow into river water sources. Dangerously high levels may result from pollution, especially from the use of fertilizers, although most farmers are too economy-conscious to deliberately use nitrogenous fertilizers so extravagantly. However, they are very much at the mercy of the weather when it comes to leaching losses of fertilizer.

All three species may be determined by colorimetric or solution spectrophotometric methods of analysis, the basic principles of which were considered in Chapter 3. As might be expected, because the selectivity of such methods depends upon the selectivity of the colour-forming reaction, the chemistry of the reactions used is rather complicated. A useful summary of the procedures used for the determination of nitrogen-containing species may be found in the book by Marczenko.[11]

4.16.1 Determination of ammonia

For several years ammonia was most commonly determined by the indophenol method or by Nessler's method, usually after separation of the analyte from concomitant species by distillation from alkaline solution. The reaction mechanism for the indophenol method is thought to be as follows:[11]

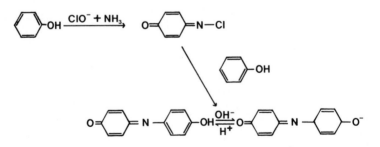

The ammonia reacts with phenol and hypochlorite to produce the blue indophenol anion in alkaline medium. In some natural waters ammonia may be determined without prior separation, provided EDTA is added as a masking agent to complex calcium, magnesium and aluminium to prevent their interference. Absorbance is measured at 625 nm, and it may be necessary to use long-path, e.g. 50-mm, cells to improve sensitivity. Addition of citrate prevents turbidity which might occur due to iron precipitation. Phosphate interferes if present in significant quantity. As with most colorimetric methods, the experimental procedure should be followed exactly, so that amounts of reagents and order of reagent addition are reproducible.

Procedure. Pipette a portion of sample solution (up to 50 ml) into a 100-ml distillation flask containing a few anti-bumping granules, add 15 ml of 30% sodium hydroxide solution (30 g sodium hydroxide pellets dissolved with cooling to give 100 ml of aqueous solution), and immerse the condenser outlet in 5 ml of distilled water containing 5 drops of 0.1 M sulphuric acid. Heat until approximately one-third of the contents of the distillation flask have distilled over. Lift the condenser outlet clear of the receiver, and allow a few drops of distillate to wash the inside of the condenser tube, collecting the washings in the receiver.

Prepare a sodium phenolate solution as follows: Dissolve 70 g of phenol in 15 ml of ethanol. Add 20 ml of acetone and dilute to 100 ml with ethanol. Immediately prior to use, pipette 10 ml of this solution into a 50-ml graduated flask, add 10 ml of 30% sodium hydroxide solution and dilute to 50 ml.

Transfer the distillate to a 50-ml graduated flask (unless the latter has been used as a receiver), and add 5 ml of fresh sodium phenolate solution, followed by 2 ml of 2% sodium hypochlorite solution. Dilute to the mark and mix thoroughly. After 30 minutes measure the absorbance at 625 nm against a reagent blank.

Prepare a series of standards containing 0–2 μg of ammonia per ml, at the final dilution, as ammonium sulphate. For precise work the recovery of the distillation apparatus should be checked regularly.

Nessler's method involves reaction between ammonia and the tetraiodo-mercury(II) anion in alkaline solution:

$$NH_3 + 2HgI_4^{2-} + 3OH^- \rightarrow NH_2Hg_2IO + 7I^- + 2H_2O.$$

In this reaction the orange-brown reaction product tends to precipitate, especially at higher concentrations, so protective colloids such as gelatin, gum arabic or poly(vinyl alcohol) are added to stabilize the suspension formed. Calcium and magnesium are masked with tartrate if the method is applied directly to natural water samples. The absorbance is measured at 400 nm.

Over the past decade there has been considerable interest in a more sensitive method for ammonia determination based upon the reaction between ammonium and a weakly alkaline mixture of sodium salicylate and dichloroisocyanurate. The rate of colour development and final intensity is enhanced in the presence of sodium nitroprusside.[12,13] Ammonia may be removed from potential interfering ions either by distillation or by gaseous diffusion through a suitable membrane. For natural waters which are highly coloured, the ammonium ions may be separated from the coloured organic matter by dialysis. The inorganic ions are able to pass through the dialysis membrane which retains the organic matter.

4.16.2 *Determination of nitrite*

The most widely-used methods for nitrite determination are based upon diazotization reactions. In acid solution, nitrite reacts with aromatic primary amines to produce rather unstable diazonium salts:

$$ArNH_2 + NO_2^- + 2H^+ \rightarrow Ar^+N\equiv N + 2H_2O.$$

The diazonium salt may then be coupled with one of a range of suitable aromatic amines or phenols to produce an intensely coloured azo dye. The absorbance of the azo dye thus produced is proportional to the original nitrite concentration under carefully controlled conditions. Older books recommended α-naphthylamine as the aromatic amine, but as this was always contaminated by the carcinogenic β-amine, some modern methods recommend instead the much purer, and also water-soluble, derivative, 1-naphthylamine-7-sulphonic acid.[11] Sulphanilamide is also widely used:

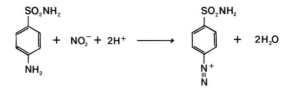

This diazonium ion may then be coupled to *N*-1-naphthylethylenediamine dihydrochloride to produce a highly absorbing, purple azo dye:

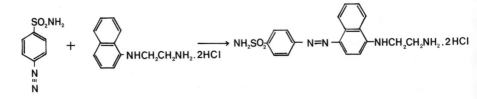

In the procedure described below, the diazonium salt from sulphanilic acid (4-aminobenzenesulphonic acid) is coupled with 1-naphthylamine-7-sulphonic acid.[11]

Procedure. Adjust the pH of a portion of up to 40 ml of sample to 7 ± 0.5, and dilute, if necessary, to *c.* 40 ml in a 50-ml graduated flask. Add 2.0 ml of sulphanilic acid solution (0.83 g in 250 ml of 20% v/v acetic acid, stored in a dark bottle), shake and stand for 10 minutes. Add 2.0 ml of 1-naphthylamine-7-sulphonic acid solution (0.83 g in 200 ml of warm water, cooled and filtered, and diluted to 250 ml with glacial acetic acid, stored in a dark bottle), dilute to volume and mix thoroughly. Measure the absorbance at 520 nm in a 40-mm cell against a reagent blank. Prepare standards covering the range $0-1 \mu g \, ml^{-1}$ (at the final dilution).

Remember to make the standard nitrite solution slightly alkaline to prevent decomposition.

4.16.3 Determination of nitrate

The determination of this anion presents some problems to which more than one solution has been offered. It is worth looking into this in a little detail and comparing the performances of the methods available. The first approach is to convert nitrate to nitrite and proceed as already described, and the second is to convert nitrate into a coloured nitrophenol and measure the absorbance of the yellow solution of its anion.

Reduction to nitrite. An older procedure[14] for this step involved shaking with zinc powder in ammoniacal solution in the presence of manganese(II) to reduce nitrate to nitrite. The sensitivity of the overall method (involving diazotization of sulphanilamide and coupling with N-1-naphthylethylene-diamine) is good, enabling 1 μg of nitrate to be detected, but the standard deviation, at 5% for 5 μg, is poor compared with that for the nitrite determination (1%) which does not involve a reduction step. The problem is that nitrogen exhibits many oxidation states, and it is difficult to ensure quantitative reduction to any one state. Better results have been claimed when a coppered cadmium reductant (in a small glass column) is used in the pH range 6–10 (below pH 5 nitrite is further reduced), with errors around 1–2% for 2 μg.[15]

Nitration of phenols. Numerous variations on this approach have been recommended at intervals since the publication of Blom and Treschow's paper in 1929.[16] The idea is simple: a reactive aromatic compound is nitrated quantitatively to give a typical yellow nitro-derivative, the colour of which is used for a photometric determination. Phenols generally are easily nitrated, but preferably one should be chosen which will give only one product. The xylenols are possible candidates.

Next, there is the problem of clean-up, since other substances in the sample may give brown or yellow products with the high sulphuric acid concentration needed (typically 70–80% v/v). A solvent extraction separation is simple and effective, the nitroxylenol being extracted from acidic aqueous solution into toluene and then washed back into aqueous alkali to give the required yellow colour.

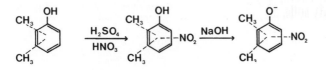

Alternatively, separation may be achieved by steam distillation: the diluted sulphuric acid solution is distilled until a few ml of distillate have been collected in a dilute alkali, giving the usual yellow colour. However, only o-nitroxylenols are steam volatile. We are now in a position to make a choice from the six possible xylenols, based upon the information summarized in Table 4.3. Of the methods surveyed, Andrews' method[17] is simple, avoids the necessity of evaporating to dryness, tolerates chloride, uses the extraction method of clean-up, and, with care, gives acceptable results in the hands of students.

Table 4.3   Nitration of xylenols

Structure and nitration positions	Number of products	Steam volatile?	Comments	Ref.	Rating
	1	no	71 % v/v acid; extraction based	17	**
			80 % v/v acid; tolerates chloride†; uses only 1 ml of sample	18	***
	2	yes/no	undesirable, two products‡	—	—
	1	yes	chloride must be removed and sample must be dried; distillation based.	19	**
			63 % v/v acid; evolved for nitrate esters; distillation based.	20	**
	2	yes/no	undesirable, two products‡	—	—
	2	yes/no	2-nitro-4,5-dimethylphenol obtained in ca. 85 % yield	21	**
	2	yes/no	undesirable, two products‡	—	—

† Carried out with added NH_4Cl to enhance sensitivity; reaction product is 4-nitroso-2,6-xylenol (Ref. 18).

‡ Also nitration adjacent to a methyl group gives poorer sensitivity because steric hindrance twists the nitrate out of the plane of the ring (Ref. 21).

Procedure.   To a 5-ml portion of water sample in a 100-ml beaker, add slowly 15 ml of sulphuric acid reagent, then cool to room temperature. Add 1 ml of 1 % w/v 2,6-xylenol in glacial acetic acid (*care!*), swirl to mix, and place the beaker in a water bath at 35° for 30 min. Cool and transfer the contents to a 250-ml separating funnel. Add 80 ml of water, 10 ml of toluene, and shake well for 1 min. Run off the lower (aqueous) layer, wash the toluene twice with 20-ml portions of water, then extract the nitroxylenol from the toluene with 20.0 ml of 2 M sodium hydroxide $(80 \, g \, l^{-1})$. Measure the absorbance in a 10-mm cell at 432 nm against a reagent blank. The standards used for calibration should cover the range up to 15 μg of nitrate.

Reagent: Dissolve 2 g of mercury(II) sulphate in 400 ml of water and cautiously add 20 ml of concentrated sulphuric acid. Each day as required, add 158 ml of concentrated sulphuric acid slowly and with cooling to 42 ml of the mercury solution. Cool to room temperature before use.

Sources of error: High quality sulphuric acid (e.g. AnalaR) must be used or the blank will be excessive. Do not overheat, and do not leave longer than 30 min, as some river samples may then give brown reaction products. It may be necessary to wait a few minutes for the phases to separate. Filter the coloured aqueous solution (through paper or cotton wool) to hold back droplets of toluene.

4.17   Determination of phosphate

Phosphate in natural waters is also determined routinely by colorimetric procedures. As mentioned earlier, phosphate is relatively immobile in all but very sandy soils, and therefore the natural levels of phosphate in waters tend to be very low. The anion does not present any particularly severe health hazard, the MAC for phosphorus being $5\,\mu g\,ml^{-1}$. It can sometimes enter watercourses from fertilizer, and sodium phosphates are used in water treatment, to precipitate calcium as finely crystalline calcium phosphate (to prevent scale formation). Much phosphorus enters in domestic effluent as detergent, and from sewage and animal waste products. One of the main problems associated with high levels of phosphorus in lake waters is the part it can play in encouraging excessive growth of algae, especially if nitrogen levels are also high.

At the low concentrations normally encountered in natural waters, a very sensitive method is necessary for its determination. Phosphate reacts with molybdate in acid solution to produce a pale yellow 'heteropoly acid', phosphomolybdic acid. This reacts with any one of a range of different reducing agents to produce an intense blue colour known as molybdenum blue. The procedure gives excellent sensitivity, and if long path cells are used in the colorimeter to increase the signal, can be used to determine the very low levels of phosphate often present. The colour of the complex is not very stable, the stability depending upon the reducing agent and the conditions of colour development. The method developed by Murphy and Riley[22] for ocean waters is not the most sensitive, but gives relatively good stability. Moreover, the reaction may be carried out by adding a single reagent solution, consisting of ammonium molybdate, ascorbic acid and potassium antimony tartrate in acid solution. The fact that the reagent may be pre-mixed is particularly advantageous in manual rather than in automated methods. In practice, less stable colours may be quite acceptable with automatic analysis systems because the colour development time is so rigidly fixed.

Procedure. Prepare the molybdate reagent solution in four parts as follows:

(i) Prepare 2.5 M sulphuric acid by dilution of 70 ml of concentrated acid to 500 ml.
(ii) Dissolve 20 g of analytical reagent grade ammonium molybdate in water and dilute to 500 ml.
(iii) Make up 75 ml of a 0.1 M ascorbic acid solution (prepare this fresh each day).
(iv) Dissolve 0.274 g of potassium antimony tartrate in water and dilute to 100 ml.

The molybdate reagent is prepared each day by adding in turn to 125 ml of solution (i), 37.5 ml of (ii), 75 ml of (iii) and 12.5 ml of (iv). Pipette up to 40 ml of sample into a 50-ml graduated flask (if necessary, dilute to *c.* 40 ml), add 8 ml of reagent and dilute to volume. Shake well and stand for at least 10 minutes. Measure the absorbance against a reagent blank at 882 nm, using 40-mm cells. Prepare standards covering the range 0–8 μg of phosphorus.

4.18 Automation of colorimetric procedures

As mentioned earlier it is generally necessary to follow procedures very carefully if reliable results are to be obtained by colorimetry. The amounts and strengths of reagents, the order of their addition, colour development time, and the time and temperature of any heating stages must all be carefully controlled. The resulting methods are often time-consuming and tedious, especially if large numbers of samples are to be processed. Although, as mentioned in Chapter 2, analysts generally produce better results when they are familiar with the procedure they are following, it is equally true that boredom may lead to careless slips and general lack of precision. Fortunately it is possible to automate the tedious manual methods of colorimetric analysis, and obtain at the end of the day results which are every bit as reliable as the manual results of a competent and careful analyst.

Essentially, what is necessary is to be able to mix reagents, samples and buffers in the required ratios and order, allowing required development times, with the required degree of reproducibility. One of two main approaches may be adopted to solving this problem. The reagents etc. may be added for pre-set periods of time from suitable rigid motorized syringes. Small vials move on a conveyor belt to pass under the appropriate syringe outlets, and the contents of the vials may be stirred automatically. Development time may be adjusted by selecting the position of the uptake tube through which the final solution is sucked to be pumped to the colorimeter cell for absorbance measurement.

Alternatively, and in practice more commonly, the solutions may be pumped through flexible plastic tubing at steady rates by means of a peristaltic pump. The principle of operation of the pump is very simple, and is shown schematically in Fig. 4.7. As the rollers rotate in the direction shown,

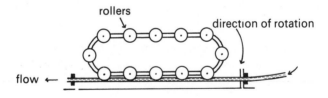

Figure 4.7   The principle of operation of a peristaltic pump.

they cause a restriction in the plastic tubing, which effectively squeezes the trapped liquid along the tube as indicated. The tubing internal diameter and wall thickness govern the flow rate of the solution being pumped. Reagents are mixed as required by the use of special T-pieces immediately upstream of mixing coils. The length of the coil (i.e. the number of turns) governs the reaction time after each reagent addition. If required, heating coils in oil baths or large delay coils are available for reactions which require heat or have long development times.

If tubing of very narrow diameter is employed and the flow rate of liquid is high, there is very little mixing between the colours developed by adjacent samples, especially if these are separated by a reagent blank. Determinations by the resulting technique, which is known as flow injection analysis, may be completed very rapidly, a rate of 120 samples per hour being fairly typical.

If tubing of a larger diameter (still however only a few mm) is employed, mixing between adjacent samples would occur, which is obviously undesirable as it would require pumping each sample for a longer period of time and thus slow down the analysis rate. The problem may be avoided by introducing slugs of air into the liquid line, thus giving segmented flow. This is the basis of the famous Technicon Autoanalyser system, the dominant automatic analyser for many years. Of course it is necessary to remove the air bubbles before the final solution is pumped into the colorimeter cell, but this is relatively simple.

Precisely how the system works will probably become clearer when a typical manifold is examined—the example chosen being for the determination of nitrite plus nitrate after reduction to nitrite. The components required and their assembly into a complete manifold are shown in Fig. 4.8.

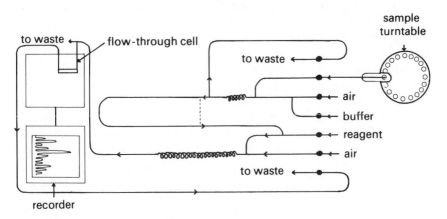

Figure 4.8 Manifold for the automated determination of nitrate plus nitrite.

The sample is pumped from a small plastic vial in the sample turntable for an appropriate period, say 20s. The take-up arm then automatically lifts out of the sample and dips into a wash solution (not shown) for an appropriate period. The turntable rotates until the next sample is under the take-up arm, which is then automatically lowered, and so on. Ammonium chloride is meanwhile pumped continuously, segmented by air, and mixed with the sample. The samples are then de-bubbled, by pumping off the air plus a small part of the sample, so that air does not impair the efficiency of the copper/cadmium reductor U-tube, through which the sample then passes. In the reductor, nitrate is reduced to nitrite. The output of the reductor is then again segmented by air, and mixed with reagent in a longer coil (to allow adequate time for colour development). The resulting coloured solution is de-bubbled and pumped through the flow-through cell of the colorimeter, where the absorbance is measured and recorded on a chart recorder. Note that if the cadmium/copper reductor is by-passed (the broken line in Fig. 4.8), the manifold would then determine nitrite, rather than nitrate plus nitrite, which is what is determined by the manifold shown. Nitrite concentrations are normally appreciably lower than nitrate in natural waters, so nitrate may be determined quite adequately by difference. If the sample nitrate levels are off-scale (i.e. too high for the standards), it is relatively simple to incorporate a dilution step. This would involve mixing water with segmented sample, de-bubbling and re-sampling the diluted sample.

Once such manifolds have been set up and their reliability established, they are relatively simple to operate, and a competent technician can easily determine nitrate and nitrite in several hundred samples with only a few hours of work spread over a week. The most time-consuming aspect in their routine use is probably the periodic replacement of tubing, the characteristics of which do eventually change. However, standards are run, dispersed through every batch of samples, to give early warning of possible problems from this source.

Most traditional chemical manipulation processes may now be automated, including for example dialysis which, as mentioned earlier, is used to prevent interference from coloured dissolved organic matter in the determination of ammonia. Even procedures incorporating solvent extraction steps may now be successfully automated. Although the cost of apparatus for automated colorimetric analysis is high, if the sample throughput is also high, the cost may be recouped after a relatively short period through saving in labour costs. The reproducibility of each individual step in the overall process is excellent.

4.19   The determination of chloride by titrimetry (visual)

Chloride in drinking water is generally regarded as relatively harmless if present in small amounts: the World Health Organization has quoted $200\,\mu g\,ml^{-1}$ as the level above which undesirable health effects may be noted. It occurs naturally in rainfall, and levels of $10\,\mu g\,ml^{-1}$ are not uncommon in areas with maritime climates, much higher levels often being observed in coastal regions. Problems of salt accumulation are of interest in irrigation water used in arid areas, and in river water used for livestock, where during abnormally dry periods tidal waters reach much further upstream than normal.

Chloride may be simply and rapidly determined by titration with silver nitrate, using potassium chromate as an indicator, and the end point is indicated by the occurrence of a permanent reddish tinge (Mohr's method). A small amount of solid sodium tetraborate may be conveniently added as a pH buffer. Bromide, iodide, cyanide and sulphide are included in the titration, but these anions are normally present at a negligible concentration compared with chloride, so these potential interferences are of little practical consequence.

Procedure: Add to 100 ml of sample in a 250-ml flask a small spatula-full of sodium tetraborate (as pH buffer, pH 9) and a small microspatula-full of potassium chromate (as indicator). Titrate carefully, dropwise at the start, in case the chloride level is very low, with 0.05 M silver nitrate solution (8.49 g l^{-1}) from a 10-ml burette until a permanent reddish tinge is seen.

Calculation. One ml of 0.05 M silver nitrate solution for 100 ml of sample is equivalent to $0.05 \times 10^{-3} \times 35.5 \times 10$ g l^{-1} of chloride = 17.7 g l^{-1} (or 29 g l^{-1} of sodium chloride). Compare the value you get with the estimate based on conductivity measurement. This will give you an idea as to whether there are significant amounts of other ions to be looked for.

4.20   Ion-selective electrodes

An alternative to a visual end-point location for the above titration (or even to titration of any kind) is to use an ion-selective electrode for the determination of chloride. This device is a development of the long-established pH glass electrode, discussed in Section 4.11. Electrodes which are selective towards other ions have membranes of many different types and materials, and mention can be made here of only a very few types.

4.20.1   *Glass membranes*

An electrode made of soda-alumina-silica glass shows good response towards sodium ions in solution at least down to 10^{-4} M, and can be a useful alternative to flame photometry for this element. A similar electrode based on a potash-alumina-silica glass responds to potassium, but also to most other monovalent ions, so has rather limited applications, particularly as there is usually more sodium than potassium in biological fluids and environmental waters.

4.20.2   *Single-crystal membranes*

Crystals of silver chloride, for example, can be used to make an electrode with a good response towards chloride ion down to the level of the solubility of AgCl, at 10^{-5} M. Ions giving less soluble salts (such as iodide and sulphide) interfere, sometimes permanently. Probably the best example of a crystal electrode is the fluoride electrode, with a single crystal of europium-doped lanthanum fluoride, LaF$_3$. As this has a low solubility, it can be used for determining fluoride comfortably to 10^{-5} M $(0.2\,\mu\text{g ml}^{-1})$ and even to

10^{-6} M under favourable conditions. However, the response tends to be slower at these low levels. As drinking water treated with fluoride for prevention of dental caries typically contains 1 μg ml^{-1} the electrode provides an attractive means of carrying out the analysis. The LaF$_3$ is doped with some europium to improve its electrical conductivity, and the membrane is cut as a 1 mm-thick disc a few mm in diameter. The disc is sealed into the end of a rigid plastic tube, which is filled with an equimolar solution of potassium chloride and sodium fluoride into which dips a silver/silver chloride electrode, as shown in Fig. 4.9. A second electrode, usually a saturated calomel

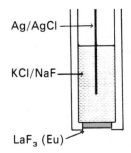

Ag/AgCl

KCl/NaF

LaF$_3$ (Eu)

Figure 4.9   A fluoride ion-selective electrode.

electrode, is inserted into the test solution along with the fluoride electrode, and the potential difference between the two is measured with a high-input resistance millivoltmeter (a modern digital voltmeter with 0.1 mV readability is suitable). The measured potential is given by:

$$E_{\text{meas}} = \text{constant} + \frac{RT}{nF} \log a_{\text{F}^-} - E_{\text{S.C.E.}}$$

$$E_{\text{meas}} = 0.058 \log [\text{F}^-] + \text{constant}'.$$

It is convenient to plot calibration measurements for a wide range of concentrations on log/linear paper, as in Fig. 4.10.

4.20.3   Determination of fluoride

It is important to remember that electrodes respond to a particular ionic species. The fluoride electrode responds to hydrated F$^-$, but not to HF nor to FeF$_6^{3-}$; it will also respond to OH$^-$ if the pH is above 9. A practical method for fluoride will therefore need to take these factors into account to yield correct answers from unknown samples. A further problem is that the electrode responds to the *activity* of the ion, not to the concentration. However, if the samples and standards are all brought to a constant ionic strength, the response will be reproducible. The use of a Total Ionic Strength

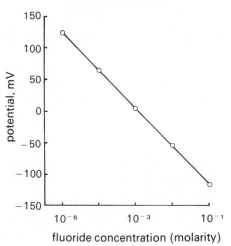

Figure 4.10 A typical calibration graph for the determination of fluoride with an ion-selective electrode.

Adjustment Buffer (TISAB) was suggested by Frant and Ross[23] for ensuring reliable performance with their original fluoride electrode and this has become standard practice. A TISAB solution containing an acetate buffer (to control pH), a complexing reagent, CDTA (to mask metals and thus release fluoride), and a salt at a high concentration, e.g. sodium chloride or perchlorate, to maintain a constant ionic strength, is added to all samples and standards before they are measured.

Procedure. Prepare the TISAB reagent as follows:[24] to 500 ml of water add 57 ml of glacial acetic acid, 58 g of sodium chloride and 4 g of 1,2-diaminocyclohexane tetra-acetic acid (CDTA) (EDTA will be nearly as good). Place the beaker in a cold-water bath and add 5 M sodium hydroxide solution slowly with stirring until the pH lies in the range 5.0–5.5. Dilute to 1 l.

Prepare a series of standard solutions by dilution of a stock sodium fluoride solution, conveniently covering the range 10^{-1} M $- 10^{-5}$ M ($1.9 \mathrm{g} \, l^{-1}$–$0.19 \, \mathrm{mg} \, l^{-1}$ of fluoride). To 10 ml of each add 10 ml of TISAB, mix, insert the electrode and a calomel reference electrode and after waiting a little while—from a few seconds in concentrated fluoride solutions to a few minutes in very dilute solutions—read the potential on a digital millivoltmeter with readability of 0.1 mV. Plot the results on log/linear paper as shown in Fig. 4.10.

Apparatus. Plastic beakers and flasks (e.g. polypropylene, polyethylene or Teflon) should be used for storing the fluoride solutions and for all measurements.

4.20.4 Polymer membranes

It has proved possible to make a wide variety of electrodes with membranes consisting of a sparingly soluble salt of the ion to be determined, such as AgCl for chloride, in a silicone rubber matrix; this is the Pungor type of electrode. Alternatively, an organic salt may be used, such as tributyl phosphate, doped with Ca^{2+} in poly(vinyl chloride) for the determination of calcium.

4.20.5 *Liquid membranes*

A viscous organic solvent, supported on a sintered glass disc and containing suitable selective reagents, can.make a very effective membrane for a working ion-selective electrode. One good example is the use of valinomycin in diphenyl ether, which gives an electrode with very good selectivity towards potassium, particularly welcome as the glass electrodes for potassium are not very useful.

4.20.6 *Selectivity*

Most electrodes respond to some extent to species besides those for which they are intended. The equation for the response of an electrode may be expressed, for univalent ions, as

$$E = \text{constant} + 0.058 \log \{a_i + K_{ij}(a_j)\}$$

where a_i is the activity of the ion i which is to be determined and a_j is the activity of an interfering ion j. Clearly, K_{ij} should be small if interferences are not to be serious. Moody and Thomas have discussed the general problems of electrodes and selectivities[25] and a number of useful texts on ion selective electrodes and potentiometry are available (see, for example, Refs. 26–29).

4.20.7 *Potentiometric titrations*

Unless an electrode is actually malfunctioning in such a way as to give an open circuit, it will always give some potential, and the operator has no direct indication as to whether the reading on the millivolt meter is meaningful or not, although common sense may suggest that there is cause for suspicion. Instead of relying on a single measurement of electrode potential, the analyst can use the electrode to monitor the course of a titration following, for example, the decrease in fluoride when titrated with thorium or in chloride when titrated with silver. The latter titration is easily (and cheaply) carried out by using a piece of silver wire in the sample solution as the silver ion-selective electrode. Since the solubility product, $K_{sp} = [Ag^+][Cl^-]$, $[Ag^+] = K_{sp}/[Cl^-]$, where square brackets denote molar concentrations. The electrode responds to silver ions:

$$\begin{aligned} E &= \text{constant} + 0.058 \log [Ag^+] \\ &= \text{constant} + 0.058 \log K_{sp} - 0.058 \log [Cl^-]. \end{aligned}$$

The sharpness of the break in the titration curve can be improved by adding an equal volume of acetone to reduce the solubility of the silver chloride formed (Fig. 4.11). If two or more ions which form insoluble silver salts are present, it may be possible to get two or more end-points from the titration curve, but it may not be easy to get correct results because of co-precipitation

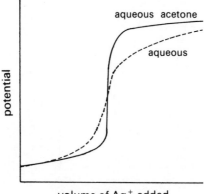

Figure 4.11 Potentiometric titration curves for chloride in water and in aqueous acetone with silver.

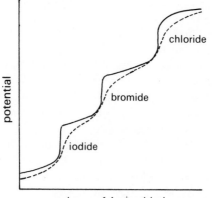

Figure 4.12 Theoretical (solid line) and experimental (broken line) potentiometric titration curves for a mixture of halides.

and adsorption phenomena. Fig. 4.12 shows the predicted and the experimentally observed curves for the titration of a mixture of halides with silver nitrate.

Procedure. Fig. 4.13 shows the apparatus required: the silver wire dips into the sample solution (diluted 1:1 with acetone) in a beaker on a magnetic stirrer. The reference electrode is a silver or platinum wire fused into the jet of a 10-ml burette, the tip of which must dip below the surface of the sample solution. Add increments of 0.05 M silver nitrate, small at first, and again small as the potential begins to change significantly, and plot potential vs. volume of titrant added. The end-point is at the point of steepest slope.

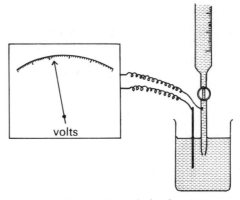

Figure 4.13 Apparatus required for potentiometric titrations.

4.21 Ion chromatography

For many years ion exchangers have been used in water analysis for the separation and/or concentration of metal cations prior to determination of individual elements. The cations from large water samples, typically up to one litre, may be absorbed on to a relatively small amount of ion exchanger, and then eluted with a much smaller amount of dilute acid. Concentrations of 20-fold or higher may be readily achieved. In recent years, however, a technique known as ion chromatography[30] has attracted much attention, particularly for the determinations of anions in natural waters.

Essentially ion chromatography depends upon the separation of anions on a column of anion exchange resin, according to their size and charge, by elution with dilute sodium carbonate/bicarbonate solution. The separated anions are then converted to the corresponding free acids by passing the eluate through a column of cation exchanger in the H^+ form. The presence of the free mineral acids, even at very low concentrations, causes a change in the conductivity of the final eluate which may be readily measured, and thus, by use of suitable standards, provides a measure of the concentrations of the individual cations. The procedure has been applied to the routine determination of sulphate, chlorate and nitrate in precipitation samples.[31] Using commercially available automated apparatus, up to 60 samples may be analysed in a working day for a wide range of anions.

4.22 The determination of heavy metals

In recent years there has been much interest in the concentrations of heavy metals in drinking water because of their possible toxicity. As the effect of consumption of contaminated water is generally cumulative, prolonged use of water containing very low concentrations is hazardous. The elements lead, cadmium and mercury are particularly undesirable, the 1980 EEC Directive MAC levels for these elements being 0.05, 0.005 and 0.001 $\mu g\,ml^{-1}$ respectively. The development of analytical methods for the determination of such low levels of these elements has played an important part in achieving recognition of the problem they present, and it may well be that when the detectability of other elements also eventually improves, their MAC values may also be reduced. The ability to analyse clinical samples for very low levels of lead was instrumental in the discovery that lead may have neuro-toxic effects at levels below those associated with clinical lead poisoning. As mentioned earlier, lead (from lead piping) is still found in the water in many older houses in the UK, and in such properties the MAC value may often be exceeded (many consider that this level is in any case too high).

To make determinations at this level is difficult. Preconcentration tech-niques are necessary if colorimetric methods or flame atomic absorption are to be used, and high reagent blanks may then create problems. Lead may be determined by atomic absorption spectroscopy only if hydride generation techniques are used, because the sensitivity of conventional flame atomic absorption is not adequate (see Section 6.15); mercury can be determined by atomic absorption or, better still, atomic fluorescence spectrometry, if cold-vapour techniques are employed. Cadmium may be determined by flame atomic fluorescence spectrometry at low concentrations. However, the deter-mination of any of these three elements by these techniques would require considerable time, operator skill and specialized apparatus. Nevertheless, there is one technique, anodic stripping voltammetry (ASV), which may be used to determine heavy metals rapidly, simply and directly in drinking water samples. In this section the well-established, but rather slow, photometric methods[32] will be compared with this sensitive electrochemical technique.

4.22.1 *Photometric methods with dithizone*

A reagent extensively used for photometric determinations of heavy metals in natural waters is dithizone,[33] a dark green compound, soluble in organic solvents, which forms red chelate complexes with many metal ions.

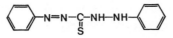

It dissolves as the anion in water at high pH, giving a yellow solution. Some 17 elements form extractable coloured chelates with dithizone, so a little chemistry has to be used to develop a method selective towards any one metal. Much use is made of pH control and selective masking reactions. The choice of solvent for extraction of dithizone and its chelates is important: it is about 30 times more soluble in chloroform than it is in carbon tetrachloride, so that, although an aqueous wash solution at pH 10 will take 90% of the dithizone out of carbon tetrachloride, one at pH 11.5 is needed for chloroform. Both solvents are used in practice but they are not always interchangeable, and procedures should be followed closely.

The commonest dithizone complexes have the formula $M(HDz)_2$ but a number of organo-metallic ions also form complexes, such as some alkyl-lead ions, $R_3Pb(HDz)$ and $R_2Pb(HDz)_2$, and some mercury ions, such as $RHg(HDz)$ and $Ar\,Hg(Dz)$ for methyl, ethyl and phenyl for example. This may be used in the determination of some organometallic compounds, but as the molar absorptivities are not the same as for the simple metal complexes, these organometallic complexes should rather be seen as possible interferents, and destroyed by acid mineralization before the extraction step. The equation which represents, at least in simple form, the formation and extraction of divalent metal dithizonates is

$$M^{2+} + 2H_2Dz_{(org)} \overset{K_{ex}}{\rightleftharpoons} M(HDz)_{2(org)} + 2H^+$$

from which one can define an extraction constant as

$$K_{ex} = \frac{[M(HDz)_2]_{org}[H^+]^2}{[M^{2+}][H_2Dz]_{org}^2}$$

or, in the logarithmic form

$$\log K_{ex} = \log \frac{[M(HDz)_2]_{org}}{[M^{2+}]} - 2\log[H_2Dz]_{org} - 2pH$$

hence

$$\log \frac{[M]_{org}}{[M]_{aq}} = pH + 2\log[H_2Dz]_{org} + \log K_{ex}.$$

The last equation gives a measure of the degree of extraction of the metal. Square brackets denote molar concentrations, and in the last equation $[M]_{org}$ indicates the metal as the dithizonate. Table 4.4 gives some values for $\log K_{ex}$, when carbon tetrachloride is used. Procedures are included below for lead and mercury, as examples of the combination of masking and pH control typically used to produce selective methods using this reagent.

General warnings!

(1) Cyanide is very poisonous: keep all solutions of cyanide alkaline, work in a fume hood, and do not pipette by mouth.
(2) Solvent vapours are also toxic: work in a fume hood and do not pipette by mouth. (With care, useful work can be done simply with measuring cylinders, otherwise use solvent-proof preset dispensers.)

Table 4.4 Extraction constants for metal dithizonates in carbon tetrachloride

Metal	$\log K_{ex}$	pH_{min} 99%	Masked by
Hg	26.8	very acid	Br, I, low pH
Cu	10.5	~0	CN, high pH
Cd	2.1 ⎫	2.9	CN, high/low pH
Zn	2.0 ⎭		CN, high pH
Pb	0.4	4.5	tartrate, citrate, low pH

(3) Dithizone-based procedures are very sensitive: all apparatus must be soaked in dilute nitric acid and then rinsed thoroughly. Reagents may have to be cleaned by extracting their solutions with dithizone in chloroform, but should always be measured out precisely to keep the blank from low-level contamination constant.

(4) Dithizone decomposes on storage in solution due to oxidation. Keep solutions cool and in the dark, purify as directed, and prepare fresh frequently.

Preparation of dithizone solution. Shake 20 mg of dithizone in 100 ml of carbon tetrachloride till most is dissolved. Extract four times with 50 ml of dilute ammonia solution (1 ml of 10% in 100 ml of water), combine these extracts, filter them, acidify with 1 ml of hydrochloric acid and extract into 100 ml of carbon tetrachloride. Wash the organic layer with three portions of water and filter. This solution, kept in the dark, is stable for a month. When required, dilute 10 ml to 200 ml with carbon tetrachloride for the following determinations.

Preparation of samples. To ensure that particulate matter in water samples is dissolved, acidify with hydrochloric acid and boil for a few minutes. To destroy organometallic species, particularly of mercury, add 10 ml of concentrated sulphuric acid to 100 ml of sample and boil under reflux for 2 hours, adding portions of saturated potassium permanganate solution so that there is still a pale violet colour at the finish.

Procedure for lead. To 100 ml of water sample add 30 ml of ammoniacal sulphite-cyanide solution (350 ml concentrated ammonia solution, 3 g potassium cyanide, and 10 g sodium sulphite, diluted to 1 l with water) and 10.0 ml of dithizone solution. Shake vigorously for 30 sec and run off some of the carbon tetrachloride layer through a cotton-wool plug into a 10-mm spectrophotometer cell. Measure the absorbance at 515 nm (the complex is red). For calibration take between 5 and 30 μg of lead through the same procedure. Then 10 μg in 100 ml = 0.1 μg ml^{-1} in the sample.

Procedure for mercury. Acidify 100 ml of sample to pH 0–1 with dilute sulphuric acid and extract twice with 10.0 ml of dithizone solution—the second extract must remain green, otherwise start again with a smaller sample. Wash the combined extracts three times with dilute ammonia solution (5 ml to 1 l of water), then once with dilute acetic acid to neutralize any ammonia left. Run off some of the extract, filter it into a 1-cm spectrophotometer cell, and measure the absorbance at 485 nm (the complex is orange). Calibration range, 5–30 μg of mercury.

4.22.2 *Polarographic determination of heavy metals*

The principle of polarography—the diffusion-controlled electrochemical reduction of species at a dropping mercury electrode—has been discussed in Section 4.13.2 in connection with the determination of dissolved oxygen. However, as there is a high over-voltage hindering the reduction of hydrogen ions on a mercury surface, it is possible to reduce many metals ions to the corresponding atoms which dissolve to form dilute amalgams in the mercury. In order to ensure that the rate of transport of the ions is purely diffusion controlled, and hence strictly proportional to the bulk concentration of the ions in the solution, a background electrolyte, such as 0.1 M potassium chloride is added, and the solution is not stirred. As the different metal ions have different electrode potentials, so they begin to be reduced at different potentials at the dropping mercury electrode (see Fig. 4.14). As complexing

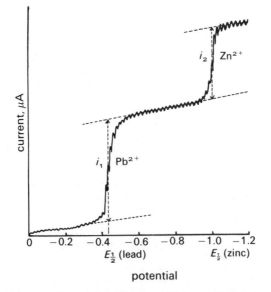

Figure 4.14 Polarographic wave for a sample containing lead and zinc.

ligands can alter electrode potentials, they can be used to alter the polarographic reduction potentials, sometimes making additional resolution of waves possible (e.g. nickel and zinc). It can be shown[34,35] that the potential half-way up the wave, called $E_{1/2}$, the *half-wave potential*, is independent of the concentration of the ion, and is also characteristic of it, making identification possible if the electrolyte is known. Some examples of half-wave potentials in various supporting electrolytes are shown in Table 4.5.

When two or more reducible ions are present in the same solution, the corresponding number of waves may be observed. The height of each is proportional to the concentration of the respective metal ion. Calibration is achieved by recording polarograms of several different concentrations of the metal ion, as shown in Fig. 4.15. The lower concentration limit for this technique is around 10^{-5} M, determined by the residual current (broken line in Fig. 4.15) and the fluctuations in the current as the mercury drop grows and then falls off. A number of instrumental developments are designed to eliminate these factors, e.g. by making the measurements only for a short time

Table 4.5 Some polarographic half-wave potentials (volts)

Metal ion	1 M KNO$_3$	1 M KCl	1 M NH$_3$/NH$_4$Cl	1 M KSCN	1 M KCN
Cadmium	−0.59	−0.64	−0.74	—	−1.18
Copper	+0.02	—	−0.20	−0.02	—
Lead	−0.40	−0.43	—	—	−0.72
Manganese	—	−1.51	−1.45	−1.55	−1.33
Nickel	—	−1.1	−1.02	−0.70	−1.40
Zinc	−1.01	−1.02	−1.21	−1.01	—

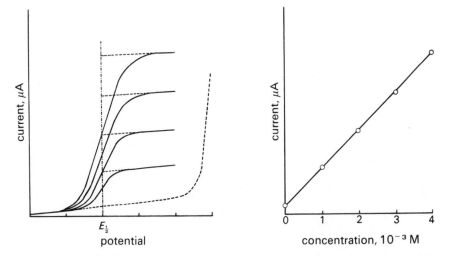

Figure 4.15 Polarographic waves for a series of standard solutions and a blank, and the calibration graph thus obtained.

just before the end of each drop-life and by allowing charging currents to subside before measurements are made, and these have improved the sensitivity of the methods, but one new group of methods has made possible very striking improvements in sensitivity. This is known as anodic stripping voltammetry (ASV).

4.22.3 *Anodic stripping voltammetric determination of metals*
In this technique[36] a stationary electrode is used, held for some specified time at a sufficiently negative potential to reduce the metal ions of interest. Diffusion control is again operative, so that the total amount of the ion reduced, i.e. deposited on and dissolved in the mercury drop (which may be hanging or sitting), will be proportional to both the bulk concentration and the time allowed. In practice, stirring the solution markedly increases the rate of transport, while still allowing it to be proportional to the concentration.

After a predetermined electrolysis time (say at $-1.0\,V$) the stirring is stopped, and the potential is then scanned at a steady rate (typically around $100\,mV\,min^{-1}$) in a positive direction (Fig. 4.16). When the applied potential is close to the half-wave potential, the accumulated metal is oxidized back

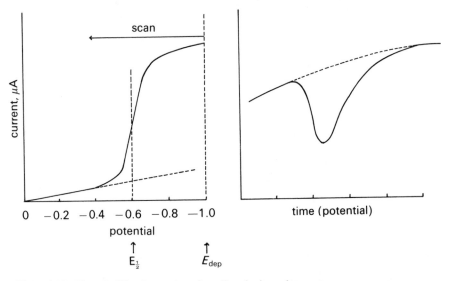

Figure 4.16   The principle of operation of anodic stripping voltammetry.

into solution as fast as it can get to the electrode–solution interface and be transported away into solution. The result is a fairly short-lived current "peak" derived from the anodic (oxidative) stripping process. The height of the peak is proportional to the original concentration of the ion in the solution. The gain in sensitivity achieved by combining the long deposition (with stirring) and the quick stripping process is impressive: Fig. 4.17 shows the stripping voltammogram recorded with simple equipment for lead at $5\,\mu g\,l^{-1}$ $(2.5 \times 10^{-8}\,M)$ in some tap water previously purified by passage through an ion-exchange resin filter. Also shown are the traces for the same sample with various standard additions of lead.

Choice of electrode.   A hanging mercury drop was used for much of the early work, because it offered the advantages of cleanliness and the ability of many metals to dissolve to form amalgams. With such an electrode, or with a sitting mercury drop on the top of a vertical capillary, the individual metals can be reoxidized quite independently, and therefore without interference on one from another. The disadvantage is that it takes a long time for all the metal atoms to diffuse out of the drop, and the resulting peak is broad (Fig. 4.16).

The mercury drop electrode gives good reproducibility (R.S.D. 1.5% for $1\,\mu g\,ml^{-1}\,Cd^{2+}$) but poor resolution from other ions.

Use of a solid electrode, such as graphite (impregnated with wax to displace oxygen) or glassy carbon, avoids the limitations of the rate of transport, so the peaks are quite sharp (see Fig. 4.17) but the possibility of

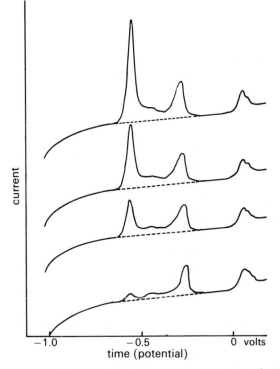

Figure 4.17 Voltammograms for a sample of water containing $5\,\mu g\,l^{-1}$ of lead before (bottom trace) and after standard additions of lead.

interference is high, as each metal tends to trap the other in the electrode. One solution to this problem which is quite often used is to add a little mercury salt to the sample and deposit a thin film—actually many tiny droplets—of mercury, into which the other metal atoms dissolve as they are co-deposited.

The standard addition technique can be used to advantage with ASV, as seen in Fig. 4.18. Here the peak heights from Fig. 4.17 have been plotted against concentration, the drinking water sample having been analysed directly and then after several additions of known small amounts of lead. Extrapolation then gives the concentration of lead in the sample.

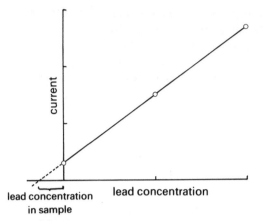

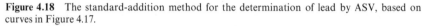

Figure 4.18   The standard-addition method for the determination of lead by ASV, based on curves in Figure 4.17.

4.22.4   *Differential pulse stripping analysis*

Although ASV is a very sensitive technique, even lower detection limits are obtained if a linear ramp with superimposed small amplitude pulses is applied instead of the steady, linear ramp, potential shift during the stripping stage. For each pulse, the current is measured immediately before the pulse and also towards the end of the pulse. These signals can then be processed to give effectively the first derivative of the normal d.c. stripping voltammetry waveform. This allows greater electronic gains to be employed, because much of the background and noise is similar for both signals and may therefore be eliminated. The resulting technique is known as differential pulse stripping analysis.

As with polarography, the advantage of stripping techniques is that several elements may be determined simultaneously, but the greatly increased sensitivity makes it possible to determine the low levels present in river- or sea water without prior chemical treatment. On the other hand, the results should be interpreted with caution, because this technique determines the dissolved ionic species only, and not the strongly bound or insoluble forms of the metals. It is still advisable to acidify the sample in good time before the determination (using high-purity acid) so as to bring most of the metal into solution.

4.23   The importance of chemical species—speciation

For trace heavy metals, most existing legislation is concerned with total amounts of a particular analyte present in a water sample. It must be remembered therefore that analytical methods which depend upon the existence of free metal ions in solution will not determine that part of the analyte which is present in the form of a complex with organic matter or as a very fine colloidal suspension. This certainly applies for example to ASV and ion-selective electrodes. In colorimetry, the situation is somewhat more complicated, because complexed metal may be partly released or colloidal species partly decomposed. Direct atomic absorption, on the other hand, tends to estimate the total amount of analyte present. In the case of the determination of lead and copper in tap water, for example, it has been shown that unless steps are taken to destroy organic matter, much of the total lead and copper is not determined by ASV.[37] In this case the organic matter could be quite easily destroyed by photochemical oxidation in acidified sample solutions, and quantitative recovery of the elements was then possible. In the analysis of natural waters, therefore, the possibility of interference from natural complexation should always be considered, even in atomic spectro-scopic methods if pre-concentration or separation techniques such as solvent extraction or ion-exchange are employed.

Recently there has been considerable interest in speciation (the distribution of elements between various chemical forms as well as the total amount of the element present). The topic has recently been reviewed by Florence.[38] The toxicity of elements is often significantly different for the different species. It seems likely that new demands will be made upon the analyst, as improved procedures become available for speciation studies, and the results of such studies are interpreted.

4.24 Trace organics in water—total organic carbon (TOC)

Interest in the types and amounts of organic pollutants in water and waste water has recently grown, much of it prompted by legislation governing what may and what may not be discharged into a river or lake, since industry must satisfy the appropriate authorities that its waste water is not likely to cause any interference with the environment.

One rapidly-determined value which serves as a starting point for an investigation of trace organics in water is Total Organic Carbon. As with oxygen demand, TOC values serve purely as an indicator of water quality. However, it is possible to make these determinations on purpose-built instruments quickly and with high sensitivity, so the approach is useful in water-quality monitoring. (In one factory known to the authors, the know-ledge that TOC determinations could detect if one bottle full of waste solvent had been emptied into the river prompted the plant operators to take much more care about recovering waste solvents. The result was that the instrument soon paid for itself in the savings on solvents, and the river became a lot cleaner!)

4.24.1   *Outline of method for TOC determination*

The water must first be acidified and purged to remove CO_2, from carbonate or bicarbonate (this may result in the loss of volatile organic compounds). A small measured volume of treated water is then injected into a gas stream passing through a heated packed tube where the organic matter is oxidized to carbon dioxide. The latter is determined either by IR absorption photometry, or is converted to methane for determination by a flame-ionization detector (see Section 3.10.6). Levels of TOC down to about $1 \mu g \, ml^{-1}$ can be determined.

4.25   Determination of some individual compounds or groups of compounds in polluted waters

The Environmental Protection Agency (EPA), in its recently-published *Sampling and Analysis Procedures for Survey of Industrial Effluents for Priority Pollutants*, lists 114 organic pollutants which may be found at (usually) very low levels in waters (see Appendix 3). Samples for analysis must normally undergo some clean-up procedure, to separate the organics from the water, since most chromatographic columns do not tolerate repeated injections of aqueous samples, and a substantial degree of preconcentration is usually needed because the concentrations in water are so low.

Two methods of clean-up are particularly useful, the purge-and-trap method for volatile compounds, and solvent extraction for the rest. In the first method, a stream of inert gas is blown through the sample and then passed through a short tube containing a solid absorbant which will hold back the volatile organics but not the water vapour. Activated charcoal is recommended by some, as the adsorbed components can be washed off with a solvent such as carbon disulphide, but a combination of a porous polymer powder (Tenax) followed by silica gel to retain very volatile components, is recommended by the EPA. The adsorbed compounds are released rapidly by heating the tube as the carrier gas flows through it, and then passed on to the chromatograph column. One group of compounds which is determined by this technique includes the halogenated solvents, which can be separated on a poly(ethylene glycol) column (Carbowax 1500) preferably with temperature programming.

Without doubt, chromatographic techniques offer the best general solution to the problem of determination of trace organics in water, but when only a total figure for compounds of a certain class is required, a chemical method based on a specific reaction of the active group may be a useful alternative. The colorimetric method for phenols may be quoted here as a typical example.

4.25.1   *Photometric determination of phenols*

Although some phenolic compounds occur naturally, phenols are common pollutants in industrial waste water, particularly in effluents from coking plants and brown coal distillation plants, even after attempts have been made to remove them.[39] They are also used in the manufacture of certain drugs, dyes, plastics, pesticides and herbicides. Phenol is lethal to fish at quite low concentrations, causing the death of trout after 3 hours' exposure at the $6 \mu g \, ml^{-1}$ level.[40]

Phenols are enriched in fish, and levels much lower than this may be sufficient to render them unfit for consumption.[38] EEC Directive 80/778 quotes an MAC value for phenols of $0.5 \mu g \, l^{-1}$ but this figure excludes natural phenols which do not react with chlorine, and exceptions are sometimes allowed for complex phenols of soil and plant origin provided they are not detectable by taste after treatment by chlorination. Some phenols can adversely affect the taste of water at very low concentrations. A number of methods have been proposed for the determination of phenols, for example a colour test with iron salts, bromination reactions and infrared spectrophotometry. While GLC of volatile derivatives of phenols (see Section 7.9.2) is now often used, the well-established aminoantipyrine colorimetric method is worth quoting as an example of a combination of clean-up and chemical reactions to give a coloured product. Phenols not substituted in the *para* position will undergo an oxidative condensation with 4-aminoantipyrine.[41]

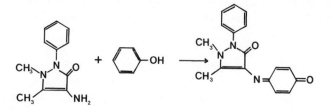

Procedure. Adjust the pH of 100 ml of sample to 10.0 ± 0.2 ($NH_3 + NH_4Cl$), add 2 ml of a $2\% \, w/v$ aqueous solution of the reagent and 2 ml of an $8\% \, w/v$ aqueous potassium hexacyanoferrate(III) solution, mixing after each addition. After 15 min measure the absorbance of the red solution at 510 nm. The calibration range covers 100–500 μg of phenol.

Clean-up procedure.   The condensation reaction also works with aliphatic amines, so a separation step is required. Steam distillation of the volatile phenols from a solution acidified with phosphoric acid (0.5 ml of 85 % acid for 500 ml of sample) and containing some copper sulphate to hold back sulphide (5 ml of 10 % m/v copper sulphate solution for 500 ml) achieves a satisfactory separation and recovery if most of the original water sample is distilled over. A suitable portion of the distillate is then taken through the procedure. As with so many other methods, the success depends as much on a carefully-performed clean-up step as on the final determination.

4.25.2   *Determination of hydrocarbons*

The EEC's MAC for hydrocarbons in water for human consumption is $0.01 \mu g \, ml^{-1}$. They may enter water supplies either from industrial waste-water or by accident or illegal storage, handling or dumping of crude oil, heating oil, fuel and lubricating oils, leaks from pipelines, etc.

One of the most useful methods for characterization of hydrocarbons is infrared spectrophotometry. In general the hydrocarbons are extracted into carbon tetrachloride at a ratio of say 50:1 water sample:solvent. The advantage of using carbon tetrachloride is that it produces little or no spectral interference in the IR spectral region of interest.

Mineral oil traces in contaminated waters may sometimes be characterized rapidly by examination of their molecular fluorescence spectra, if necessary after concentration. If the type of oil is known, then simple quantitative determination is also possible.

For the identification and quantitation of hydrocarbons in the environ-ment, gas-liquid chromatography is certainly the most powerful and most sensitive tool. It is sometimes difficult for students trained in traditional inorganic analysis to accept the concept of determining a group of com-pounds rather than an individual member, and as the composition of accepted hydrocarbon fractions may vary considerably, quantitation by comparison with standards introduces some awkward problems. But often the question an environmental analytical chemist will be asked is "Is this a spillage of petrol, diesel fuel, or kerosene?" The longer the sample has spent floating on top of a stagnant ditch slowly evaporating, the more difficult this question is to answer.

Composition of hydrocarbon fractions.   It is helpful to summarize (Table 4.6) the boiling ranges of the common hydrocarbon fuel fractions. Fig. 4.19 shows some typical gas chromatograms, which illustrate the complexity of these common mixtures, but also that it is nevertheless feasible, indeed relatively simple, to distinguish between them. Complete analyses of gasolines have been achieved by the combination of gas chromatography and mass spectrometry (see Section 4.27): over 250 components have been identified.

Table 4.6   Boiling ranges of hydrocarbon fuels

Aviation spirit	30°–150°
Petrol (gasoline)	30°–200° (rich in aromatics)
White spirit (solvent naphtha)	140°–200°
Kerosene	$\begin{cases} 175°–275° \text{ (JP5 jet fuel)} \\ 30°–270° \text{ (JP4 jet fuel)} \end{cases}$
Fuel oil, diesel oil	250°–400°
Lubricating oil	>400°

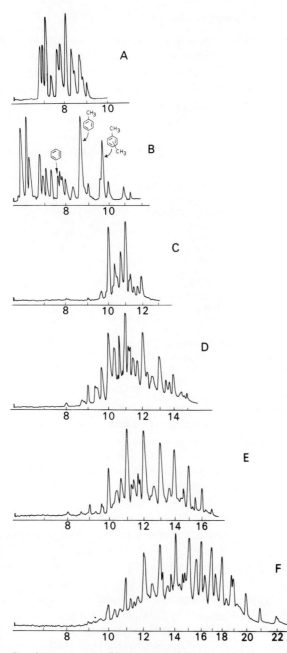

Figure 4.19 Gas chromatograms of hydrocarbon fractions analysed on a silicone oil column with programming: 2 min at 50°C, 10°/min to 250°C. *A*, light petroleum solvent, boiling range 60–120°C; *B*, petrol (gasoline); *C*, white spirit (solvent naphtha); *D*, jet fuel (JPA); *E*, paraffin (kerosene); *F*, diesel oil. Numbers indicate length of chain of *n*-alkanes.

Solubilities of hydrocarbons in water.   The solubilities of most hydrocarbons in water are low, but nevertheless cover a wide range of values. This poses a practical problem for the analyst: does he try to distinguish between true dissolved hydrocarbons and suspended or surface-film hydrocarbons? And if he is concerned with the true dissolved concentrations, is his procedure going to be sensitive enough? Some values for solubilities are given in Table 4.7.[42,43] It is significant for the environmental analyst that the aromatic hydrocarbons, particularly benzene, considered to be the most toxic, are also

Table 4.7 Solubilities of hydrocarbons in water at 25°C, $\mu g\, g^{-1}$

n-pentane	38
n-octane	0.66
iso-octane	2.4
1-pentene	150
1-octene	2.7
cyclohexane	55
cyclohexene	213
benzene	1780
toluene	515
ethylbenzene	152
naphthalene	32
anthracene	0.04
phenanthrene	1.0

much more soluble in water than the aliphatic hydrocarbons of similar molecular weight. The polynuclear aromatics (PAH's) on the other hand, have very low solubilities indeed, and are less likely to create a problem of immediate toxicity.

Gas chromatographic determination of hydrocarbons.[44]   A large volume of water (typically 1 l) is extracted with 50 ml of solvent for 15 min. Diethyl ether is recommended by some: after extraction the extract must be washed with dilute acid and then with dilute alkali to remove bases and acidic substances. It is then shaken over silica gel to remove other polar compounds. Carbon tetrachloride is also used as an extractant, and can likewise be cleaned by shaking with silica gel. The extract should then be concentrated by evaporation to a small volume, (e.g. 1 ml) by blowing a stream of nitrogen gas through it (not laboratory compressed air!) and then a suitable aliquot (e.g. 5 μl) is injected on to the column. Temperature programming (see Section 3.10.8) is desirable for chromatographic examination of these extracts, and a silicone oil column is usually recommended for petroleum hydrocarbons.

Evaporation of extracts.   Conical vessels or tubes drawn down to a narrow bore at the bottom are convenient, so it is then easy to insert the hypodermic syringe to take the sample for analysis. The apparatus shown in Fig. 4.20

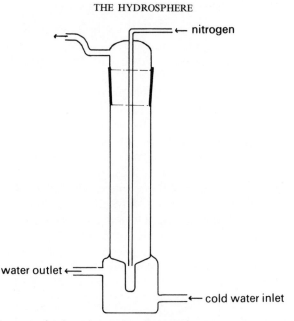

← nitrogen

water outlet ←

← cold water inlet

Figure 4.20 Apparatus for the concentration of extracts by evaporation.

allows 5 ml to be taken down to 100 μl quickly and easily and only very volatile constituents are lost.

4.26 Gas chromatography/mass spectrometry (GC/MS)
While analysis by gas chromatography has much to offer in terms of resolution of mixtures and sensitivity of detection of individual components, it is not the solution to the problem of identification of these components. There are two main reasons for this, both deriving from the fact that identification is based on measurement of retention time (it may be assisted by noting differences in the responses of alternative detectors to any one peak; see Sections 3.10.6 and 7.8.2).

First, it is quite likely that another compound may be present in the sample which exhibits the same retention time as the compound being investigated. Running the analysis on a second column of very different polarity may help to resolve the awkward pair, but in unfortunate cases the rogue peak may simply move to hide behind another one. This phenomenon was responsible for the apparent absence of acrylic acid in samples of animal stomach fluids (it was hidden under the peaks either of propionic or of isobutyric acids, both also present) and therefore a true picture of the metabolic pathways involved could not be constructed.[45]

Second, if temperature programming (see Section 3.10.8) is used in conjunction with capillary columns for high resolution GC of complex mixtures, the reproducibility is not always adequate to ensure positive identification by comparison with standards.

The solution to this problem is to couple the chromatograph to a second analytical tool which will give information leading to identification of the individual components. Fast scanning infrared spectrometry (see Section 3.8.1) may be helpful, but the most popular approach is to use a mass spectrometer, as the information content of a mass spectrum is high enough to permit identification of one compound by comparison with spectra in libraries holding data for tens of thousands of compounds. The comparison of spectra is best done by computer, and the more sophisticated programmes are designed to provide the user with a "good guess" for unknown compounds not on file, as well as simply identifying compounds which the user expects to find and has in the library. The application of the technique to water pollution analysis has been reviewed by Hites.[46]

4.27 The EPA survey procedure: priority pollutants

The EPA protocol referred to in Section 4.26 makes use of a number of solvent-extraction steps, under different conditions, separating the trace organics into four subgroups, each of which is in turn subjected to chromatographic analysis on an appropriate column. The first category — the volatiles — has already been mentioned, but the five classes are summarized in Table 4.8.

The EPA Guidelines for procedures in pollution analysis include summaries of 15 methods: 12 are based on GLC or HPLC separations, and three require the use of a GC/MS system in order to positively identify trace con-

Table 4.8 EPA-listed priority pollutants

Class	Separation from water	Column	Detector
Volatiles	purge-and-trap	Carbowax 1500	FID
Acidics (phenols)	extract into methylene chloride from sample at pH 2	Tenax (porous polymer) Supelco 1240 DA deactivized polycote	FID
Base-neutrals	extract into methylene chloride from sample at pH 11	Silicone (methyl-phenyl)	FID
Pesticides, PCB's	extract from water into 15% methylene chloride in hexane, distil off methylene chloride	Silicone	ECD
Acrolein, acrylonitrile	direct injection of aqueous sample if > 1 ppm	Porapak-Q (porous polymer)	FID

stituents.[46] The methods cover the determination of volatile solvents (601, 602), acrolein and acrylonitrile (603), phenols (604), benzidines, HPLC, (605), phthalate esters (606), nitrosamines (607), organochlorine pesticides and PCB's (608), nitroaromatics (609), polynuclear aromatics, HPLC, (610), haloethers (611) and chlorinated hydrocarbons (612). The newer GC/MS methods are for dioxin (613), volatile organics (624) and extractables (625). The EPA has attempted cost analysis of these different methods: 1979 figures were in the range $100–300 per sample per analysis for methods 610–612, and between $1000 and $2000 for the GC/MS methods. Appendix 3 lists the 114 priority pollutants, labelling them as volatiles, acid extractables, base-neutral extractables or pesticides (nearly all the compounds are available from Supelco Inc.).

References

1 Mellanby, K. (1972) *The Biology of Pollution*, Edward Arnold, London.
2 Wood, L. B. and Richardson, M. L. (1978) *Chem. Brit.*, **14**, 491.
3 King, D. L. (1971) In *Water and Water Pollution Handbook*, Vol. 22, Ciaccio, L. L. (ed.), Marcel Dekker, p. 451.
4 Wilson, A. L. (1974) *The Chemical Analysis of Water: General Principles and Techniques*, The Society for Analytical Chemistry, London.
5 Herschell, C. (1913) *Frontinus and the Water Supply of the City of Rome*, Longmans, London, p. 67.
6 *Standard Methods for the Examination of Water and Wastewater* (1975) 14th edition, American Public Health Association.
7 Mackereth, F. J. H. (1964) *J. Sci. Inst.*, **41**, 38.
8 Wilcock, R. J., Stevenson, C. D. and Roberts, C. A. (1981) *Water Research*, **15**, 321.
9 Rodier, J. (1975) *Analysis of Water*, Halsted, p. 460.
10 *Die Untersuchung von Wasser* (1975) 9th edition, Merck, Darmstadt, p. 42.
11 Z. Marczenko (1976) *Spectrophotometric Determination of the Elements*, Ellis Horwood, Chichester.
12 Reardon, J., Foreman, J. A. and Stacey, R. L. (1966) *Clin. Chim. Acta*, **14**, 403.
13 Pym, R. V. E. and Milham, P. J. (1976) *Anal. Chem.*, **48**, 1413.
14 Fries, J. (1971) *Spurenanalyse, Erprobte photometrische Methoden*, Merck, Darmstadt.
15 Karlsson, R. and Torstensson, L. G. (1975) *Talanta*, **22**, 27.
16 Blom, J. and Treschow, C. (1929) *Z. Pflanzenernaehrung, Duengung Bodenkultur*, **13A**, 159.
17 Andrews, D. W. (1964) *Analyst*, **89**, 730.
18 Montgomery, H. A. C. and Dymock, J. F. (1962) *Analyst*, **87**, 374.
19 Norwitz, G. and Gordon, H. (1977) *Anal. Chim. Acta*, **89**, 177.
20 Yagoda, H. (1943) *Ind. Eng. Chem. Anal. Ed.*, **15**, 27.
21 Holler, A. C. and Huch, R. V. (1949) *Anal. Chem.*, **21**, 1385.
22 Murphy, J. and Riley, J. P. (1962) *Anal. Chim. Acta*, **27**, 31.
23 Frant, M. S. and Ross, J. W. (1968) *Anal. Chem.*, **40**, 1169.
24 *Instrumentation Manual for Orion Fluoride Electrode* (1973).
25 Moody, G. J. and Thomas, J. D. R. (1972) *Talanta*, **19**, 623.
26 Whitfield, M. (1971) *Ion-Selective Electrodes for the Analysis of Natural Waters*, Australian Mar. Sci. Assoc. Handbook No. 2.
27 Veselý, J., Weiss, D. and Štulik, K. (1978) *Analysis with Ion-Selective Electrodes*, Ellis Horwood, Chichester.
28 Rossotti, H. (1969) *Chemical Applications of Potentiometry*, Van Nostrand, London.
29 Bates, R. (1963) *Determination of pH*, Wiley, New York.

30 Small, H., Stevens, T. S. and Bauman, W. C. (1975) *Anal. Chem.*, **47**, 1801.
31 Crowther, J. and McBride, J. (1981) *Analyst*, **106**, 702.
32 Burger, K. (1973) *Organic Reagents in Metal Analysis*, Pergamon, Oxford, p. 122.
33 Irving, H. M. N. H. (1977) *Dithizone*, Chemical Society, London, p. 50.
34 Crow, D. R. and Westwood, J. V. (1968) *Polarography*, Methuen, London, p. 25.
35 Kolthoff, I. M. and Lingane, J. J. (1941) *Polarography*, Interscience, New York.
36 Vydra, F., Štulik, K. and Julakova, E. (1976) *Electrochemical Stripping Analysis*, Ellis Horwood, Chichester.
37 Harrison, R. M. and Laxen, D. P. H. (1980) *Nature*, **286**, 21.
38 Florence, T. M. (1982) *Talanta*, **29**, 345.
39 Leithe, W. (1973) *The Analysis of Organic Pollutants in Water and Waste Water*, Ann Arbor, Michigan.
40 Mills, D. H. (1971) *Salmon and Trout, a Resource; its Ecology, Conservation and Management*, Oliver and Boyd, Edinburgh, p. 158.
41 Emerson, E., Beacham, H. H. and Beegle, L. C. (1943) *J. Org. Chem.*, **8**, 417.
42 McAuliffe, C. (1966) *J. Phys. Chem.*, **70**, 1267.
43 May, W. E. (1980) in *Petroleum in the Marine Environment*, Petrakis, L. and Weiss, F. T. (eds.), Advances in Chemistry, **185**, American Chemical Society, Washington, p. 143.
44 Whittemore, I. M. (1979) in *Chromatography in Petroleum Analysis*, Altgett, K. H. and Gouw, T. H. (eds.) Marcel Dekker, New York, p. 41.
45 Noble, R. C. and Czerkawski, J. W. (1973) *Analyst*, **98**, 122.
46 Hites, R. A. (1977) in *Advances in Chromatography*, Giddings, J. C. (ed.), **15**, Marcell Dekker, New York, p. 69.
47 Environmental Protection Agency (1979) Federal Register (U.S.) **233**, No. **44**, Dec. 3rd, 69464.

5 The lithosphere

5.1 Introduction

Strictly speaking the term "lithosphere" is applied only to the mantle of rocks which make up the earth's crust. Purely for convenience in this book it is also taken to include the soil which, in many places, covers the rock crust. Some scientists prefer to regard soil separately, as a complex interface between the lithosphere (from which it originates) and the hydrosphere, the atmosphere and the biosphere. Rocks may be weathered by rain, shattered by freezing and thawing or heating and cooling, moved by wind, rain and ice and attacked by lichens. The primitive soil thus formed soon comes to be colonized by higher plant species, and plant debris returns to the soil as the plants die or leaves fall. The organic matter is decomposed by a host of microorganisms, and the whole biologically active mass is often thoroughly mixed by the soil fauna (the soil animals). Meanwhile the processes of chemical and physical weathering continue steadily. Since, however, the soil stems from the rock mantle, though weathered and moved to a greater or lesser extent, it is appropriate to include the analyses of soils and rocks in one chapter, especially as much of the methodology employed is common to both.

5.2 The need for chemical analysis of soils and rocks

Much of the characterization of rock samples is based upon optical microscopy rather than elemental analysis. The individual crystalline mineral grains which constitute the rock are examined in a very thin section under the microscope and identified from their physical properties. The same approach may be applied to the characterization of the sand-size fraction of soil (i.e. the mineral particles between 2 mm and 0.05 mm in "diameter" in the soil—see Section 5.4). It should be remembered, however, that classification on the basis of microscopic examination still depends upon the results of chemical analysis, but in this instance the analysis has been completed previously by the mineralogists who worked out the mineral structures in the first instance.

The mineralogist is interested not just in the elemental composition of samples, but also in the mineral structure, that is, the spatial distribution of the atoms of different elements within the crystal lattice. The structures of the relatively abundant minerals are now well known, having been elucidated primarily from the results of X-ray diffraction studies (see Section 3.7.3) and from elemental analysis. Knowledge of mineralogical composition is important because it may throw light upon the probable mode of formation of a rock or the parent material of a soil, and also upon the probable physical and chemical processes occurring in the rock or soil. If the elements released upon weathering are known, then it is possible to make predictions about the natural fertility of the soil and, to a limited extent at least, about the likely long-term lime and fertilizer requirements of that soil at any particular site.

Although approximate elemental compositions may normally be deduced for samples whose mineralogical compositions are known, chemical analysis is still often necessary if a more precise knowledge of composition in terms of the major elements is required. It is particularly important if the trace-element content of samples is of interest, as it may be in geochemical prospecting, for example. An example of the use of trace analysis in geochemical prospecting is sediment analysis. The sediment in natural water samples reflects the nature of the mineral material through which the water has passed, so that if a large number of sediment samples from an area are analysed for a particular element, the variation in the concentration of that element in sediments over the area may be mapped. Such maps may permit quite accurate location of zones where its concentration is significantly higher than usual and which may then be investigated in more detail with a view to locating potential mining sites.

The total elemental analysis of soils is of interest in some of the more fundamental branches of soil science, such as pedogenesis, in which the factors of soil formation are investigated in detail. If a hole is dug in a soil to a depth of a metre or more, it is often found that the soil is not uniform in appearance to any great depth, but rather consists of various layers, known as *horizons*, as shown in Fig. 5.1. The exposed face of the pit is known as the *soil profile*. The example shown is typical for the soil under deciduous forest in an area with a climate such as that in the UK. The profile which is

dark, organic-rich horizon

lighter horizon

weathered parent material

unaltered parent material

Figure 5.1   A typical soil profile.

observed depends upon climate, topography, the nature of the parent material, drainage, past and present land use and the period of time over which the profile has been developing. The interested reader should refer to a standard text on soil science or pedology (see for example Ref. 1) for further discussion of this topic. For the purposes of this book, it is enough to note that a study of the distribution of elements throughout a soil profile may be invaluable in elucidating the physical and chemical processes occurring down the profile.

5.3 Available elements

There is more interest in soil as a medium for plant growth than there is in the fundamental processes of soil formation. The soil not only acts as anchorage and support for the parts of plants visible above the ground, but also provides the elements and their ions which are essential for healthy plant growth. These include nitrogen, phosphorus, potassium, calcium, magnesium, sulphur, copper, zinc, iron, manganese, boron, molybdenum and chlorine. This immediately raises an important question, namely: How can we assess the amount of an element present in the soil in a form in which it may be readily taken up by plants? If part of the element of interest is contained in relatively stable and inert mineral structures, this obviously will not be easily taken up by plants. Similarly, elements such as nitrogen, phosphorus and sulphur present in organic matter as part of large organic molecules may also be unavailable. It is therefore necessary to find an extractant which has an extracting power comparable to that of plant roots.

One approach to this problem is to evaluate different extracting solutions on an empirical basis for the element of interest. A wide range of soils with different properties is selected, and used to grow a small amount of a test crop in pots under standardized conditions. The same soils are then extracted with different extractants, for example dilute acetic acid, ammonium acetate solution, dilute hydrochloric acid or EDTA solutions, and the extracts analysed for the element of interest. The concentration of the element in plant tissue grown on each soil and its concentration in the extract from the same soil are then compared. The extractant which gives the best correlation coefficient may then be used to assess the amount of *available nutrient element* in other soils. The concentration of any element in a soil extract corresponding to deficiency of that nutrient in the soil may be assessed experimentally— by studying the effects of nutrient added to various different soils and seeing for which soils the added nutrient element acts as a fertilizer.

As a result of many years of such investigations, extractants have now been recommended for all the nutrient species of interest in assessing fertilizer requirement and diagnosing deficiencies and toxicities. It should be emphasized that there is no universal agreement as to the best extractant for any given nutrient—this is because the extractant producing the best correlation depends to some extent upon the soil type, and hence upon the part of the world where the determinations are being completed.

In some instances there is a theoretical basis underlying the choice of extracting solution. Potassium chloride solution, for example, may be used to extract available nitrogen from soils. Most of the nitrogen in soils is present in the organic matter fraction, and is unavailable to plants; ammonium, nitrate and nitrite are available, but typically constitute only around 2% of the total nitrogen. Nitrate and nitrite are very readily leached out of soil and could be extracted with water, but the positively-charged ammonium ion is absorbed on to negatively-charged sites on the organic matter and inorganic colloidal material (the clay fraction—see Section 5.4) in the soil, the so-called exchange sites. A large excess of another cation is therefore required to displace this absorbed ammonium by ion exchange, and so potassium chloride effectively displaces all three of the main forms of inorganic nitrogen.

5.4 Particle size distribution in soils

One of the most important properties of a soil is the size distribution of its particles. The sizes are arbitrarily split into three (or sometimes more) size ranges—slightly different ranges are still used in different countries of the world, but the classification of the US Department of Agriculture is the most common. Because soil particles are irregularly shaped, the sizes are expressed in terms of *equivalent spherical diameters* (e.s.d.), the diameters of spherical particles which, if they had the same density as the soil particles, would settle at the same velocity. This is a reasonable concept, since the procedures used to investigate the distributions of soil particle sizes are invariably based upon sedimentation. The USDA size ranges are shown in Table 5.1.

Table 5.1 Size ranges for soil particles

name	size range (μm)
coarse sand	2000–200
fine sand	200–50
silt	50–2
clay	<2

The clay content of soils is very important. Because clay particles are small, their surface area, and hence their surface charge, is often very large, so they play an important role in the ion exchange properties of soils (see Section

5.3). The mineral particles of the clay fraction are too small to be identified by optical microscopy, and the minerals constituting the clay fraction must be identified by X-ray diffraction and thermal methods of analysis, as discussed briefly in Section 5.13. Their contribution to the total amount of ion exchange which the soil may exhibit, the cation exchange capacity of the soil, depends upon the amount and the type of each clay mineral present.

5.5 Soil analysis versus visual symptoms shown by plants

When plants are receiving an inadequate supply of one or more of the nutrient elements essential for healthy growth, their growth is reduced compared to that of the same plants grown under identical conditions but where no nutrient is limiting. Associated with this reduced growth there are characteristic visible symptoms for each major or trace nutrient deficiency. The experienced observer may examine chlorotic plants (with yellowish leaves), and quite reliably diagnose nitrogen deficiency. However, the situation is complicated by the fact that different plant species may exhibit slightly different symptoms for the same elements, and because, on the other hand, rather similar symptoms may be associated with different deficiencies. Moreover, plants may simultaneously show symptoms of more than one deficiency. Agricultural advisers, however, often use visual symptoms as a basis for deciding which chemical analyses should be done. Plant tissue analysis may confirm deficiency or toxicity (Chapter 6), but, while this may identify the nature of problems in established crops, it does not allow deficiencies to be remedied before the crop is adversely affected, so it is in this respect less suitable than the assessment of the amount of available nutrient present in the soil.

When deciding what analyses need to be done, the agricultural adviser also calls upon his knowledge of the behaviour of nutrients in soil and of local soil conditions. He might expect to find manganese deficiency in plants on alkaline soils with a high organic matter content for example, or copper deficiency in plants on peaty soils. However, whereas many soil analyses are completed in response to recognized specific problems, many others are carried out on a purely routine basis, even when no visual symptoms or problems are known to exist, with a view to optimizing crop yields. The determination of soil pH and lime requirement, nitrogen, phosphorus and potassium often fall into this category. In areas with arid climates, salt accumulation in upper soil horizons may have a serious adverse influence upon plant growth. In such areas the water-soluble salt content of the soil is also monitored routinely, often by measurement of the conductivity of an aqueous extract of the soil.

5.6 Sampling problems with rocks and soils

One aspect of the analysis of rock and soil samples which requires particular attention is sampling and sub-sampling technique. The chemical composition of rocks, and even more so that of soils, may vary considerably over quite small distances, both horizontally and vertically, so that obtaining a representative sample in the field presents special problems which, if ignored, may render all subsequent analytical work worthless. Because of the lateral variation in soil, it is normal practice to collect several separate samples from randomly distributed points over the sampling area. These are then combined, air-dried, ground to pass through a 2 or 3-mm sieve, and sub-sampled for analysis.

Other problems are associated with collecting samples of soil from the field. The first is the choice of depth over which samples should be collected. The composition of soil varies with depth (see Figure 5.1 and Section 5.2). Samples for assessment of available nutrients are often collected only from the region of the soil influenced by ploughing. This is easy to do, if difficult to justify. However, plant roots may penetrate to much greater depths (three-quarters of a metre is not uncommon). From the few careful comparisons which have been made, it appears that, where the soil is deep, sampling to much greater depth can considerably improve the predictive value of available-nutrient assessments.

A second problem is that soil is not only not homogeneous, but its chemical properties also vary considerably with time. Thus the naturally available nitrogen in soils depends at any particular time upon the season of year, the recent and long-term temperature and rainfall, the crop in the field, drainage, and several other less important factors. This type of variation has far-reaching consequences when field work which will involve comparisons of different sites is planned. Similar problems are encountered in foliar analysis; these are discussed briefly in Chapter 6.

A third problem is that it is not always acceptable to dry soils before analysing them, primarily because a soil sample is biologically active. Drying drastically affects the ammonifying and nitrifying microorganisms in soils. The longer a soil is stored in an air-dry condition, the greater is the amount of organic nitrogen found converted to inorganic nitrogen (primarily nitrate nitrogen) when the soil is re-wetted for analysis. Oven-drying, on the other hand, kills nitrifying bacteria, and tends to lead to increased ammonium-nitrogen on re-wetting. The levels of available phosphorus, potassium, sulphur and manganese may also change after air drying—a specialized text[2] on soil analysis should be consulted for the nature of the changes.

The reader may well ask why samples are air-dried at all if drying leads to these difficulties. The answer, of course, is that reliable sub-sampling of some soils in the field-moist condition is virtually impossible. The advantages of air-drying therefore greatly outweigh the disadvantages. Nevertheless, available ammonium and nitrate must be determined on field-moist soils. Moreover the samples for this determination must be stored below freezing point if it is not possible to analyse them immediately, to minimize the effects of microbial activity during storage, and subsampled while still frozen for analysis. A separate determination of the soil moisture content is made, so that results may be expressed on an oven-dry basis. This is essential if meaningful comparisons are to be made between the results for a diverse range of samples.

5.7 Subsampling

Once a bulk sample has been dried and sieved, it must then be subsampled for analysis. This may be done by careful cone and quartering technique. Scoop sampling from bottles should be avoided, since samples in bottles often undergo a partial fractionation according to particle size, which may introduce serious systematic error. If quite large samples are to be split, a chute splitter or spinning riffler is useful. The chute splitter (Figure 5.2) consists of

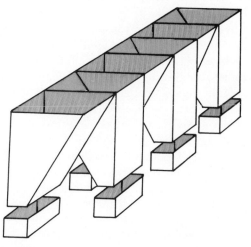

Figure 5.2 A chute splitter.

a series of triangular funnels with a rectangular cross section, arranged in such a way that the spouts of alternate funnels are to the left and the right. A subsample collection box fits accurately under each funnel spout. To split a bulk sample the sample is poured into the funnel mouths from a bottle which is moved to and fro so that the bulk sample falls randomly through the funnels. Each box then contains a representative subsample, which may be further subdivided if required by repeating the entire process. The spinning riffler is conceptually similar, but in this device the sample falls on to a single or double rotating chute. As the chute rotates the sample falls sequentially through a series of funnels arranged in a circle, into a series of subsample boxes under the funnels. Such subsampling devices typically split a sample 12-fold in a single pass, or 144-fold in a double pass.

When the analytical procedure to be followed requires only a fraction of a gram of sample, special care is needed to make certain that a truly representative subsample is taken for analysis. Many soil analyses are performed on 20–30 g subsamples of soil which has been air-dried and sieved to pass through a 2- or 3-mm sieve. Very small subsamples of 2- or 3-mm sieved soil may not however be adequately representative. Therefore, when <2 g is required for analysis, a larger subsample, typically 20 g, should be ground to pass totally through a much finer sieve, say 100 mesh, and the finely ground material then further subsampled for analysis.

5.8   Dissolution for total elemental analysis

Soils and rocks are clearly not very easily dissolved, but one of two approaches may be adopted. The sample may be dissolved in a suitable acid mixture, such as $HF/HClO_4$. The hydrofluoric acid is essential to dissolve silicates, but means that the apparatus used for dissolution must be of an inert material such as platinum or Teflon. Teflon-lined bombs are very suitable, and eliminate the possibility of loss of volatile elements (see Section 2.6.1). For soils rich in organic matter, the sample should be ignited before digestion, although nitric acid predigestion may be preferable for the destruction of organic matter if loss of volatile elements must be prevented.

Alternatively, the sample may be fused with a suitable alkaline flux, such as sodium carbonate, in a platinum crucible. If the soil contains much manganese oxide, the manganates formed on fusion liberate chlorine when the melt is subsequently dissolved in hydrochloric acid, and the chlorine will attack the platinum. The melt should therefore be removed from the crucible, or ethanol added, before digestion with the acid. Iron oxide, if present in large amounts, also attacks platinum crucibles if the oxide is reduced to the metal during the fusion step, since iron forms an alloy with platinum. The oxide should therefore be dissolved in aqua regia (not in the crucible!) before fusion. Not all minerals are attacked by sodium carbonate. Chromite, for example, is not attacked either by sodium carbonate fusion or sulphuric/ hydrofluoric acid digestion. In this case, the sample may be fused with potassium hydrogen sulphate, but since this does not attack silica, a second, alkaline fusion or an acid digestion must then be carried out if complete analysis is required. Fusion with sodium peroxide or sodium hydroxide in nickel crucibles may be useful for the determination of certain elements such as arsenic or barium.[2] In any case, fusions on reagent blanks are essential for most trace element analyses.

5.9 Some selected chemical methods in soil analysis

5.9.1 *Determination of soil pH*
The definition and measurement of pH of waters is covered in Section 4.11. The pH value of a soil cannot be as precisely defined as that of a solution because it is the pH of a soil-water equilibrium system which must always be measured. In spite of this, pH is the most commonly measured single parameter of soils.

The main value of a soil pH measurement is not that it shows a soil to be acid or alkaline, but that it yields useful information about element availabilities, base status (the amount of exchangeable calcium, magnesium, potassium and sodium relative to exchangeable acidity), etc. Almost all agricultural soils have pH values between 5 and 8. Elements such as zinc, copper, manganese and iron are more mobile in more acid soils, and at very low pH values, a soil may contain toxic quantities of certain elements (a common example is aluminium toxicity, which stunts and deforms roots, and thus restricts growth of the whole plant. A high soil pH on the other hand can induce trace element deficiencies. Microbial activity is also strongly pH-dependent.

The pH value of a soil is a measure only of the intensity of acidity, and not of the total amount of acid present. Soils with high clay contents have far greater reserves of acidity than sandy soils. Peaty soils often also have large reserves of acidity. These soils are said to be well-buffered, as appreciable quantities of base must be added to raise their pH significantly. The nature of buffering action in soils is far more complicated than that in simple buffer solutions familiar in chemistry (e.g. acetic acid–ammonium acetate). Organic acids may make a contribution towards soil buffering capacity; aluminium is also partly responsible for the buffering action of soils, because as the pH of a soil is increased, aluminium dissociates hydrogen ions from coordinated water molecules in the clay. The series of reactions may be represented in a simplified form as follows:

$$Al^{3+} + OH^- \rightleftharpoons [Al(OH)]^{2+}$$
$$[Al(OH)]^{2+} + OH^- \rightleftharpoons [Al(OH)_2]^+$$
$$[Al(OH)_2]^+ + OH^- \rightleftharpoons Al(OH)_3$$

When the water content of a soil is at or below the point at which plants growing in it would wilt, the electrical resistance of the soil is too high for pH measurements to be made. The problem for the soil analyst is therefore that, although pH measurements must be carried out on a moist soil, the value obtained will vary with the amount of water added. Normally the pH of an equilibrium soil–water system increases as more water is added. Since most soils yield salt solutions when shaken up with water, dilution reduces the salt concentration. The pH also tends to rise when the soil contains an appreciable amount of dissolved carbon dioxide (i.e. dilution of the carbonic acid).

Another important factor when measuring the pH of soil pastes is the existence of an electric double layer around the small suspended charged soil particles. The surface charge on the colloid particles attracts a layer of ions, which in turn attracts a further layer of ions. Thus the concentration of free ions in solution is less than might be expected. If, however, the soil paste is made up with a salt solution, such as potassium or calcium chloride, the added ions reduce the depletion of hydrogen ions in the bulk solution through the double layer effect.

Using a specified ratio of soil : salt solution, it is possible to obtain highly reproducible results for soil pH measurement. This offers the advantage of simplifying comparison of results obtained in different parts of the world. However, much less solution needs to be added to a sandy soil than to a clay soil or a peaty soil. Therefore, in many studies, the amount of salt solution added is adjusted according to the soil texture. This has an adverse affect upon precision, but the results are probably more significant. Sufficient solution is added to produce a very stiff paste on thorough mixing. Different approaches are adopted in different countries, so it is important to specify the exact procedure adopted when results of soil pH determinations are quoted in reports.

The pH may be measured with a glass/calomel electrode and a pH meter, as outlined in Section 4.11, and in the laboratory most soil pH values are determined in this way. The soil pastes are left to equilibrate for a standard time, typically one hour, before measurement. Battery-powered pH meters are available for use in the field, although in remote areas the associated paraphernalia (beakers, distilled water, etc.) may make the method inconvenient.

Soil pH may also be determined using standard acid-base indicators. Most readers will be familiar with the use of indicators in acid-base titrations. The colour of a single indicator changes over approximately 2 pH units. If standard buffer solutions containing the indicator are prepared with their pH values increasing in steps of 0.2 pH unit, a steady gradation in colour is observed. Comparison of soil extracts containing added indicator with the standards allows the pH to be ascertained to within ± 0.2 units. This is perfectly adequate for most practical purposes, because of the natural field variation which is always observed. By mixing indicators which exhibit suitable colour changes over different pH ranges, it is relatively simple to produce a mixed indicator which changes colour more than once in a series of steps between say pH 3.5 and pH 8, the range of normal soils. Such solutions may be used to assess pH to c. ±0.5 units, and the only equipment required is a small white plastic spoon and the solution. The spoon is first rinsed with 1–2 ml of solution, soil is scooped directly out with the spoon and then the indicator is added. The mixture is mixed by gentle swirling for a few minutes and the colour compared with a colour chart or table. This technique is well suited to rapid field observation, and again may be quite adequate for many practical purposes.

5.9.2 *The assessment of lime requirement*
As should be clear from Section 5.9, the pH of soil is important because of its direct influence on plant growth, and also because of its effect upon trace nutrient availability and microbial activity. If the soil pH is too low for optimum yield of a crop to be obtained, it may be raised by adding a suitable liming material. The analyst must then be able to answer the question: "How much lime must be added?"

As mentioned briefly in Section 5.9.1, soils are buffered to a greater or lesser extent. Soils with a high cation exchange capacity, i.e. those with high clay content or organic matter content, are usually highly buffered: sandy soils are only weakly buffered. Measurement of pH alone therefore gives no indication of the amount of lime required to change a soil pH to a desired value. The most widely used procedures for assessing lime requirement involve determination of the exchange acidity.

Procedure. Extract 5 g of soil with 50 ml of 1.0 M ammonium acetate solution at pH 7.[2] After a one-hour equilibration period read the pH value to ±0.02 units. Measure a separate 100-ml portion of ammonium acetate into a beaker, and check its pH value. Add acetic acid (0.02 M) dropwise with stirring, and read the pH and volume after each addition. Draw a graph of pH against millimoles of hydrogen ion added, and read off this graph the H^+ concentration corresponding to the sample extract. The exchange acidity may then be calculated in millimoles kg^{-1}. Lime requirement is then calculated in kg ha^{-1}, assuming values for the soil bulk density and that the pH is changed down to the depth affected by ploughing.

Many other methods, mainly similar in general principle, may be found in the literature.[2,3] Different procedures give somewhat different results. Newcomers to the field of soil analysis may at first be perturbed by the apparent lack of universally accepted procedures. It must be realized that highly precise determinations would often in any case be of limited value. What happens when ground calcium carbonate is added to a soil depends upon the type and particle size of the carbonate, the climate and any subsequent cultivation. The rate at which the soil is neutralized improves with the fineness of the liming material, but in an area where rainfall exceeds evaporation and transpiration, the calcium starts to be leached from the soil more or less immediately. Thus additional factors based upon local knowledge and experience must be taken into account. Once a procedure has been shown to give satisfactory results from the practical viewpoint, it will not be easily displaced by a new method, however superior the latter may be in theory.

5.9.3 *Determination of available phosphorus*

As is the case for most available-nutrient assessments, various different extractants are currently in use for the determination of available phosphorus in soils throughout the world. The most widely used is probably 0.5 M sodium bicarbonate solution at pH 8.5.[3]

Procedure. Extract 5 g of soil with 100 ml of 0.5 M sodium bicarbonate solution adjusted to pH 8.5. Determine the extracted orthophosphate by colorimetry or solution spectrophotometry, using a method such as that described for water analysis in Section 4.17. Use a 5-ml aliquot of filtered or centrifuged extract, and neutralize the bicarbonate by addition of up to 5 ml of 0.25 M sulphuric acid, before proceeding with the phosphate determination as described in Section 4.17. If the extract is coloured, add 1 g of carbon black to a fresh 5-g subsample of soil and repeat the extraction. Standards should be put through the entire procedure.

Automatic analysers are generally used if a large number of determinations are made routinely. However, analysis of soil extracts poses a new problem, as mentioned above; alkaline solutions such as sodium bicarbonate extract an appreciable amount of organic matter from soil, and the extracts are often quite a dark brown, which would interfere in the subsequent colorimetric analysis. The problem may be avoided by using a suitable extract blank, or, better still, by adding a teaspoonful of carbon black to the soil before extraction of the phosphate. The charcoal should be a grade low in phosphate, such as Darko G60—animal charcoal contains large amounts of phosphate and gives very high blanks.

5.9.4 *Determination of available nitrogen*

As mentioned in Section 5.3, the available nitrogen in soils is primarily in the form of ammonium and nitrate, and these species may be extracted from the soil with potassium chloride solution. They may be determined by distillation of ammonia from alkaline extracts, followed by titration of the distillate with dilute sulphuric acid, the nitrate being first reduced with titanium(III) sulphate, for example. If many samples are to be analysed, automated colorimetric analysis is very suitable, the organic matter being removed by dialysis (see Section 4.18).

Procedure. Extract 20 g of fresh, field-moist soil (from which the stones have been carefully removed) with 200 ml of 2 M potassium chloride solution, by shaking (intermittently if a shaker is not available) for 2 hours. Filter and retain the filtrate.

A Hoskin's apparatus, such as that shown in Fig. 5.3, is very convenient for the analysis of large numbers of extracts because it is self-cleansing, but any suitable macro-steam distillation

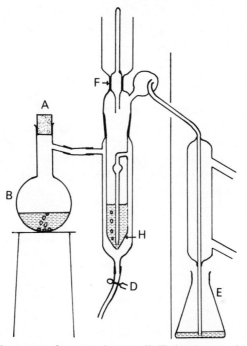

Figure 5.3 Hoskin's apparatus for ammonia steam distillation. Letters refer to the text.

apparatus will suffice. With bung *A* removed, tap *D* closed and the acidified water in flask *B* boiling gently, pipette 25 ml of extract into the inner chamber of the Hoskin's apparatus, and add 5 ml of pH 9.6 borax buffer (0.5 M sodium hydroxide containing $50\,g\,l^{-1}$ of borax). Insert the bung *A* and stopper *F*, and immediately place the receiving flask *E*, containing 10 ml of boric acid indicator solution under the condenser. The *indicator solution* is prepared as follows: dissolve 10 g of boric acid in 350 ml of hot water, cool, and add to 100 ml of ethanol and 10 ml of mixed indicator solution (bromocresol green (0.16 g) and methyl red (0.08 g) in 250 ml of ethanol) in a 500-ml flask. Dilute to volume). Heat to steam distil *c.* 40 ml in 5 minutes. Lower the receiving flask (*E*), stop heating and at once open clip *D* and stopper *F*. Remove the bung *A* and resume heating flask *B*, leaving the contents of the inner chamber (*H*) to cool slightly. Replace *E* with a fresh flask of indicator solution, add 5 ml of titanium(III) sulphate solution (5 % freshly prepared, in sulphuric acid) to the contents of the inner chamber, and rapidly insert stopper *F*, close tap *D* and insert bung *A*. Collect a second 40 ml of distillate, which contains ammonia corresponding to the reduced nitrate, and lower *E*. Remove the source of heat from flask *B* and *H* empties automatically as the steam in *B* condenses. Rinse *H* with 25 ml of water and allow this to siphon off too.

Titrate the ammonia collected in the two receiving flasks with 0.003 M sulphuric acid in turn. Calculate the ammonium-N and nitrate-N contents, applying suitable corrections for reagent blanks. For precise work the recovery of the apparatus should be checked with a fresh standard ammonium nitrate solution.

5.9.5 *Determination of total nitrogen*

Although the available (mineralized) nitrogen is most important for healthy plant growth, this typically constitutes only about 2 % of the total nitrogen present. The determination of total nitrogen is of interest because it gives an indication of the reserves of organic nitrogen capable of undergoing mineralization under suitable conditions.

Organic nitrogen may be converted to ammonium ions by prolonged boiling with concentrated sulphuric acid—this is the basis of the Kjeldahl method. The reaction may be speeded up by adding potassium sulphate to raise the boiling point of the sulphuric acid, and a suitable catalyst (selenium or mercury are most widely used in soil analysis). It still takes several hours, however. Water is added to the soil first to wet it, and to prevent charring and associated low recoveries of nitrogen through too rapid a reaction in the early stages. The ammonium formed may be determined by distillation/titration or by colorimetry (see Section 5.9.4).

Procedure. Weigh *c.* 8 g of sandy soil, 5 g of clay or 3 g of peaty soil into a clean, dry 300-ml Kjeldahl flask. Add 10 g of potassium sulphate catalyst mixture (100 K_2SO_4 : 5 $CuSO_4 \cdot 5H_2O$: 2 Se, readily available as 5 g tablets) and *c.* 25 ml of water. Swirl to wet the soil thoroughly and add 30 ml of concentrated sulphuric acid. Heat gently in a fume hood, preferably with an additional fume extraction manifold. When the frothing subsides and the water has boiled off, heat more strongly until the long neck of the flask is acting as an air reflux condenser. Continue heating for at least 2 hours after the oxidation appears complete (5 hours is preferable). Cool, add about 50 ml of water, shake to dissolve any salt cake, and cool again. Transfer to a 250-ml graduated flask and dilute to the mark, making sure the final dilution is made when the solution has attained room temperature.

Determine the ammonium content of the digest, and hence the nitrogen content of the soil, by steam distillation/titration with 0.01 M sulphuric acid. The digest is more acidic than the potassium chloride extract used in Section 5.9.4, so 15 ml of 40% sodium hydroxide should be used in place of the 5 ml of pH 9.6 borax buffer, and of course the titanium(III) addition and second distillation are unnecessary.

5.10 Flame atomic absorption spectroscopy

For the determination of the major and many of the minor metallic elements in soils and rocks, very extensive use is made of flame atomic absorption spectroscopy (AAS). Indeed much of the important pioneering work on the evaluation of AAS was conducted in soils laboratories. This is not surprising, because elements such as potassium, calcium, sodium and magnesium are not readily determined in such complex matrices by the techniques described so far in this text without time-consuming and tedious separation techniques. For the determination of other metallic elements too, the matrix is always complex, so that a sensitive and selective method of analysis is desirable. AAS is just such a method.

Although the fundamental principles of atomic absorption are similar in many respects to those of molecular absorption (see Section 3.8.1) there is one essential difference. When atoms absorb light, only photons with exactly the right amount of energy to produce an allowed electronic transition of the element of interest may be absorbed. As mentioned in chapter 3, when molecules absorb, there are whole series of rotationally and vibrationally excited states associated with both the electronically unexcited (ground-state) molecule and the electronically excited state. A whole series of transitions may therefore be possible from rotationally or vibrationally excited or unexcited energy levels in the electronic ground state to rotationally or vibrationally excited or unexcited energy levels in the electronically excited state. The absorption spectra for absorbing gases therefore appear as close-lying series of bands. In solution, any slight excess of energy may be absorbed by collisional interaction with solvent molecules, and broad band spectra are produced, covering 200 nm or more of the visible or ultraviolet spectrum. The absorption bands due to electronic transitions coupled with rotational or vibrational transitions which are observed in molecular spectra are absent in pure atomic spectra, and one observes instead a series of narrow absorption lines, typically only 0.005 nm wide, each corresponding to one specific electronic transition for the atom in question.

If attempts are made to measure the fraction of light from a continuum source, such as a deuterium or hydrogen arc lamp, which is absorbed by a cloud of analyte atoms, the narrow width of the absorption line poses a problem. Suppose the monochromator used to isolate the region of the spectrum in the vicinity of the line is capable of isolating a band of wavelength 0.05 nm wide. As shown in Fig. 5.4A, most of the light passing on to the detector would not be absorbed. The absorbance, $-\log_{10} I_t/I_0$ (see Section 3.8.1) would therefore always be low, and the sensitivity poor.

The major breakthrough in the development of the use of measurement of atomic absorbance as an analytical technique came in the 1950's when Sir Alan Walsh[4] realized that it was possible to use *line sources*, which emitted very narrow lines at the same wavelengths as those at which atomic absorption occurred, rather than a continuum source. As may be seen in Fig. 5.4, very much better sensitivity should then be attainable. Moreover, the resulting technique should be highly selective from the point of view of spectral interference, because precise overlap of very narrow absorption and emission lines is necessary.

The line source most commonly used in AAS is the hollow-cathode lamp, a typical design being shown in Fig. 5.5. The source consists of a high voltage, low current, low pressure electrical discharge. The cylindrical cathode is made from the analyte element or one of its alloys, and fixed rigidly at the centre of the lamp. A small, flag-like anode, usually made from tungsten, is fitted to one side. To confine the hollow cathode discharge to the central region of the cathode, insulating sheets of mica are often inserted as shown. The lamp is filled with an inert gas, usually neon, at low pressure (e.g. 5 mm of Hg). The glass envelope of the lamp is fitted with a silica end-window if the main lines of the analyte element occur at UV wavelengths.

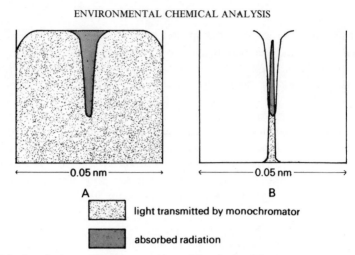

light transmitted by monochromator

absorbed radiation

Figure 5.4   Atomic absorption using a continuum (*A*) and a line (*B*) source.

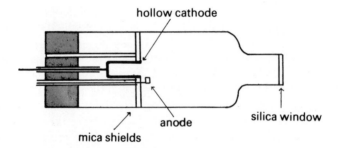

Figure 5.5   A typical hollow cathode lamp.

The sample is broken up into atoms (atomized) in a flame. Most commonly an air-acetylene flame is used, although for elements which tend to form refractory oxides (which are stable at high temperatures), such as silicon, aluminium or titanium, the hotter, nitrous oxide-acetylene flame is employed. The flame atomizer is usually long and thin, since a long path length favours better sensitivity. Flame lengths of 50–60 mm and 100–120 mm are typical for nitrous oxide-acetylene and air-acetylene flames respectively. The sample is introduced into the flame as a fine mist or aerosol, which is produced by a pneumatic nebulizer. A concentric flow of air or oxidant along the outside of a steel capillary tube creates a low pressure zone at the end of the capillary. This sucks the sample through the capillary, a process known as *aspiration*. The oxidant then expands very rapidly, setting up shock waves which cause the thread of liquid leaving the capillary to break up into fine droplets. The production of aerosols in this way is known as *pneumatic nebulization*. It is desirable that only the smaller aerosol droplets should reach the flame to minimize signal instability (noise) and limit the production of larger solid particles, after the solvent has evaporated, which may not be totally volatilized in the flame.

Figure 5.6 is a diagram showing the main components of a typical atomic absorption spectrometer. Light from the hollow-cathode lamp is focused to produce a narrow beam passing through the flame in which the sample is atomized. The light beam is further focused on to the entrance slit of the monochromator. The latter serves to isolate the line of interest from any

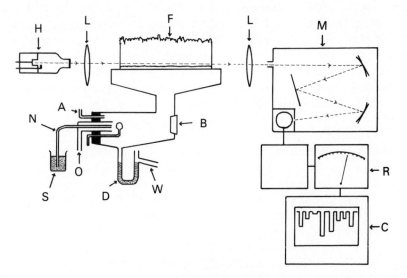

Figure 5.6 Components of an atomic absorption spectrometer. *A*, acetylene inlet; *B*, blow-out bung; *C*, chart recorder; *D*, drain; *F*, flame; *H*, hollow cathode lamp; *L*, lens; *M*, mono-chromator; *N*, nebulizer capillary; *O*, oxidant inlet; *R*, meter read-out; *W*, waste outlet; *S*, samples.

other less sensitive or insensitive analyte lines or neon lines emitted by the source. Light at the isolated wavelength passes through the monochromator exit slit on to a photomultiplier, where it is converted to an electrical signal.

To allow electronic discrimination between light emitted by the hollow-cathode lamp and any thermally-excited atomic or molecular light emission from the flame, the power supply to the lamp is modulated, so that the source is effectively flashing, and produces an a.c. signal. Emission from the flame produces a d.c. signal, and it is relatively simple to separate the two signals. In practice synchronous demodulation of the lamp signal is used: the amplifier is in effect switched on and off at the same frequency and in phase with the source. This allows random a.c. signals (noise) to be rejected, and thus improves the signal-to-noise ratio, giving steadier signals and blanks which may be read more precisely.

5.10.1   Interferences in AAS

By far the greater portion of the free atoms produced in the flames used in AAS are in the ground state rather than the excited state. It follows that sensitive atomic absorption is generally only observed for transitions in which the lower energy level involved is the ground state. Therefore absorption occurs at far fewer wavelengths for each element than does emission. *Spectral overlap* of an atomic absorption line of a concomitant element with the emission line of the analyte being used is rare, although examples are known. The platinum line at 271.9038 nm, for example, overlaps the iron line at 271.9025 nm so large amounts of platinum interfere in the determination of iron at this wavelength.[5] This has never presented any real problem to the authors! There are other wavelengths for the determination of iron by AAS which give superior sensitivity.[6,7] It is, however, important to recognize the existance of such overlaps. Problems were found, for example, in the determination of zinc in iron meteorites, which were attributed partly to line overlap and partly to *molecular absorption*.[8]

Molecular absorption tends to occur in flames only when a matrix element is present at a very high concentration. The absorption bands are generally broad, and a correction may be made by using a continuum source after the line source. The difference between the two absorbance signals gives a corrected value for the absorbance attributable to analyte atoms. Some modern atomic absorption spectrometers provide facilities for simultaneous automatic background correction. The two beams from the continuum and the line source are passed sequentially through the flame, and the two signals from the photomultiplier are separated by synchronous demodulation and subtracted electronically to give a corrected absorbance read out. Scattered light, from solid salt particles, which also may be observed at high dissolved salt concentrations, may be corrected for by the same approach. Alternatively both effects may be eliminated by careful matching of the matrices of both standards and samples if chemicals of sufficient purity are available. This approach is not easily applied to soil and rock samples if total element analyses are being performed, however, because the matrix may vary too much from sample to sample.

Although spectral interferences are rarely a problem in flame AAS, *chemical interferences* are more common. These occur when the analyte forms a thermally stable compound with a concomitant species present in the sample. For example calcium in the presence of phosphate tends to form stable calcium phosphate, so that phosphate suppresses the absorbance of calcium. Silicate similarly suppresses the absorbance of calcium, magnesium or iron. These effects may be greatly reduced, and often eliminated by using a hotter flame, such as nitrous oxide-acetylene, or by dilution of the sample, if the sensitivity allows this. Alternatively an element which forms a more stable compound with the interferent may be added to samples and standards. Lanthanum acts in this way in the examples quoted above for example. The reagent added is known as a *releasing agent*.

Another type of interference which may occur is known as *incomplete volatilization interference*. This happens when matrix components form stable compounds in the flame which simply physically trap the analyte, thus suppressing its absorbance. The effect may be reduced by dilution or by using a hotter flame.

A drawback to using hotter flames is that some of the analyte atoms may be ionized, thus lowering the absorbance, e.g.:

$$K_0 \rightleftharpoons K^+ + e^-. \tag{5.1}$$

This in itself is of no consequence, because atoms from samples and standards would be ionized to a similar extent. However, suppose the analyte contains a second easily ionizable element, sodium say. This is also partially ionized:

$$Na_0 \rightleftharpoons Na^+ + e^-. \tag{5.2}$$

This second ionization increases the electron concentration in the flame and hence suppresses the ionization of the potassium, the equilibrium represented by equation (5.1) moving from right to left because of the mass action equation:

$$\frac{[K^+][e^-]}{[K_0]} = \text{a constant} \tag{5.3}$$

where square parentheses denote molar concentrations. Thus the easily-ionized concomitant element interferes by suppressing the ionization of the analyte and increasing its absorbance. This is an example of an *ionization interference*. Ionization interference effects may be eliminated by adding a large excess of an easily ionized element, which is then known as an *ionization buffer*. This effectively maintains the electron concentration at a constant high level, the small concentration from concomitant species becoming negligible. The buffer must obviously be added to both samples and standards.

There is one further type of interference which should be considered here before we leave this topic, namely *physical interference*. This occurs when the density, surface tension or viscosity of samples and standards are not adequately matched. Viscosity difference in particular may cause variation in the aspiration rate, and differences in all three parameters may cause changes in the size distribution of the aerosol droplets produced by the pneumatic nebulizer. This in turn may cause a change in the nebulization efficiency, by changing the proportion of the aerosol which reaches the flame. These effects, which are common when organic solvents are mixed with the aqueous solutions, are eliminated by careful matching of the matrices of sample and standard solutions.

It is worth emphasizing here that atomic absorption, like colorimetry, is a secondary method of analysis in that it is based upon comparison of unknowns with standards. Any pipetting or dilution error in the preparation of standards therefore leads to a systematic error in all subsequent determinations. From the discussion in the preceding pages it is also clear that careful matching of matrices in samples and standards may also be very important in the elimination of physical, chemical, ionization, incomplete volatilization and even spectral interferences if systematic errors are to be avoided.

5.10.2 Applications of flame AAS to soil and rock analyses

Very widespread use is made of AAS in the elemental analysis of soils and rocks. Total or available (in soils) calcium, magnesium, sodium and potassium are determined in an air-acetylene flame, a releasing agent being added in the case of calcium and magnesium to prevent interference from silicate, phosphate and aluminium. Total iron, aluminium, silicon and manganese may be determined in a nitrous oxide-acetylene flame, potassium being added as an ionization buffer for aluminium. Extractable or total zinc, copper, lead, cadmium, nickel and cobalt may be determined in air-acetylene, if necessary after prior concentration and separation by solvent extraction. Some organic solvents, particularly methylisobutylketone (4-methylpentan-2-one) and ethyl acetate, are well suited to AAS. They are nebulized with a higher efficiency than water, giving 2- to 3-fold enhancement in sensitivity. Moreover, solvent extraction may be used as a concentration step, whilst at the same time it may be used to separate analyte from potential interferences.[9] From time to time the authors have determined various other elements, including strontium and barium (in nitrous oxide-acetylene with an ionization buffer), chromium (in nitrous oxide-acetylene) and gallium (in air-acetylene after solvent extraction).

Flame AAS is not suitable for elements with their only absorbing lines at wavelengths below about 193 nm. These include the halogens, sulphur, carbon, nitrogen, oxygen and phosphorus. However some of these elements may be determined by indirect methods. For example, sulphate in soil extracts may be precipitated with barium, and the precipitate dissolved, after careful washing, in a solution of ammonia and EDTA. Determination of the dissolved barium by AAS then gives an indication of the sulphate content of the original extract. The conditions for the determination of the elements most often determined by flame AAS are summarized in Table 5.2.

Table 5.2 Elements commonly determined in soils and rocks by flame AAS

Element	Wavelength (nm)	Detection limit*	Flame	Requirements
Al	309.3	0.04	N_2O/C_2H_2	fuel-rich; ionization buffer
Ca	422.7	0.002†	air/C_2H_2	releasing agent (La or Sr)
Cd	228.8	0.002	air/C_2H_2	solvent extraction‡
Co	240.7	0.02	air/C_2H_2	solvent extraction‡
Cu	324.8	0.004	air/C_2H_2	solvent extraction‡
Fe	248.3	0.03	air/C_2H_2	releasing agent (La or Ca) or use N_2O/C_2H_2
K	766.5	0.006	air/C_2H_2	ionization buffer $<1\,\mu g\,ml^{-1}$
Mg	285.2	0.0002	air/C_2H_2	releasing agent (La or Sr)
Mn	279.5	0.003	air/C_2H_2	releasing agent (La) or use N_2O/C_2H_2
Na	589.0	0.003	air/C_2H_2	ionization buffer $<1\,\mu g\,ml^{-1}$
Ni	232.0	0.01	air/C_2H_2	good resolution; solvent extraction‡
Pb	283.3	0.02	air/C_2H_2	solvent extraction‡
Si	251.6	0.1	N_2O/C_2H_2	very fuel-rich flame (critical)
Zn	213.9	0.003	air/C_2H_2	solvent extraction‡

* Typical value in $\mu g\,ml^{-1}$ for aqueous solution.

† Detection limit depends on flame stoichiometry and matrix—may be poorer for some matrices.

‡ Solvent extraction may be necessary to improve sensitivity. For higher concentrations, if a fuel-lean flame and the greatest possible dilution is used to minimize interferences, then solvent extraction is not normally necessary. However a check should be made in total element analyses for background absorption.

5.10.3 The determination of exchangeable cations by AAS

Soil scientists are very interested in the cation-exchange properties of soils, because the distribution of the exchangeable cations indicates the relative abundance and availability of some major nutrient elements and of the lime requirement of the soil. The exchangeable cations may be displaced from a soil by leaching with a solution containing a large excess of a cation not of immediate interest, such as ammonium. The leachate may then be analysed by AAS for calcium, magnesium, sodium and potassium, the major basic cations.

Procedure. Pack 25 g of 3-mm sieved, air-dried soil (5 g mixed with 20 g of acid-washed fine sand if the soil has a high clay content) into a leaching tube as shown in Fig. 5.7. Place a plug of cotton-wool on top of the soil, place the tube in a conical flask, and invert a 500-ml volumetric flask containing 500 ml of 1 M ammonium acetate at pH 7 as shown (make sure everything fits first!). The solution should leach through over at least 2 hours. If the leaching rate is too high, push down on the cotton-wool plug to pack the soil more tightly and slow the rate. Transfer the leachate to a 500-ml graduated flask, and dilute to mark with the 1 M ammonium acetate.

Prepare standards containing 0–$4\,\mu g\,ml^{-1}$ sodium and potassium in 0.1 M ammonium acetate; also prepare standards with 0–$20\,\mu g\,ml^{-1}$ calcium and 0–$1\,\mu g\,ml^{-1}$ magnesium in 0.05 M ammonium acetate containing, at the final dilution, $5000\,\mu g\,ml^{-1}$ of lanthanum. Dilute the leachate 10-fold for the determination of sodium and potassium; dilute it 20-fold, adding sufficient lanthanum to give a final concentration of $5000\,\mu g\,ml^{-1}$, for the measurement of calcium and magnesium. Determine the sodium, potassium, calcium and magnesium contents of the leachate by AAS, following the instrument manufacturer's instructions carefully when setting

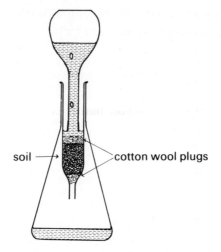

Figure 5.7 Apparatus for leaching soil.

up the equipment. Different dilution factors may be necessary for some soils, but remember to keep the ammonium acetate and lanthanum levels of samples and standards constant.

Ammonium acetate is not a suitable extractant for all soils. Calcium carbonate, for example, dissolves to a significant extent, limiting the value of the results for calcareous soils. For a discussion of the merits of alternative extractants see Refs. 2 and 3.

5.11 Flame emission spectroscopy

A technique which was established and used extensively before the introduction of AAS is that of flame emission spectroscopy (FES). Since the technique is still used for some elements, it is worth a brief discussion here. When atoms are produced in a flame, some of the atoms are thermally excited. The number of excited atoms, N^*, is proportional to the number of ground state atoms, N_0, and depends upon the flame temperature, T, and the excitation energy, E

$$N^* \propto N_0 \exp(-E/KT). \tag{5.4}$$

Clearly the lower the required excitation energy and the hotter the flame, the greater is the number of excited atoms. Some of the atoms lose their electronic excitation energy via collisional deactivation, but part is also lost by radiative deactivation, i.e. the excited electrons return to lower energy levels with the emission of light. The intensity of the emitted light depends upon the number of excited atoms, and hence upon the number of ground state atoms. Thus the concentration of analyte element in a sample solution may be determined by nebulization of the sample solution into a flame, and the comparison of the resulting thermal emission with that of suitable standards. This is the basis of FES.

The instrumental requirements of FES are very similar to those of AAS, i.e. a pneumatic nebulizer/spray chamber/burner system, a monochromator, a photomultiplier, an amplifier, and a read-out system. Of course the amplifier must now be capable of responding to d.c. signals, or the latter must first be modulated electronically. In practice many FES determinations are now made using atomic absorption spectrometers. Special circular burner heads may be used (although these are not really necessary, slot burners generally being perfectly adequate.) Many atomic absorption spectrometers have monochromators capable of giving perfectly adequate spectral resolution for sensitive and selective emission measurements. Moreover, they perform well in the UV, so that elements emitting at lower wavelengths, such as silver (328.1 nm) or magnesium (285.2 nm) may be monitored. The field of view of most AA monochromators is narrow, so that they only see the low background, central region of the interconal zone of the flame, and not the much more intensely emitting secondary diffusion flame (the outer zone of the flame).

Any factor which interferes in the production of atoms in the flame will constitute an interference in FES. Thus physical, chemical, incomplete volatilization, and ionization interferences are similar in incidence and extent in FES and AAS. The techniques differ considerably with respect to spectral interferences, however. Consider the transitions in a simplified typical energy diagram, shown in Fig. 5.8. The wavy arrows represent thermal excitation processes and the straight arrows radiative excitation (absorption) or de-activation (emission) processes.

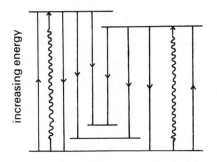

Figure 5.8 Simplified energy diagram to illustrate spectroscopic transitions.

Even in this very simple case six lines would be observed in the emission spectrum, but only two in the absorption spectrum, where only transitions originating from the ground state are generally significant. Thus there may be many more lines to contend with in emission techniques. Moreover, whereas the function of the monochromator in AAS is merely to isolate the line of the analyte element which gives the best sensitivity from other lines of the analyte and perhaps of neon or argon, in FES the monochromator must isolate the analyte line from the lines and molecular band emission of all possible concomitant elements. Therefore a monochromator of high resolution is necessary for the selective analysis of complex matrices such as rocks and soils.

It is possible in emission spectroscopy to use low-temperature flames such as air/propane or air/natural gas. In this case, T in equation (5.4) is low, and N^* is only significant when E is also low. Thus only elements with low excitation potentials emit significantly from cool flames. A low value of E corresponds to emission at long wavelength, λ, since:

$$E = hc/\lambda \qquad (5.5)$$

where c is the velocity of light and h is a constant. Relatively few elements emit at these longer wavelengths ($>420\,\text{nm}$), so those that do may be determined with good selectivity, even if a simple interference filter is used to isolate the radiation of interest.

If a filter is used rather than a monochromator, then a simple photocell detector may be used in place of a photomultiplier. The resulting instrument,

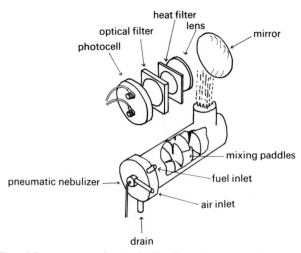

Figure 5.9 Essential components of a simple filter flame photometer (by courtesy of Corning Medical and Scientific).

known as a filter flame photometer, is clearly smaller, simpler and much cheaper than an atomic absorption spectrometer, as Fig. 5.9 shows. It may be used to determine sodium, potassium, lithium, calcium and barium. However, for soil and rock analyses, flame photometry is primarily used for the determination of the amount of potassium available in soils in assessments of potassium fertilizer requirement. If sodium is determined in the presence of an excess of calcium (as is frequently the case in soil analysis), interference from CaO band emission presents a problem on filter instruments. It may be eliminated either by a separate determination of calcium, and then subtraction of the CaO emission signal at the sodium wavelength corresponding to this concentration of calcium from the combined emission signals, or by chemical separation of the calcium.

5.12 Other emission techniques

Whereas AAS scores over FES with respect to selectivity, emission techniques offer the advantage of simpler simultaneous multi-element determinations. The monochromator of an emission spectrometer is simply replaced by a poly-chromator, with a separate exit slit and photomultiplier for each of several analytical wavelengths. If such spectrometers are coupled with hotter exci-tation sources such as arcs, sparks or, more recently, inductively coupled plasmas (ICP), then most elements of interest are excited and may be deter-mined simultaneously. Typically thirty or more elements may simultaneously be routinely determined in this way. The data are usually processed directly by a computer, and such systems are very expensive, but are cost-effective in cases where large amounts of data are to be obtained. Photographic detection may be used to record emission spectra from arcs and sparks, the technique then being generally known as *emission spectrography*. The advantage of this technique, apart from its multi-element capability, is that it may be used for the total element analysis of finely powdered rock or soil samples without prior dissolution, leading to a significant saving in time in the sample preparation stage.

The IPC is similar to a flame in so far as sample introduction is usually via a pneumatic nebulizer, but the fuel and oxidant are replaced by argon or argon/nitrogen. If the argon is ionized in a powerful radio frequency field, (r.f.) applied to a copper coil around a quartz tube (see Fig. 5.10), the argon absorbs most of the r.f. energy, and as the ions and electrons are accelerated to and fro at high speed, collisions cause the gas to reach a very high temperature indeed, and a plasma is formed. The aerosol is introduced into the centre of the plasma, where it is very rapidly desolvated, and the residual solid particles are volatilized and atomized. At the high temperature of the plasma, very intense atomic emission is observed, but ionization is so extensive that many ionic emission lines are also readily detectable.

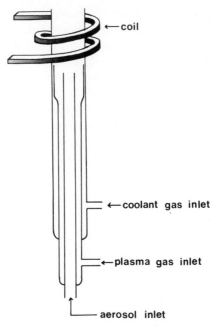

← coil

← coolant gas inlet

← plasma gas inlet

— aerosol inlet

Figure 5.10   A typical r.f. plasma torch.

Not only is the ICP an excellent excitation source for multi-element emission spectroscopy, it also offers the possibility of simple and direct determination of some of the elements in soils at levels not accessible by simple AAS because sensitivity is inadequate. These include boron, molybdenum and phosphorus. Because of its high temperature, chemical interferences do not present serious problems, but interferences stemming from factors which change the aspiration rate or aerosol production still occur. Spectral interferences are more probable at the elevated temperatures of plasmas, so that high resolution monochromators are necessary.

5.13   Identification of minerals

5.13.1   X-ray diffraction

Before leaving the subject of rock and soil analysis, brief mention should be made of the instrumental methods used to identify mineral structures. Much use is made of *X-ray diffraction*, which was discussed briefly in Section 3.7.3, particularly for clay-sized mineral particles which cannot be identified by optical microscopy. In many clay minerals the spacings between layers of units are variable, depending upon the associated cations, so it is necessary to saturate the minerals with a particular cation during sample preparation. Because of the similarities in spacings for certain different minerals, additional information may sometimes be obtained by saturation with different cations, or by examination of the collapse (if any) of the mineral lattices when heated at different, known temperatures.

5.13.2   Thermal methods of analysis

Thermal methods are also widely used in mineralogical analysis. *Differential thermal analysis* exploits the change in rate of temperature increase of a sample being heated at a steady rate when it undergoes a chemical or physical change such as dehydration or a structural change. The sample and a suitable inert standard are heated side by side in a pair of small crucibles of an inert metal such as platinum in a furnace designed to give a very uniform heating rate. The temperatures of the two crucibles are monitored with a pair of matched thermocouples. If an exothermic reaction occurs, the sample temperature rises more rapidly than that of the standard, whereas if endothermic reaction takes place it rises more slowly. Thus a positive or negative peak is obtained for each reaction involving a change in energy state if the temperature difference is plotted vs. temperature. The peak positions are characteristic of the minerals involved. Typical traces for two minerals are shown in Fig. 5.11.

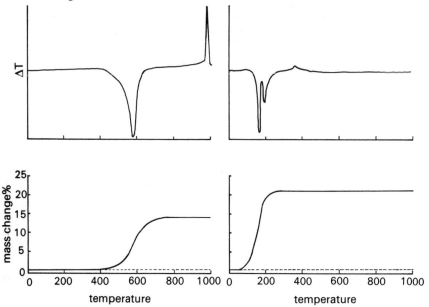

Figures 5.11 (upper) and **5.12** (lower)   Differential thermal analysis and thermogravimetric analysis traces for kaolinite (left) and gypsum (right).

An alternative approach is to follow the change in mass of a sample being heated at uniform rate with time—the basis of *thermogravimetric analysis* (or thermogravimetry). In this case a single small crucible fixed to the arm of a recording microbalance is heated at a uniform rate in a furnace. The temperature is monitored simultaneously, so the temperature at which each mass loss occurs may be read off. Unlike DTA, only changes in the sample involving mass loss are detected. Figure 5.12 shows the mass loss traces for the two minerals whose DTA traces are given in Fig. 5.11. Clearly mass loss curves are rather simpler to interpret, but they are not always as informative as DTA traces. Usually thermal methods are used in conjunction with X-ray diffraction data, and sometimes with IR spectroscopy too to build up a complete picture.

References

1 Fitzpatrick, E. A. (1971) *Pedology. A Systematic Approach to Soil Science*, Oliver and Boyd, Edinburgh.
2 Hesse, P. R. (1971) *A Textbook of Soil Chemical Analysis*, John Murray, London.
3 Black, C. A. (ed.) (1965) *Methods of Soil Analysis. Part 2: Chemical and Microbiological Properties*, American Society of Agronomy, Madison, Wisconsin, USA.
4 Walsh, A. (1955) *Spectrochim. Acta*, **7**, 108.
5 Fassel, V. A., Rasmuson, J. O. and Cowley, T. G. (1968) *Spectrochim. Acta*, **23b**, 579.
6 Kirkbright, G. F. and Sargent, M. (1974) *Atomic Absorption and Fluorescence Spectroscopy*, Academic Press, London and New York.
7 Price, W. J. (1972) *Analytical Atomic Absorption Spectrometry*, Heyden & Son, London.
8 Kelly, W. R. and Moore, C. B. (1973) *Anal. Chem.*, **45**, 1274.
9 Cresser, M. S. (1978) *Solvent Extraction in Flame Spectroscopic Analysis*, Butterworths, London.

6 The biosphere

6.1 The nature of the biosphere

The previous chapter concentrated upon the analysis of samples of soil or rock. Here we are concerned with the host of living organisms, from the simple amoeba to the complex mammal, which inhabit the outer part of the lithosphere, or live on or above the earth's surface. Chapter 5 emphasized that soil must be regarded as biologically active, but for convenience it was considered as a part of the lithosphere. Here botanical or zoological samples are considered together because of the many common problems they pose to the analyst. Collectively they constitute what may be termed the biosphere. This chapter emphasizes plant materials, primarily because they are more readily available for laboratory exercises than are animal samples, but still illustrate some of the problems peculiar to all biologically active samples.

6.2 The need for plant analysis

There are numerous routine problems which may necessitate plant analysis. The most important of these are the following:

1. *Nutrient deficiencies*: looking for elements which are essential to healthy plant growth, but are present in the soil at inadequate levels or in unavailable forms.
2. *Species toxic to plant growth*: seeing if excessive amounts of an undesirable element or ion have been made available to the plant.
3. *Understanding plant growth processes*: studying the distribution or take-up of a particular element or group of elements by plants.
4. *Presence of particular organic compounds*: these may be beneficial, e.g. vitamins, or potentially hazardous, e.g. residues from pesticides, fungicides, etc. Analyses coming into this category often fall within the remit of Chapter 7 (foods).
5. *Chemical species in pasture* at levels which may be injurious or toxic to grazing animals. Strictly speaking these too could be discussed in Chapter 7. They are included here on the grounds that the analytical procedures followed are indistinguishable from those used under (2) and (3).

6. *Economically important elements in plants*: these may be present in the soil or rock where the plant is growing, and are extracted by the plants (this is the basis of *biogeochemical prospecting*).

6.2.1 Deficiency problems

Most of the nutrients essential for plant growth were mentioned in Chapter 5, where it was seen that the amount of nutrient available in a soil may be estimated by treating the soil with a suitable extractant solution. Alternatively, plant tissue, usually foliage, may be analysed, on the basis that a growing plant should be the best indicator of its own nutrient requirements. Chemical analysis should prove to be a more reliable indicator of a particular deficiency problem than diagnosis by visual symptoms such as discoloration patterns and trends, or changed growth patterns, such as reduced stem elongation between leaves, or stunted root growth. Table 6.1 shows the

Table 6.1 Typical concentrations of elements in dried healthy foliage

Nitrogen, %	0.8–3.0
Potassium, %	0.5–2.5
Calcium, %	1.5–2.8
Magnesium, %	0.15–0.45
Phosphorus, %	0.08–0.35
Iron, $\mu g\,g^{-1}$	40–150
Manganese, $\mu g\,g^{-1}$	30–100
Boron, $\mu g\,g^{-1}$	10–50
Copper, $\mu g\,g^{-1}$	5–12
Zinc, $\mu g\,g^{-1}$	30–200
Molybdenum, $\mu g\,g^{-1}$	0.1–1.5
Cobalt, $\mu g\,g^{-1}$	0.1–0.5

typical range of concentrations of elements found in healthy foliage, based upon the authors' experience, and Refs. 1–3. Results below the lower level quoted in Table 6.1 may indicate possible deficiency problems, but unless they are grossly lower, they should be interpreted with caution. 'Normal levels' depend very much upon the plant. For example, in an extreme case two different species found growing side by side in mixed pasture species differed 20-fold in their manganese content;[4] also, as discussed later, nutrient levels vary throughout the growing season. Further, plant analysis in some instances may give no indication of deficiency of a particular nutrient, even although a fertilizer response to added nutrient is observed. This is the case, for example, for the copper in the aerial parts and grain of cereals.[1]

6.2.2 Toxicity problems

A number of toxicity problems occur quite naturally. On soils derived from serpentine, for example, the very high levels of magnesium may cause severe stunting. Associated with this there may sometimes be nickel and/or chromium toxicity, though it is not usual to find much chromium in foliage, because the element tends to be retained and concentrated in the plant roots. However, the majority of toxicity problems occur as a result of man's impact upon his environment. A common cause is the disposal of sewage sludge on land, especially if the practice is carried out at the same location over many years. In one survey the ranges of concentrations of trace metals in 42 sludge samples were found to be $800-49\,200\,\mu g\,g^{-1}$ of zinc, $200-8000\,\mu g\,g^{-1}$ of copper, $20-5000\,\mu g\,g^{-1}$ of nickel and $40-8800\,\mu g\,g^{-1}$ of chromium, the precise values for a particular sample being dependent upon the types and levels of industrial activity in the area.[3] Illegal, and sometimes even legal, dumping of chemical wastes may interfere with plant growth, due to inorganic and organic toxicities, as may prolonged exposure to pollution from airborne particulates, in the vicinity of smelters for example, or from "acid rain" from gaseous emissions. In some areas, toxicity symptoms may be found where water drains into the soil from nearby slag or mine spoil dumps. Sometimes waste dumped apparently quite safely in an old mine may later contaminate water nearby, causing toxicity symptoms.

6.2.3   Pasture analysis
Vegetation may be analysed in order to ascertain its suitability as animal feed, and herbage may be found either deficient in essential elements or toxic. Cattle may suffer from zinc or cobalt deficiency, for example, in spite of the fact that the vegetation on which they have been feeding appears to be completely healthy. On the other hand, cattle fed on selenium-rich pasture may suffer from the staggers, a result of severe selenium toxicity. Selenium accumulator plants may be abundant in such mixed pasture and these can contain very high concentrations of the element (e.g. $2000\,\mu g\,g^{-1}$ in *Astragalus*).

6.2.4   Biogeochemical prospecting
Our attention so far has been concentrated on elements which are essential or toxic to plants. Such analyses are important to the agricultural scientist or plant physiologist. Other scientists, particularly geologists, are also interested in the fact that plants take up elements from differing soils to different extents. Sometimes advantage can be taken of this fact to assist in the exploration for commercially viable mineral deposits.

Geobotanical prospecting is based on the observation that certain plants grow only where there is a significantly high concentration of some trace element. For example *Viola calamineria lutea* is used in many parts of Europe as an indicator for zinc, and species of *Astragalus* in western north America for selenium, and, by association, for uranium. This prospecting technique requires much care and experience, as well as sound botanical training, to ensure accurate identification of different varieties of indicator plant species.[5]

Biogeochemical prospecting depends on the analysis of plant matter— usually leaves or twigs—for supplying information about the soil below the plants. The plants are seen as extractors of trace metals from minerals in the soil or the bedrock: whether they sample from surface soils or from deeper-lying rocks will depend on the growth habits of the root systems. *Xerophytes* are plants with shallow root systems collecting surface waters— mostly rain—but *phreatophytes*, which send their roots down to considerable depths in search of the natural water table (10–15 m is not uncommon), can yield information about underlying rocks and ore bodies.

There are difficulties associated with this prospecting technique. Some trace metals are precipitated in the roots of plants and never reach the leaves, while others may be accumulated as far as a particular concentration regardless of the concentrations in the soil. Ideally, a plant would accumulate a given element (or preferably several elements) to reach levels strictly proportional to the concentrations in the soil, but this is rarely found in practice. When it is, the relationship may hold for only one element. Further complicating factors are the pH of the soil, the drainage, the geographical situation and so on, quite apart from the problem of deciding what species of plant to collect and which part of the plant to analyse. It has been said that there is also the psychological difficulty of persuading geologists to collect parts of plants instead of rocks!

One approach which attempts to overcome some of the problems associated with the wide variability of plant behaviour is to determine the *ratio* of two elements in plant material rather than their absolute concentrations. For instance, typical zinc levels in ash from different species of plants may vary by a factor of ten or more, but Warren and Delavant[6] found that the Cu : Zn ratio was much more constant, even for very different plant species, and concluded that ratios below 0.07 and above 0.23 would indicate the presence of high zinc or high copper levels respectively in the bedrock.

We may conclude that it is not always easy to interpret the results of chemical analysis of plant ash in terms of underlying rock composition, and while it may be easier to collect and analyse plant matter than to dig holes for rocks and analyse them, the flowering season, when the plants are most easily identified, is short, and collecting would involve a short spell of great activity. Brooks[7] has written a useful account of these prospecting techniques.

6.3   The need for analysis of zoological specimens

A list of reasons for analysing samples of animal origin would closely resemble the list for plant tissue samples (Section 6.2). Zoological specimens may be analysed to detect trace element deficiencies or trace element toxicities, to study the distribution and movement of elements in animals, to detect the presence of particular organic compounds, or of toxic levels of elements or compounds in animal products to be used as food. Here too, analyses in the latter two categories interest mainly those concerned with food production. However, there are some notable exceptions to this general rule. It may be regarded as important, for example, that chemicals used to control undesirable organisms or insects do not adversely effect desirable predators such as lady bugs or other natural agents of biological control, or other desirable creatures, from bees to hedgehogs.

Manufacturers of pesticides, fungicides and herbicides are continuously engaged in research into the fate of both existing and possible new control chemicals, as well as into the nature and fate of their metabolic breakdown products. Such research often includes studies of their effect upon micro-organisms, insects and appropriate higher animals, and may involve extensive analyses of materials of animal origin. Frequently particular species may be concentrated in a specific organ, and this is then used for analysis.

6.4 The merits of treating the biosphere as a whole

As mentioned briefly in Chapter 1, much environmental analysis is completed in studies of ecological processes. For example, a pesticide applied to vegetation may enter the human food chain directly, or indirectly after consumption by a herbivore which is in turn eaten by man, and so on. It may be absorbed as airborne particles from aerosols after spraying, or from contaminated water supplies. The same complex pattern occurs for toxic heavy metals. It follows that the analysis of plant tissue used as food may be of as much value in investigations of animal toxicity problems as the analysis of animal tissue. This, together with the similarity in analytical techniques used, more than justifies treating the biosphere as a whole.

6.5 Sampling problems

6.5.1 *Plants*

One of the difficulties posed by vegetation sampling is illustrated by the problem of collecting foliage samples from a 50-foot high tree. The question deserves more serious consideration than it was given by one of the authors' students ("Wait for autumn"). It is possible to obtain long-handled pruning shears for sampling from a distance, and trees may be climbed. It has even been suggested that a shotgun may be used to effect pruning, with fielders strategically placed to collect the falling samples[8]—these leaves were required for physical measurements, and not for trace lead determinations! In the case of deciduous trees, it is relatively easy to be confident that the current year's growth is being sampled, but for evergreen species, sampling procedures must be carefully followed to make sure that current growth is collected from near the top of the tree. For an area of woodland, samples should be collected from a number of typical trees and bulked, before drying and grinding. Atypical, stunted trees should never be selected simply because they facilitate sample collection, since this could obviously introduce a significant systematic error.

Plants, like all biologically active samples, present particular sampling problems in that their chemical composition changes with time. Figure 6.1

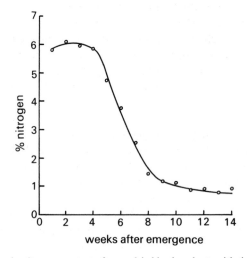

Figure 6.1   Change in nitrogen content of oven-dried barley plants with time after emergence.

shows, for example, how the nitrogen content of barley plants changes over a period of fourteen weeks after germination. The precise level of nitrogen found can therefore depend upon the plant species and the variety, the sampling time, the soil, the climate over the growth period, the climate prior to germination (which influences soil nitrogen availability at germination) and any nitrogenous fertilizer added. Furthermore, the level of a particular nutrient element may well depend upon the amounts of one or more other nutrients which may be present, because many complex interactions occur. These interactions, together with the dynamic nature of plants, serve to demonstrate how carefully field sampling programmes must be thought out if meaningful comparisons are to be made of the results obtained either from different sites or from similar sites at different times.

Plant samples other than trees may be much more readily accessible, but still pose problems.

1. Elemental composition varies with time, as discussed already.
2. Contamination may seriously affect short plant material. This is discussed in Section 6.6.1.
3. Should the whole plant be sampled, or selected parts? The distribution of major and trace nutrients is not uniform throughout the plant.
4. Care must be taken to collect representative samples, and not a sample from just inside the gate which may be benefiting from liberal doses of manure, or suffering from compaction by excessive trampling. Because of defecation by farm animals, areas around field boundaries and drinking troughs may also be atypical.

6.5.2 *Animals, etc.*

Many analyses of small animals and insects are carried out on specimens which have been bred under carefully controlled laboratory conditions alongside controls which provide reference levels. Sampling in this case presents fewer difficulties, provided that adequate sample populations are available to indicate the extent of natural variability. Single, or small numbers of, dead specimens are nevertheless sometimes brought into the laboratory from their natural environment. If samples are to be collected from the field by trapping, however, it is important to try to avoid a biased sample—poisoned, half-dead rabbits, for example, are a good deal easier to catch than healthy ones.

6.6 Sample preparation problems

6.6.1 *To wash or not to wash?*

Growing plant material is likely to be covered by dust from air-borne contamination. This is specially true for rough-textured surfaces such as hairy leaves. Low-growing material is also likely to be contaminated with soil from soil splash, which occurs during heavy rainfall. Clearly if attempts are being made to determine the amounts of elements taken up from the soil, the presence of soil dust on the plant is undesirable. Much gross contamination may be removed from broad-leaved plants by soft brushing, or the plant material may be washed under running water or by successive dipping in dilute detergent solution and deionized water. This raises two important questions:

1. Is there any possibility of analyte being leached out?
2. When is washing really necessary?

The answer to the first question is yes, at least for some ions and elements. Nitrogen is particularly susceptible to leaching, even on quite gentle washing.[9] Potassium may also be lost, particularly from cut material. To decide if a reduction in analyte found on washing indicates genuine removal of contamination, rather than loss of part of what the analyst was in fact trying to determine, requires the use of isotopic tracers. For example, a plant growing in a soil labelled with radioactive iron will absorb some of that iron into its leaves. If care is taken to avoid splashing, and the soil surface is covered with a protective barrier, losses in activity on washing the cut plant material would clearly indicate loss of part of the intended analyte. Losses in total iron without loss in radioactivity would, however, indicate removal of contamination.[10]

The answer to the second question can be found in Table 6.1. Under normal circumstances, no serious contamination would be expected from the major nutrients, or from boron, molybdenum, copper, cobalt, or zinc, unless they were present at abnormally high levels in the soil dust. The concentrations of these elements are generally rather similar in soils and plants, so that only severe contamination with soil dust should present serious problems. For iron and (to a lesser extent) manganese, however, the levels in soils tend to be much higher than those in plants, and even minor contamination could be serious. The same is true for aluminium, which is much more abundant in soils than in foliage. For most analyses, therefore, only removal of obvious dust is advisable, but before iron, aluminium and manganese determinations, plant material should be washed, and then dried and ground.

For root samples the same contamination problems are encountered, but they are very much more severe. In the authors' experience it is virtually impossible to clean up roots adequately, even using vigorous washing procedures involving ultrasonic cleaning baths. Again the problem is particularly severe for elements present at much higher levels in soils than in plant tissue.

In the case of many animal samples, contamination is not a serious problem, because samples of animal internal organs or blood are generally well protected, although care should be taken during dissection and other sample preparation stages to avoid the introduction of any species to be determined. Sometimes decisions must be taken as to what precisely constitutes the sample. For example, should the solid lead from fishing weights sometimes found in swans be included in trace lead analyses (see Section 1.2)? Lead (as lead shot) may also be found in grouse feeding on much-used grouse moors. Should this be included, since it may, or may not, be contributing to toxic effects? Including analyte contained in undigested food may lead to an overestimate of what is actually retained by the animal. The analysis of earthworms is another good example of this problem.

For samples such as hair, too, it is not always easy to decide what is part of the sample, especially for human hair, where trace elements may be retained from shampoos or a variety of grooming aids. These may not be readily removed by washing, and the problem of needing to confirm that no analyte is lost during the washing process arises once again.

6.6.2 Drying
If biological samples are to be dried at all, then they should be dried quite rapidly to eliminate the possibility of microbial degradation. Large samples of plant material should be well spread out on trays, and ideally dried rapidly in a stream of warm air. The possibility of losses of volatile constituents should be borne in mind. Selenium may be lost from plant material dried at temperatures above 90°C, for example. Containers in which samples are to be dried should be made from material free from analyte elements, and drying rooms should, ideally, be sited away from grinding rooms. Sometimes samples may be more easily subdivided into required parts after they have been dried. For example, needles may be very easily separated from twigs once branches of coniferous species have been dried. Samples containing volatile analyte species may need to be freeze-dried.

6.6.3 Grinding
Many plant and animal tissue samples are relatively soft, and quite easily ground once they have been dried. It is sometimes tacitly assumed that contamination from grinders is not likely for soft sample material, but this is not always the case in practice: contamination from grinder blades and built-in sieves may still be a problem.

6.6.4 Homogenization
Because wet or dry oxidation procedures are so time-consuming, tissue homogenization in the presence of suitable organic bases has recently attracted considerable attention as a method of sample preparation, particularly before determinations by atomic spectroscopy. High-speed blenders or ultrasonic dispersion systems are necessary to disperse most samples satisfactorily and not all sample types may be adequately treated in this way.

6.6.5 Sample preparation for plant pigment determinations
Whereas for most biological sample types and determinations the samples are stable provided the possibility of microbial degradation is minimized, when plant material is being extracted before determination of chlorophylls or carotenoids, the possibility of photochemical degradation must also be considered. The samples should be ground with an appropriate solvent,

usually aqueous acetone, under the minimum possible light level or using a red safelight, and extracts should be stored in darkness. Wet ball-milling in dark, sealed bottles is therefore a very suitable procedure for sample preparation.[11] For the determination of organic compounds, the possibility of chemical or photochemical changes should always be considered, as well as the possibility of biological degradation.

6.7 Sample dissolution

The most time-consuming stage in the trace element analysis of biological materials is that of sample dissolution. The three main methods, wet acid oxidation, dry ashing, or combustion in a stream of oxidizing gas, were considered in chapter 2, and need not be discussed again here. However, the possibility of multi-element analysis on a single, simple digest is worth consideration.

6.7.1 *Scope for digestion for multi-element analysis*

Because the sample dissolution rate often limits the rate at which samples may be analysed, digestion procedures which allow subsequent simultaneous or sequential multi-element analyses are potentially very attractive. In plant analyses the determination of nitrogen is often required, so that a Kjeldahl-type digestion may be regarded as necessary. However, if selenium or mercury is used as a catalyst for the conversion of organic nitrogen to ammonium, problems may be encountered in the determination of elements other than nitrogen in the same digest. For example, in the measurement of phosphorus, mercury or selenium may be precipitated when attempts are made to reduce phosphomolybdic acid to molybdenum blue. Plant material is more readily oxidized than is soil organic matter, and a digestion with concentrated sulphuric acid, with a few microlitres of perchloric acid added in the final stages to complete the oxidation is quite adequate.[12] The single digest may then be used for the determination of nitrogen, phosphorus, potassium, calcium, magnesium, sodium, iron and manganese. This digestion procedure may be used to produce 50 ml of solution from up to 200 mg of plant material. Larger samples may not be used, because then so much perchloric acid is required that some loss of ammonium occurs at the higher perchloric acid concentration. Thus $1 \mu g g^{-1}$ of a trace element in plant material would give a solution containing $0.2 \mu g$ in 50 ml or $0.004 \mu g ml^{-1}$. Table 6.1 shows that the concentrations of most trace elements would therefore be too low for this digest to be suitable for their determination. Even manganese may only be determined because its determination by flame AAS is very sensitive.

6.7.2 Acid digestions for trace analysis

If nitrogen is not to be determined, then larger subsamples may be digested with sulphuric acid/perchloric acid mixtures, because loss of ammonium is no longer important. Alternatively, nitric/perchloric acid mixtures may be used. With such systems it is possible for example to dissolve 1 g of plant material and dilute to a final volume of only 10 ml. The resulting solution, although quite strongly acidic, may be used for the determination of a range of trace elements by flame AAS. If colorimetric procedures are to be followed, however, the need for control of pH may lead to greater dilution, and, at the low concentrations thus obtained, to poor precision. For elements present at levels below $1 \mu g\,g^{-1}$, acid digestion may lead to excessive blanks, and dry ashing is the preferred technique. Perchloric acid is in any case potentially quite dangerous, and the hot concentrated acid must not be allowed to come into contact with fatty or waxy organic materials or partially charred organic matter, or a violent explosion may ensue. Moreover, the acid tends to collect in ducting, producing potentially dangerous perchlorates, so that special fume cupboards which are sprayed down with water during the digestion are required for routine use. For safety reasons too, then, dry ashing may be deemed more desirable. It is, however, not suitable for the determination of elements such as selenium, which are lost at elevated temperatures.

6.7.3 Problems of dry ashing

Although dry ashing is simple, and allows samples of 10–20 g to be dissolved in a small volume of relatively dilute acid, it is not without drawbacks. Some trace elements, particularly copper and cobalt, tend to be retained by the siliceous residues of the ashing process, so it is necessary to heat the residue with acid and to repeat the ashing, and finally to use quite vigorous heating to take the trace elements completely into solution.[10] A further problem lies in the quantity of organic vapours evolved when many large samples are heated. If samples are heated too rapidly to too high a temperature, they may catch fire, leading to possible loss of analyte or cross contamination between samples. Longer ashing at relatively low temperature (e.g. 8 hours at 460°C) is often preferred.

6.7.4 Fusion techniques

For the determination of silicon, fusion of ash residues with sodium hydroxide or sodium carbonate is generally necessary. Acid digestions involving perchloric acid can dehydrate silicates to silica, unless hydrofluoric acid is added at the final stage, and then care must be taken that the element is not lost by volatilization as SiF_4.

6.8 Analysis of plant tissue for N, P, K, Ca and Mg

As mentioned in Section 6.7.1, it is possible to determine all of the above nutrient elements in a single acid digest. Provided the sample mass does not exceed 200 mg, then the procedure described below is simple and rapid, and no potassium or calcium is lost (as precipitated potassium perchlorate or calcium sulphate).

6.8.1 Digestion procedure

Weigh (to ± 0.1 mg) up to 200 mg of oven-dried, ground plant material into a dry, clean 100-ml Kjeldahl flask. If solid adheres to the neck of the flask tap it gently with a metal spatula. Add 5 ml of concentrated sulphuric acid and a few grains of quartz sand (which have previously been boiled with fresh concentrated acid at least twice) to limit bumping. Swirl gently and leave to stand for 20 minutes, then heat to boiling over 5 minutes, taking care to avoid excessive frothing. Boil gently for a further 30 minutes. Stop heating, and add 1 ml of a 4% v/v solution of 62% perchloric acid in concentrated sulphuric acid. Heat gently for 10 minutes, by which time the digest should be clear and colourless. Cool, transfer with washings (*caution*—high concentrations of H_2SO_4!) to a 50-ml volumetric flask, and dilute to the mark. Prepare duplicate reagent blanks, putting them through the entire digestion procedure.

6.8.2 Nitrogen by distillation/titration

Determine nitrogen on duplicate 10-ml aliquots of digest as outlined in Section 5.9.5. Use 10-ml aliquots of the blank digests to make a blank correction, and 0.005 M sulphuric acid as titrant.

6.8.3 Phosphorus by spectrophotometry

Prepare a mixed reagent solution as described in Section 4.17 in 1 M sulphuric acid. The acidity needs to be considered carefully because the digests are already $c.$ 1.8 M in sulphuric acid, and the final acidity must lie in the range 0.15 to 0.30 M[7]. Use a 2-ml aliquot of digest for the determination in the first instance (although any volume up to 2.8 ml may be used if necessary) and 10 ml of mixed reagent for a final volume of 50 ml. Prepare standards containing 0–50 μg of phosphorus and 2.0 ml of blank digest, proceeding as described in Section 4.17.

6.8.4 Potassium by flame photometry

Prepare a series of standards containing 0–5 μg ml^{-1} of potassium and 2.5 ml of blank digest per 500 ml of standard. Determine the potassium contents of the sample digests after 20-fold dilution, by flame photometry or flame emission spectrometry, as described in Section 5.11.

6.8.5 Calcium and magnesium by AAS

Prepare a series of standards containing 0–15 μg ml^{-1} of calcium, 0–2.5 μg ml^{-1} of magnesium, 10 ml of digest blank per 100 ml of standard solution and 5000 μg ml^{-1} of lanthanum as a releasing agent. Pipette 5 ml of digest and 25 ml of 10 000 μg ml^{-1} lanthanum solution into a 50-ml volumetric flask and dilute to volume. Determine the calcium and magnesium contents of the diluted digest by flame atomic absorption spectroscopy in an air/acetylene flame. (For flame emission measurements with the EEL flame photometer the range should be 0–50 μg ml^{-1} Ca).

6.9 Boron in plant tissue

The determination of boron is important, because while the element is essential at a low concentration for healthy plant growth, it is toxic to plant growth at a level only slightly above this concentration. The symptoms of boron deficiency are particularly marked in root vegetables, where severe dark brown discoloration around the crown of the vegetable renders it totally unmarketable.

The determination of boron by flame spectroscopic methods is not very sensitive, and because of the low levels of the element occurring naturally in plant tissue, a solvent-extraction preconcentration step may generally be necessary if flame atomic absorption or emission is to be used. Colorimetric methods are available and are fairly sensitive and selective. One of the best known is based upon the coloured complex formed with curcumin (1,7-bis(4-hydroxy-3-methoxyphenyl)-1,6-heptadiene-3,5-dione) in ethanolic solution in the presence of oxalic acid. A slightly simpler and more rapid method is the determination by spectrofluorimetry, based upon the fluorescent complex formed by reaction of boron with carminic acid. This procedure is simple, sensitive and rapid.[14]

6.9.1 *Spectrofluorimetry*

When most small molecules absorb light, the electronic excitation energy they acquire is rapidly dissipated via intermolecular collisions or internal redistribution. For some larger organic molecules with relatively rigid structures, however, the molecules pass very rapidly to the lowest possible rotational or vibrational excitation state of either an excited singlet state (in which the electrons involved have their spins paired), or, if intersystem crossing has occurred, an excited triplet state (unpaired spin). Further deactivation may then occur by the dissipation of energy as described above, or else by the emission of light. Light emission from an excited singlet state occurs virtually instantaneously, and is known as fluorescence. However, excited triplet states are metastable, and the light emission occurs after a delay of anything from a microsecond to ten seconds, depending upon the emitting species. This emission is known as phosphorescence.

As discussed in Section 3.8.1, the relationship between the incident radiant power, P_0, and the transmitted radiant power, P_t, for monochromatic light passing through a solution of concentration c in a cell of path length l is given by

$$\log \frac{P_0}{P_t} = \varepsilon c l \qquad \text{or} \qquad P_t = P_0 10^{-\varepsilon c l}. \qquad (6.1)$$

The radiant power absorbed is given by $P_0 - P_t$, or $P_0(1 - 10^{-\varepsilon c l})$, and the radiant power of emitted fluorescence depends upon the radiant power absorbed, and the probability of deactivation by fluorescence emission. If we define a term ϕ, the quantum efficiency, as the ratio of the fluorescence radiant power, P_f, to the absorbed radiant power, then:

$$P_f = \phi P_0(1-10^{-\varepsilon cl}).\tag{6.2}$$

The right-hand side of equation may be expanded to

$$\phi P_0\left[2.3\varepsilon cl - \frac{(2.3\varepsilon cl)^2}{2!} + \frac{(2.3\varepsilon cl)^3}{3!} - \cdots\right]\tag{6.3}$$

At low values of c, the second and subsequent terms of the factorial expression are negligible compared to the first, so to a close approximation

$$P_f = 2.3\phi P_0\varepsilon cl.\tag{6.4}$$

Thus the radiant power of fluorescence emission, or, at fixed excitation and emission wavelengths, the intensity of fluorescence emission, is proportional to the intensity of the exciting radiation and to the concentration of the fluorescing species. Thus fluorescence provides the basis of a method of analysis, provided the analyte fluoresces, may be converted to a fluorescent species, or may be made to suppress the fluorescence of a fluorescent species.

It is worth emphasizing one important difference between fluorimetry and absorption spectrophotometric techniques. In fluorescence the intensity of the fluorescence emission signal increases with the intensity of the excitation source, so that sensitivity, and to a large extent detectability, improve with the source intensity. One other important difference is that calibration graphs take the form shown in Fig. 6.2A. In simple terms, this happens because at high analyte concentration most of the exciting radiation is absorbed very close to the surface of the irradiated face of the cell, as in Fig. 6.2B. Although

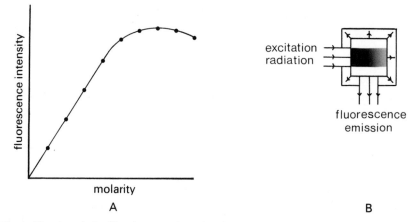

Figure 6.2 A: typical calibration curve for spectrofluorimetry.
B: change in fluorescence emission intensity across the cell for a concentrated solution.

intense fluorescence emission from this region may be visible to the eye, it does not reach the monochromator which isolates the fluorescence emission. This is rarely a problem in trace analysis, however.

Instrumentation for fluorimetry.   To avoid problems from scattered incident radiation it is normal practice in fluorimetry to employ monochromatic exciting radiation and measure the fluorescence emission intensity at a single, longer wavelength. The use of monochromatic exciting radiation also reduces the possibility of photochemical decomposition of the analyte. Thus spectro-fluorimeters or fluorimeters may be based upon either two filters, one filter and one monochromator, or two monochromators. This, together with the fact that a photomultiplier and its associated stabilized high voltage power supply are necessary to make the technique a sensitive one, tends to make fluorimeters rather more expensive than UV-visible absorption instruments. Typical optical arrangements for the simplest (twin-filter) and more complex (dual-monochromator) instruments are shown in Fig. 6.3.

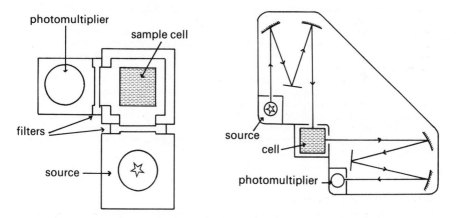

Figure 6.3   Optical components of twin-filter and dual monochromator spectrofluorimeters.

Selectivity of fluorimetry.   As far as trace elemental analysis is concerned, it might be expected that fluorimetry should be more selective than colorimetry, because relatively few metals form fluorescent complexes with organic reagents. However, any species which absorbs at either the excitation or the emission wavelength constitutes an interference, so that in fluorimetry too it is not always easy to develop selective and sensitive procedures. Often separation or masking techniques are used. Instructions appertaining to reagent concentrations, order of addition, development time, etc., must again all be followed closely. Extensive use is made of fluorimetry in organic analysis, as might be expected from the discussion of the types of molecules which fluoresce. Examples of its use in organic analysis may be found at various points in this book. Two elements which are often determined by fluorimetry are selenium and boron, and a procedure for the determination of boron in plant material is included below.

It should be remembered that boron may be extracted from borosilicate or pyrex glassware, so that plastic or pure fused silica apparatus must be used. Ordinary glassware may sometimes be used after it has been very thoroughly leached by being passed through a sample preparation procedure many times.

6.9.2   Dissolution procedure for boron determination

Ash 2 g of oven-dried, finely ground plant material for at least six hours at 450°C in a silica crucible. Cool, and digest the ash with 20 ml of 1 M nitric acid for 1 hour on a water bath. Neutralize with 1 M sodium hydroxide, filter, and dilute to 100 ml in a 100-ml plastic volumetric flask. Prepare reagent blanks from separate 20-ml aliquots of the nitric acid.

6.9.3   Fluorimetric determination[14]

Prepare a 10^{-3} M solution of carminic acid by dissolving 0.246 g of reagent in 10 ml of 0.1 M sodium hydroxide, neutralize to pH 7 with dilute acetic acid or sodium hydroxide as appropriate, filter, and dilute to 500 ml. Prepare a buffer solution by dissolving 35 g of disodium hydrogen phosphate in about 400 ml of deionized water, adjusting the pH to 7 and dilution to 500 ml. Prepare a stock boron solution by dissolving 0.286 g of recrystallized boric acid in water and diluting to 500 ml; this solution contains $100 \mu g \, ml^{-1}$ of boron. Prepare a $10 \mu g \, ml^{-1}$ boron solution from this when required. Also prepare a 0.1 M disodium EDTA solution.

Pipette 0, 1, 2, 3, 4 and 5 ml of stock $10 \mu g \, ml^{-1}$ boron solution and an appropriate volume of digest (25 ml is a useful volume to start with) and reagent blank into a series of 50 ml plastic graduated flasks. To each add 2.5 ml of 0.1 M EDTA, 5 ml of pH 7 buffer solution and 5 ml of 10^{-3} M carminic acid. Dilute to volume, mix well, and leave to stand for one hour.

Measure the fluorescence emission intensity at 556 nm, using an excitation wavelength of 467 nm, or appropriate filters.

6.10   Cobalt in plant tissue

The importance of cobalt in plant tissue used as animal feed has already been mentioned briefly (Section 6.2.3). Because of the low levels of cobalt which must be determined, around $0.1 \mu g \, g^{-1}$ for pasture which is suspect, the determination of plant cobalt requires the dissolution of a relatively large amount of plant material into a relatively small amount of solution. To avoid high blanks, ashing is therefore the preferred technique. However, care is then necessary to ensure that the element is not retained by the ash residue. Solvent-extraction may be used to enhance the sensitivity of the subsequent determination by flame AAS, as described by Gelman.[13]

6.10.1   Ashing procedure

Heat 10 g of sample in a silica evaporating dish (c. 75 mm diameter) over an electric heater in a fume cupboard to char without ignition. Then ash for 9 h (or overnight) in a furnace at 460°C (if these relatively large organic samples are not preheated, the muffle furnace will be contaminated).

Moisten the ash with distilled water, add 5 ml of concentrated nitric acid and evaporate to dryness, preferably under infra-red lamps. Re-ash for 5 h at 460°C, cool, and treat the residue with 8 ml of 5 M hydrochloric acid. Evaporate to dryness under an infrared lamp.

6.10.2   Dissolution and solvent extraction
Dissolve the residue in 20 ml of 0.1 M hydrochloric acid with warming (30 min on a water bath should suffice). Cool, and filter into a 100-ml separating funnel. Wash the residue with hot 0.1 M hydrochloric acid, to give a final volume of c. 50 ml in the funnel. Cool, add 2 ml of ammonium tetramethylene dithiocarbamate solution (APDC, 2 g/100 ml) and mix thoroughly. Add 5 ml of MIBK (4-methylpentan-2-one or methylisobutylketone) and shake vigorously for 1 min. When phase separation is complete, run the aqueous layer to waste, and the organic layer into a 10-ml test tube for the determination of cobalt by flame AAS. Prepare a series of standard cobalt solutions containing 0 to 3 μg of cobalt in 50 ml of 0.1 M hydrochloric acid and proceed as above. Also prepare a reagent blank, starting from the 5 ml of concentrated nitric acid-addition stage, put through the entire procedure.

6.10.3   Determination of cobalt in organic extract
Determine the cobalt by AAS at 240.7 nm using an air-acetylene flame. Zero the instrument using MIBK rather than water, and adjust the acetylene flow to give a non-luminous flame.

6.11   Sulphur in plant tissue
At the present time there is considerable interest in the measurement of the sulphur content of plant material. Decreasing levels of atmospheric SO_2 pollution and the large amounts of N, P and K fertilizer applied to increase crop yields mean that sulphur deficiency in plants is becoming more prevalent (see also Section 4.1). Organic sulphur must be converted quantitatively to a single inorganic form prior to determination; sulphate is the most widely chosen. This may be done by a wet oxidation with nitric and perchloric acids, or alternatively by an oxygen flask combustion, in which the organic sulphur is converted to SO_2, and then to sulphate (see Section 2.6.3).[15]

6.11.1   Oxygen flask combustion: procedure
Weigh accurately 50–100 mg of plant material on to a suitably shaped piece of filter paper, wrap the paper around the material, and enclose it in the platinum mesh sample holder of an oxygen-flask (Schöniger flask) combustion apparatus (see Fig. 6.4). Place 9 ml of 3% hydrogen peroxide in the flask as an absorbent, and ignite the sample. After 30 min remove the stopper and warm to remove the excess of hydrogen peroxide.

6.11.2   Turbidimetric determination of sulphate
Many methods are available for the determination of sulphate. The turbidimetric procedure outlined here is that of Hunt.[15] It is simple, rapid, sensitive and selective. Turbidimetry is a method of analysis based upon measurement of the apparent absorbance of light due to scatter by a suspension of the analyte species rather than to true absorption. In this instance sulphate is converted to a suspension of barium sulphate by reaction with barium

Figure 6.4   A Schöniger flask for combustion in oxygen. A thick-walled 250 ml flask is used.

chloride. The suspension is stabilized by the addition of the surfactant Tween 80.

Procedure.   Acidify the absorbent solution by the addition of 1 ml of 1 M hydrochloric acid. Pipette 5 ml of the acidified solution and of appropriate standards (0–20 μg ml^{-1} sulphate in 0.1 M hydrochloric acid) into a series of clean, dry test tubes. To each add 3 ml of a solution of Tween 80 and barium chloride (66 ml of Tween 80 and 13.4 g of barium chloride per litre), mix, and leave to stand for 30–45 min. Shake thoroughly again and measure the absorbance at 420 nm in a 10-mm cell.

A novel feature of Hunt's procedure[15] is that potentially interfering cations are retained in the ash, which is held by the platinum mesh of the sample holder.

6.12   Simultaneous multi-element analysis

6.12.1   *Emission spectrography*
Where large numbers of samples are to be analysed for a range of elements, simultaneous multi-element analysis becomes attractive, and direct analyses of ashed biological materials by emission spectrography with polychromator systems such as those described briefly in Section 5.12 have been widely used for many years. The ash is mixed with pure powdered carbon, typically on a 1:1 basis, and the mixture is packed into the hollow end of one of a pair of carbon electrodes. An arc is then struck between the two electrodes and the spectrum recorded for the required period. The emission intensities observed are compared with those from suitable synthetic standards or of certified reference materials. The method is relatively rapid when several elements are

estimated simultaneously, but not particularly precise. Better precision is attainable using an ICP excitation source after sample dissolution.

6.12.2 *Plasma emission spectroscopy*

Inductively coupled plasmas have recently been increasingly widely used for the simultaneous multi-element analysis of biological samples after dissolution. The excellent sensitivity and wide working range for many elements, together with the low level of interferences, make ICP emission spectroscopy an almost ideal method so long as sample throughput is high enough to justify the initial capital outlay. The recent text edited by Boumans[16] is an excellent comprehensive account of the use of ICPs.

6.13   The role of trace elements in living systems

Some metals are required, particularly by animals, in substantial quantities: calcium is necessary for building bones, for example, and iron for forming haemoglobin, the oxygen-transferring system in the blood. Other elements are, as we have seen, essential at low levels only: these are usually bound to special protein molecules to constitute the enzymes which catalyse and control the biosynthetic pathways in living systems.

6.13.1   *The nature of enzymes*

One of the simple early models of enzymes is that developed by Cloetens[17] which treats an enzyme as a large three-dimensional molecular structure with a number of groups or active centres (G_1, G_2, G_3).

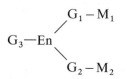

In this model, G_3 is not bound to a metal, but is free to bind the small molecules taking part in the reaction in such a way as to offer a stereospecific reaction pathway of low activation energy. Groups G_1 and G_2 bind to metal ions—G_1 rather loosely, G_2 rather more strongly. Only where the appropriate metal ions are present does the enzyme function as a biological catalyst.

6.13.2   *Rates of enzyme-controlled reactions: kinetic methods of analysis*

For a general reaction of the type $A + B \rightarrow C + D$, the rate of reaction can be expressed as the rate of disappearance of A, i.e.

$$\text{Rate} = \frac{d[A]}{dt} = -k[A][B]. \tag{6.5}$$

The reaction is first order with respect to A and B, i.e. the rate is proportional to the two concentrations. In the presence of a large fixed excess of B, the rate varies only with the concentration of A, and remains reasonably constant at the beginning of the reaction until $[A]$ has decreased significantly. Separate experiments carried out with different initial concentrations of A yield different initial rates which are proportional to the initial concentrations of A.

Consider now an enzyme-controlled reaction, $B + \text{enzyme} \rightarrow C + D + \text{enzyme}$: The enzyme is recycled, and so remains at a constant concentration. Thus the rate of reaction is constant for a large part of the reaction and is proportional to the enzyme concentration.

$$\frac{d[B]}{dt} = -k\,[\text{enzyme}][B] = \frac{-d[C]}{dt}. \tag{6.6}$$

The reaction can be followed for solutions with different enzyme concentrations by monitoring the production of C (say by spectrophotometry or spectrofluorimetry) as in Fig. 6.5A, or the disappearance of B. From such data it is simple to plot $[C]$ at a given time, t_m, against concentrations of enzyme, as in Fig. 6.5B. If the rate of formation of C is then measured for an

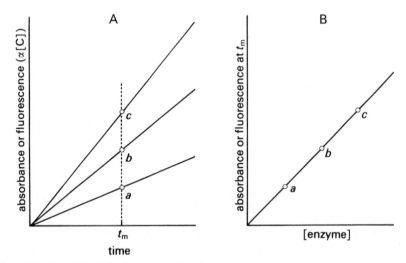

Figure 6.5 Principle of kinetic methods of analysis.

unknown sample, the concentrations of enzyme in it may be determined. This is the basis of *kinetic methods* of analysis.

The compound B is called the *substrate* and is chosen because either it or its product C may be easily measured at low concentration. Thus *p*-nitrophenylphosphate can be hydrolysed at pH 8–10 by the enzyme alkaline phosphatase to yield the *p*-nitrophenolate ion which is intensely yellow and easily measured by spectrophotometry. Careful temperature control is necessary for reproducible results.

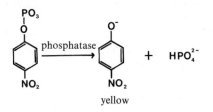

A still more sensitive method is to use fluorimetry to measure the product of the hydrolysis: α-naphthyl phosphate(I) and umbelliferone phosphate(II) both give fluorescent products which have been used for assaying phosphatases.

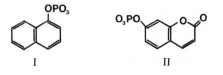

Many different substrates have been recommended for the determination of a wide range of enzymes, particularly in clinical analysis: the topic has been reviewed by Guilbault.[18]

6.13.3   *Deactivation of enzymes*

It was stated earlier that the metal ions are essential for the enzyme to operate. It is possible to remove the metal ions by dialysing a solution of the enzyme against a solution of some metal-complexing ligand separated by a thin cellophane membrane. The enzyme solution then shows no catalytic activity and is said to be *deactivated*. The process is reversible, so that by adding very small amounts of metals to the enzyme solution we can restore its activity. If the amount of metal ion added is less than was removed, the activity (measured as before by following the rate of reaction) is proportional to the concentration of metal added. We now have a potentially very sensitive method for the determination of trace metals—say at the 10–100 ng level—though there are problems of selectivity since various metals can be used to reactivate the enzymes. Townshend has described the determination of ng amounts of zinc by using alkaline phosphatase which has been first completely deactivated, and then partially reactivated by a controlled excess of magnesium.[19]

6.13.4 *Inhibition of enzymes*

Heavy metals are known to poison many living organisms: they do so by blocking enzymes and thus blocking metabolic pathways. The heavy metal ions often form more stable complexes than the lighter ones (e.g. Pb^{2+} and Hg^{2+} form very stable EDTA complexes while Ca^{2+} and Mg^{2+} form much weaker ones), and so displace ions such as Zn^{2+} and Mg^{2+} from the enzymes. The enzyme is said to be *inhibited*, and the decrease in reaction rate can be taken as a measure of the concentration of the heavy metal ion. It is difficult to make the system selective towards only one heavy metal, but on the other hand it can sometimes be useful to have a system responding to "poisonous heavy metals" in total. This application has been extended to cover blocking of enzyme systems by various pesticides. Guilbault et al.[20] have shown that cholinesterase, which hydrolyses acetate groups, can be inhibited by traces of various pesticides, and that the same type of enzyme extracted from different animals shows markedly different response to different groups of pesticides. For instance, cholinesterase from human serum is very sensitive to traces of organophosphorus pesticides, and that from bees is particularly sensitive to organophosphorus compounds but not to the organochlorine pesticides.

In some ways this type of approach to an environmental analytical problem is particularly satisfying, as we are making use of the undesirable phenomenon observed in the environment in living creatures, to determine the compound or even the group of compounds at the root of the problem. We are nearly back full circle to the problem of the river water supposedly toxic to fish: putting a fish in the water to see if it dies is hard on the fish, but adding a little of the water to a solution of an enzyme and determining its activity by kinetic measurements may well be the next best thing.

6.14 Trace element determinations on very small samples

A useful attribute of many instrumental methods of analysis is their relatively small sample requirement. Whereas classical methods require typically mg quantities of analyte, or more, some instrumental methods require only a few μg or less. Provided a representative sample may be obtained for analysis, this capability opens exciting new possibilities in many branches of biological science, especially in clinical science. Thus for example, it is possible to determine several elements in single hairs or finger nail clippings, or in a few μl of whole blood. One development in particular is worthy of mention, namely the introduction of electrothermal atomizers in AAS.

6.14.1 *Electrothermal atomization*

Although many elements may be determined at low concentrations by flame AAS (see Section 5.10), nebulization even for only 15 seconds at an aspiration rate of 4 ml min^{-1} requires a sample of 1 ml. If, however, the flame is replaced by a small graphite rod or furnace which is heated electrically, then a much smaller sample may be used, typically c. 10 μl. Whereas generally only 10% of analyte reaches a flame, all of the analyte in the sample may be atomized very rapidly by electrical resistive heating, thus giving excellent sensitivity.

Typical rod and furnace atomizers are shown in Figs. 6.6 and 6.7 respectively. The sample is introduced to the atomizer while it is still cool, and the atomizer is then heated in several stages. First the temperature is

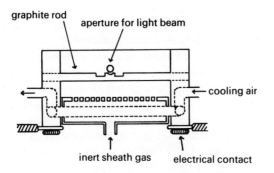

Figure 6.6   A typical graphite-rod atomizer.

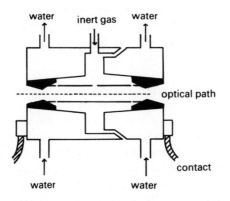

Figure 6.7   A typical graphite-furnace atomizer.

raised just enough to cause the solvent to evaporate without sputtering, and then it is raised further in one or two stages to destroy any organic matrix components. Finally the atomizer is heated to a high temperature, the analyte is atomized, and the absorbance peak is recorded. The individual heating temperatures and times may be controlled individually and automatically.

Modern atomic absorption spectrometers usually have facilities for measurement of both absorbance peaks and the areas under the absorbance vs. time traces. Many also have facilities for simultaneous automatic background correction using a separate continuum source to compensate for background absorbance attributable to molecular absorption or scattering. Provided adequate care is taken to prevent interferences, which are rather more prevalent with this type of atomization device, very low detection limits may be obtained using very small samples. For further discussion of the use of rods or furnaces a more specialized monograph should be consulted.[21]

The availability of methods for the direct determination of trace elements in clinical samples of only a few μg has had a tremendous impact upon trends of research into the distribution and accumulation of potentially toxic heavy metals. Blood samples of $50\,\mu$l volume are easy to obtain, and this, coupled with the speed and simplicity of the subsequent analyses, has caused an enormous increase in published results based largely upon AAS determination using electrothermal atomization. However, in some instances, published results should be treated with caution, particularly those obtained when electrothermal atomizers had first become commercially available but signal processing, knowledge of possible interferences and background correction systems were all far less evolved than at present. Often there is insufficient information given in papers where novel analytical procedures have been employed to assess the validity of the analytical methodology used. We will return to this point in Chapter 8, but it is mentioned here to stress the importance of an intelligent interest on the part of the environmental scientist in the work of the analyst, and vice versa.

6.15 Cold vapour and hydride generation systems in AAS

A limited number of the elements which are routinely determined by AAS readily form volatile hydrides. Among those that do are germanium, tin and lead in group IV of the periodic table, arsenic, antimony and bismuth in group V and selenium and tellurium in group VI. If the elements in solution are converted to the corresponding hydrides they may be swept from the solution by a stream of argon or nitrogen into a heated cell. There, because they are not very stable thermally, the hydrides may be broken down into free atoms, and the atomic absorption signals recorded. The atomization cell is a silica tube, heated electrically or by a flame.

Hydride generation techniques, like electrothermal atomization, avoid the problem of poor nebulization efficiency and, because the hydride may be displaced from the sample solution very rapidly, may give quite dramatic improvements in detectability. An improvement of 2–3 orders of magnitude (100- to 1000-fold) is not atypical.

Of all the metallic elements of the periodic table, mercury is unique in that it exists as a monatomic vapour at room temperature. The sensitivity of the determination of this element may therefore be improved substantially by reducing mercury salts to the free element, and displacing the latter by a stream of inert gas as described above. It has been claimed that problems from condensation and water vapour may be best avoided by allowing the solution to equilibrate with the atmosphere above it, and displacing the latter with the inert gas stream, rather than by bubbling the gas through the test solution,[22] but the authors have found the simple apparatus shown in Fig. 6.8 to be satisfactory.

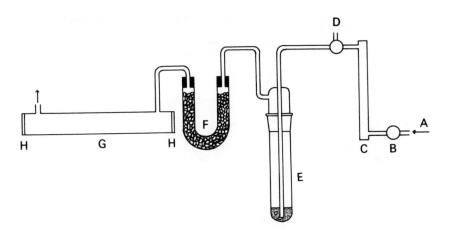

Figure 6.8 Apparatus for the cold vapour determination of mercury. *A*, air inlet; *B*, needle valve; *C*, flow meter; *D*, three-way valve; *E*, sample tube; *F*, calcium chloride drying tube; *G*, absorption cell; *H*, silica windows.

6.15.1 *Determination of mercury in urine*

Mercury has been recognized for several years now as a potentially dangerous environmental contaminant—high levels of mercury are an occupational hazard to dentists and electrochemists who fail to take sufficient care, and mercury-containing fungicides on cereal seed have sometimes found their way into food at times of famine, with catastrophic consequences. The mercury content of urine may be determined quite simply by cold-vapour AAS.[23]

Procedure. Pipette 2 ml of urine or mercury standard $(0–0.2 \mu g\, ml^{-1})$ into a series of tubes with ground glass joints. Cool the tubes in cold water and to each add cautiously 0.4 ml of concentrated sulphuric acid and mix. Add 3 ml of potassium permanganate solution $(60\,g\,l^{-1})$ swirl gently to mix, and leave the tubes loosely stoppered overnight at room temperature. After at least 12 hours, add 0.6 ml of hydroxylammonium chloride $(20\,g/100\,ml)$ to reduce the excess of permanganate.

Add 5 ml of stannous chloride solution (20 g $SnCl_2 \cdot 2H_2O$ in 100 ml of 6 M hydrochloric acid) to the first tube and immediately fit the tube to the apparatus as shown in Fig. 6.8, with the air flow vented to the atmosphere at D. Turn D to pass air through the sample and on through the absorption cell at $31 min^{-1}$. Record the mercury absorbance peak, measuring at 253.6 nm. Replace the tube containing the sample with one containing 20 ml of distilled water, and flush air through the system until the baseline absorbance returns to its initial value. Continue with the remaining samples and standards.

References

1 Mitchell, R. L. (1964) *The Spectrochemical Analysis of Soils, Plants and Related Materials*, Tech. Comm. 44A of the Commonwealth Bureau of Soils, Commonwealth Agricultural Bureau, Farnham Royal, England.

2 *International Methods for Chemical Analysis, Report on Activities, 1971–1973* (1973) IUFRO Subject Group S1.02, Working Party 3.

3 *Trace Elements in Soils and Crops*, Ministry of Agriculture, Fisheries and Food Technical Bulletin 21 (1971) HMSO, London.

4 Archer, F. C. (1971) Factors Affecting the Trace Element Content of Pastures, in *Trace Elements in Soils and Crops*, MAFF Technical Bulletin, **21**, HMSO, London.

5 Cannon, H. L. (1960) *Science*, **132**, 591.

6 Warren, H. V. and Delavant, R. E. (1952) *Trace Elements in Geochemistry and Bio-geochemistry, Scient. Monthly, New York*, **75**, 26.

7 Brooks, R. R. (1972) *Geobotany and Biogeochemistry in Mineral Exploration*, Harper and Row, New York.

8 Waring, R. H. and Running, S. W. (1978) *Plant, Cell and Environment*, **1**, 131.

9 Boswell, F. C. (1972) *Commun. Soil Sci. Plant. Anal.*, **3**, 243.

10 Nicholas, D. J. D., Lloyd Jones, C. P. and Fisher, D. J. (1957) *Plant and Soil*, **8**, 367.

11 O'Neill, E. J. and Cresser, M. S. (1980) *Analyst*, **105**, 625.

12 Cresser, M. S. and Parsons, J.W . (1979) *Anal. Chim. Acta*, **109**, 431.

13 Gelman, A. L. (1972) *J. Sci. Fd. Agric.*, **23**, 299.

14 Gabriëls, R. and Van Keirsbulck, W. (1977) *Lab. Pract.*, **26**, 620.

15 Hunt, J. (1980) *Analyst*, **105**, 83.

16 Boumans, P. W. (1982) *Analysis by Inductively Coupled Plasma Atomic Emission Spectrometry*, John Wiley, New York.

17 Cloetens, R. (1941) *Biochem. Z.*, **307**, 353.

18 Guilbault, G. G. (1970) *Enzymatic Methods of Analysis*, Pergamon, Oxford.

19 Townshend, A. and Vaughan, A. (1970) *Talanta*, **17**, 289.

20 Sadar, M. H., Kuan, S. S. and Guilbault, G. G. (1970) *Anal. Chem.*, **42**, 1770.

21 Fuller, C. W. (1977) *Electrothermal Atomization for Atomic Absorption Spectrometry*, The Chemical Society, London.

22 Ure, A. M. and Shand, C. A. (1974) *Anal. Chim. Acta.*, **72**, 63.

23 Lindstedt, G. (1970) *Analyst*, **95**, 264.

7 Food

7.1 Introduction

Food may be seen as the last link in the chain which we have been examining in this book, when the living products of the environment fed by the air and the water and grown on the rocks and soils are served up as nourishment for human sustenance. Over the very long period of his evolution, man has learned which plants and which parts of which animals may be eaten, but only in comparatively recent times has he had to cope with food which was not of the purest and most natural composition. There are two main reasons for our present-day need to examine and control the quality of food offered for sale to the public—adulteration and contamination. The former is the deliberate admixture of other substances, usually with a view to marketing an apparently high-quality product from cheap and low-quality starting materials, while the latter is usually unintentional, arising when undesirable trace substances in the environment find their way into the food chain of man (Fig. 7.1). The food chemist is thus faced with a very wide range of types of

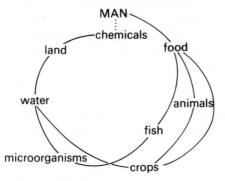

Figure 7.1 The food chains culminating in man.

sample and nearly as wide a range of substances which may have to be determined.

7.2 Food legislation

Since the beginning of the growth of the cities in the early industrial revolution (18th century) there has been an increasing dependence of a larger fraction of the population on a smaller number of farmers for the production of food and also on middlemen who buy from the farmers and in turn sell to the public. By the middle of the 19th century the extent of adulteration of food bought in the cities had reached quite intolerable limits, and there seemed little that could be done about it. One reason was the difficulty of proving that a food sample was indeed adulterated; the need to exchange information and experience on such matters led to the formation in 1874 of the Society of Public Analysts, and to the publication of their journal *The Analyst* in March 1876. The reports in the early volumes make fascinating reading today, but we sometimes forget the formidable difficulties faced by these pioneering chemists.

The second reason was the absence of comprehensive legislation. In Britain, this was put right in 1875 with the introduction of the Sale of Food and Drugs Act, 1875, the core of which lay in Section 6 (now Section 2 of the Food and Drugs Act, 1955) which

> prohibits the sale of any food which is not of the nature, substance or quality demanded, if to the prejudice of the purchaser

but just as important is Section 1 which

> prohibits additions to or subtractions from food which might render it injurious to health.

A possible misinterpretation (that someone purchasing food with a view to analysing it rather than eating it was expecting it to be adulterated and was not therefore being prejudiced) was clarified in an amending Act in 1879. In the 1955 Act, Section 91 relates to the powers of an officer to purchase samples of food for analysis, Section 4 empowers a minister to make regulations relating to the composition of food, Section 5 is concerned with obliging manufacturers to supply information about their products, and Sections 6 and 7 deal with labelling.

The working details of the Act are to be found in the various Regulations which have been published since the Act was passed. The examination of samples is in the hands of Public Analysts who, according to Section 89, are to be appointed by every food and drugs authority, and who must be specially qualified.

British legislation relating to food has followed a new path since 1973 when the UK joined the European Economic Community, one of whose aims is to rationalize and standardize the laws concerning food in the member states. A number of EEC Directives and Regulations are now in operation in the UK, and work is in progress to prepare many more. In some cases the recommendations of WHO Expert Committees are adopted, e.g. for permitted levels of pesticides in foods. The former Society for Analytical Chemistry in London published an extensive compilation of approved methods in 1974[1] and the whole field is most readably and thoroughly surveyed by Pearson,[2] though for instrumental methods, Macleod[3] is more helpful, and has an extensive bibliography as well.

In the United States, the Association of Official Analytical Chemists (AOAC) was founded (originally as the Association of Agricultural Chemists) in 1884 by Federal and State chemists. The scope of that organization has steadily broadened to cover all aspects of food and agricultural chemistry in recent years, and the regularly updated handbook *Official Methods of Analysis*[4] describes in detail methods which have been accorded preferred status in Federal and State courts.

7.3 The composition of food

While we have accepted that air, natural waters, soils and plants are all complex mixtures, we have in previous chapters concentrated on the determination of specific components, usually at low levels, either as elements or as compounds. But the food chemist is often required to make pronouncements on the bulk composition of some commodity and to classify major constituents into a few broad categories. The answer supplied to the person submitting the sample for analysis is often simply a number arrived at by following a particular test procedure, rather than a value for the concentration of one specific compound.

Water, for example, may be determined by heating the sample to dry it, or by distilling the water along with a suitable carrier such as dichloromethane or xylene: in both cases volatile oils are likely to be carried over with the water, so the water itself should be determined subsequently rather than being equated to the weight-loss of the sample.

Fats are determined by a solvent-extraction procedure followed by evaporation of the solvent. This is suitable for the oil content of peanuts, but tells us nothing about the type or source of the fat or oil in a sample of processed food. It might also be necessary to distinguish between free fat and bound fat: for the latter to be determined, the cell structure must first be broken down before the fat can be extracted. The analysis of fats and oils becomes of much greater interest to the analyst when the individual long-chain fatty acids are determined. Such analyses—by GLC or GC/MS—can tell us much about the sources of fats and oils and even reflect on the diet of the animals from which the fats were obtained (see Section 7.9).

The determination of protein is another problematical area. There are many different substances in animal tissue called proteins, but all have in common the peptide link of the combined amino acids —NH·C(:O)—. Routine determinations convert such materials to ammonium ions by boiling in concentrated sulphuric acid and then separating the ammonia by alkaline distillation and finally estimating the ammonia by acid-base titration or colorimetric reaction (see Section 5.9.4). The nitrogen content is multiplied by a factor appropriate to the type of sample, e.g. 5.7 for flour, 6.25 for meat and 6.38 for milk, so as to give a figure for protein content.

When we come to consider the minor components of foods, it is convenient to divide them under two headings: permitted additives and non-permitted contaminants (Table 7.1). In the remainder of this chapter we shall look at

Table 7.1 Additives and contaminants in foods

Additives	Contaminants
Preservatives	Solvents
Anti-oxidants	Packaging additives
Colourings (specified)	Pesticides
Emulsifiers and stabilizers	Hormones
Vitamins	Toxins
Flavourings	Trace heavy metals

examples of determinations of some of these minor components, paying special attention to the problems of clean-up—of separating the traces from the very complex bulk of the food matrix.

7.4 Preservatives

Compounds in this class are added to foods to inhibit bacterial degradation. The Preservatives in Food Regulations, 1975, list a number of permitted substances and specify what may be used and up to what levels, in many different kinds of foods (see Appendix 1 of Ref. 2).

Sulphur dioxide inhibits growth of yeasts, moulds and aerobic bacteria, and is used, for example, in fruit products and sausages. It is commonly determined by titration with iodine, either directly, or after preliminary separation by distillation.

Benzoic acid, when undissociated (pH < 5), also inhibits the growth of yeasts and moulds. Extraction from the acidified sample into ether may be followed by UV spectrophotometry, or even by evaporation to dryness and weighing, but in both cases additional clean-up steps are required.

biphenyl   o-phenylphenol

Biphenyl and o-*phenylphenol* are also used as fungicides to prevent growth of moulds, but are only used for citrus fruits, where it is assumed that the skins are not (normally) eaten. Fruit may be dipped into an alkaline solution of the o-phenylphenol, or wrapped in paper impregnated with biphenyl. It seems there is negligible transport of these fungicides into the inside of the fruit, and when treated oranges are boiled to make marmalade, the fungicides will be lost by steam-distillation. The permitted levels in citrus fruits are 70 and 12 μg g^{-1} respectively for the two compounds.

The separation by steam distillation is convenient for their determination: both are carried over from acid solutions, but the phenol is held back in alkaline solution, and this property can be made use of when the assay is based on UV spectrophotometry (at 251 and 290 nm respectively).[5] They can also be determined by GLC[6] in a procedure which makes an interesting laboratory exercise.

7.4.1 Determination of fungicides on citrus fruit peel

Chop up about 20 g of orange skin into 5-mm pieces and transfer to the sample tube of the apparatus shown in Fig. 7.2, along with 20 ml of water and 1 ml of syrupy phosphoric acid. Boil

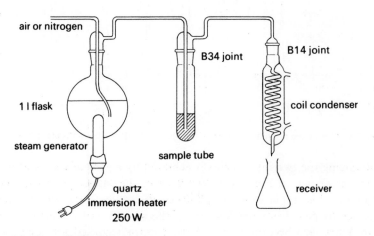

Figure 7.2 Steam distillation apparatus.

the water in the steam generator and pass a slow stream of air or nitrogen through the system. The sample tube will be heated by the steam passing into it, and after a few minutes, when 5–10 ml of distillate has been collected (and the water condensing in the condenser is clear and no longer milky) the heating may be stopped. Extract the distillate with two 4-ml portions of ether which are then combined, dried by the addition of a spatula-full of anhydrous sodium sulphate, then transferred to a 10-ml standard flask. Add 1 ml of a 1 mg ml^{-1} solution of naphthalene in ether as internal standard and make to the mark with ether. Evaporate 5 ml down to 0.1 ml and inject a 10-μl portion on to a silicone oil column in a gas chromatograph running at 160°C, equipped with a flame ionization detector. A temperature programme of 2 min at 150° followed by 10°/min gradient to 220° gives a faster and better separation of the fungicides from the natural oils (see Fig. 7.3).

7.4.2 Identification of the chromatographic peaks by GC/MS

The chromatogram in Fig. 7.3 has quite a number of peaks, and the ones of interest are rather small. While identification by retention time is satisfactory for biphenyl, it is not conclusive for o-phenylphenol because there is often a naturally-occurring constituent which elutes at the same retention time. Two separate steam distillations from different pH's will help here, but by far the best method for identifying peaks is the combination of gas chromatography and mass spectrometry—GC/MS.[7]

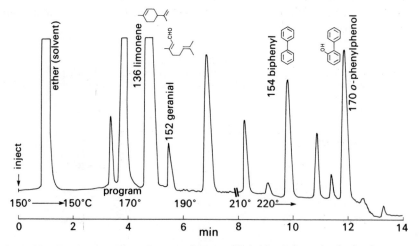

Figure 7.3 Gas chromatogram of extract of orange skin (with m/e for molecular ions).

Interfacing the two instruments is achieved by means of a separator such as the one shown in Fig. 7.4, where most of the carrier gas (it should be helium for this application) is pumped off leaving most of the sample molecules to pass from the first jet to the second and on into the mass spectrometer (see Section 3.10.6). Mass spectra recorded for some of the peaks in the sample chromatogram shown in Fig. 7.3 confirmed the presence of biphenyl (m/e = 154) and also showed that several peaks corresponded to

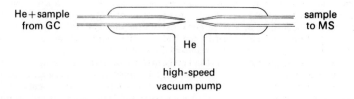

Figure 7.4 Molecular separator for GC/MS.

molecular ions with m/e = 136: these are all terpene isomers from the orange oil, of which limonene is the most abundant.

7.5 Anti-oxidants

Chemicals in this class are added to foods containing fats and oils, particularly pre-cooked meals, to prevent their degradation during processing. If the manufacturer has got the quantities right and also the processing conditions, there should be very little left by the time the food is packaged.

Butylated hydroxyanisole (BHA), butylated hydroxytoluene (BHT) and certain alkyl gallates are permitted in edible fats and oils. BHA can be

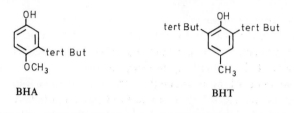

BHA   BHT

separated by steam distillation from melted fats (such as lard) and determined directly in the aqueous distillate by spectrofluorimetry[8] (see Section 6.9.1).

7.5.1 *Determination of BHA in fats by spectrofluorimetry*
Transfer 5 g of fat to the sample tube shown in Fig. 7.2 and add 5 ml of 0.2 M sulphuric acid. Steam-distil to collect 50 ml of distillate and measure its fluorescence, using 293 nm excitation, at an emission wavelength of 323 nm. Checks should be made on the recovery of BHA as a function of the volume of distillate collected, by comparison with the linear section of a log–log calibration based on standards with 1, 3, 10, 30 and 100 μg ml^{-1} of BHA in water (similar to the curve in Fig. 6.2). The permitted levels are 200 μg g^{-1} in edible fats and oils, and 160 μg g^{-1} in butter. Such levels can be determined by this method, but anything much lower will prove difficult. Try to make an estimate of the limit of detection of this procedure based on standard additions.

7.6 Vitamins

Many different vitamins are present in raw foods, but some of them will be destroyed to a greater or lesser extent during processing. In certain cases the Regulations prescribe that essential vitamin(s) be made up to specified levels, e.g. at least 0.24 mg/100 g for vitamin B_1 in flour. Some vitamins such as D and riboflavin (B_2) are determined by microbiological assay of their activity, but others can be determined by chemical colour reactions or even by direct spectrophotometry after a suitable clean-up procedure.

One interesting reaction involves the conversion of vitamin B_1 (thiamine) to thiochrome, which is fluorescent and can be determined with good sensitivity. Simple column chromatography is used to isolate the vitamin from solution following its release by hydrolysis from combination with other species such as sugars. Oxidation by alkaline potassium hexacyanoferrate(III) then produces the thiochrome and elutes it from the column. It is determined by its fluorescence at 365/445 nm. The full working details are given by Pearson (Ref. 2, p. 217); spectrofluorimetry is discussed here in Section 6.9.1.

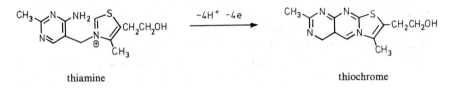

thiamine   thiochrome

7.6.1 Determination of vitamin C

A vitamin much easier to assay by chemical means is ascorbic acid (vitamin C). This is present in many fruits, particularly citrus fruits, blackcurrants, rose hips, and papaya. It is particularly interesting to see just how much of the vitamin survives on cooking to make jam: the authors have found wild rose hips to contain as much as 4 % w/w of vitamin C, and a jam made from them to contain about 1 %. The assay can be by titration with potassium hexacyanoferrate(III), or with 2,6-dichlorophenolindophenol(I), a deep blue dye which oxidizes ascorbic acid to dehydroascorbic acid, being itself reduced to a colourless species (II):

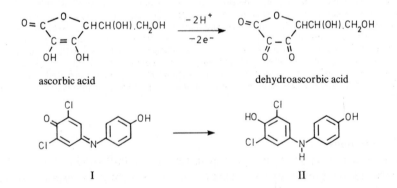

ascorbic acid   dehydroascorbic acid

I   II

Procedure.   Dissolve 50 mg of reagent in 100 ml of water and filter. Standardize by titrating 10-ml aliquots of ascorbic acid solution (50 mg dissolved in 60 ml of 20 % metaphosphoric acid then diluted to 250 ml with water: the acid is to prevent aerial oxidation of the ascorbic acid) to a pale pink colour. Add 2 ml of 25 % metaphosphoric acid and 5 ml of water to 5 ml of fruit juice or extract (diluted if needs be) and titrate with the indophenol solution as before. Work out the content of ascorbic acid by simple proportion of the titres. The titration can be done on coloured samples (such as proprietary blackcurrant drinks) as one only needs to see a colour change in the titration, whereas in a photometric method the colour of the blackcurrant would interfere. Citrus fruit juices contain typically 30–50 mg of vitamin C per 100 ml.

7.7   Volatiles in foods: head-space analysis

Under this heading fall two main groups of substances: the essential oils and flavouring components of foods, and solvents, used either in processing the food or in preparing the packaging material. Gas chromatography would suggest itself as an obvious analytical technique for such determinations, but there are two problems: one is that there is so much non-volatile matter present in foods that the chromatographic columns would quickly become quite unusable if no clean-up step were used, and the second is that it is difficult to find suitable volatile solvents which can be used for a clean-up separation but will not mask the peaks of the sample components. The elegant answer lies in the technique known as head-space analysis.

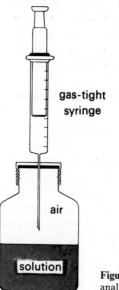

gas-tight
syringe

air

solution

Figure 7.5   Equilibrium jar for head-space analysis.

The sample solution is equilibrated with the air space above it in a sealed bottle at a slightly elevated temperature (see Fig. 7.5). A volatile solute will partition itself between the solution and the air with a partial pressure p_i proportional to the mole fraction x_i in the solution.

$$p_i = p_i^0 \cdot x_i \cdot \gamma_i$$

where γ_i is the activity coefficient of the solute in the solution and p_i^0 is the vapour pressure of the pure solute. At low concentrations of solute the mole fraction of the solvent is always very close to unity and does not vary significantly, so we can use concentration of solute instead of mole fraction:

$$p_i = k \cdot p_i^0 \cdot C_i \cdot \gamma_i. \tag{7.2}$$

The value of p_i is determined by analysing a known volume (say 1 ml) of the air over the solution, by sampling with a gas syringe through the rubber septum closing the bottle. The area (A) of the chromatographic peak is then found (though peak-height may often be used instead):

$$A_i = k' \cdot p_i^0 \cdot C_i \cdot \gamma_i. \tag{7.3}$$

Calibration is best done by standard additions after withdrawing the initial air sample for analysis (or a series of bottles can be prepared, one with sample and others with sample spiked with known amounts of the compound being determined and possibly also with a second compound known not to be present, to be used as an internal standard). This gets over the problems of possible variation in p_i^0 due to fluctuations in temperature, or in γ_i due to variable composition of the solution, particularly if salts are present. Close control of the temperature is therefore essential if good reproducibility is to be achieved.

If several volatile components are present in the sample, then each can be determined from the one chromatogram, as each should partition independently of the others between the gas and the liquid phases. An additional advantage of this technique is that analysis times are short, since negligible amounts of higher-boiling compounds will be present in the vapour. The sensitivity depends on the insolubility of the volatile compound in the sample: hydrocarbons and chlorinated hydrocarbon solvents can be determined at very low level in aqueous samples, while acetic acid in pickled herrings or petrol in lubricating oil are rather more difficult.

One might ask where the solvents in foods come from: in a few cases they are used in the processing, particularly to clean up certain fats (acetone) or to decaffeinate coffee (dichloromethane) but more usually they migrate from packaging materials into the food. The solvents or residual monomers in plastics (styrene or vinyl chloride) or, more commonly, the solvents from printing inks (tetrahydrofuran, toluene or ethyl acetate) can be investigated simply by putting a piece of the plastic wrapper into the jar and equilibrating it at say 60°C, then analysing the air plus solvent vapour by gas chromatography, on a poly(ethylene glycol) column. Quantitation is difficult when solid samples are handled, but for qualitative work the technique is excellent. Crompton's book[9] on the migration of polymer additives into foods is a useful reference source on this topic.

When large numbers of samples have to be analysed, a dedicated head-space analyser* will not only carry out the full cycle of operations automatically, but will also give a much better precision than can be obtained by manual operation.

7.8 Pesticides

As examples of the very large number of compounds which may be encountered in environmental samples and therefore also in foods, two classes will be considered very briefly—the organochlorine (OC) and the organophosphorus (OP) pesticides.

7.8.1 Organochlorine pesticides

Products in this class, including DDT, Aldrin, Dieldrin and Heptachlor, have been manufactured and dispersed on an enormous scale all over the world since the 1940's. Because they are particularly stable molecules they have very long half-lives in the environment and are transferred from one living species to the next through nature's complex food chains, terminating in man.

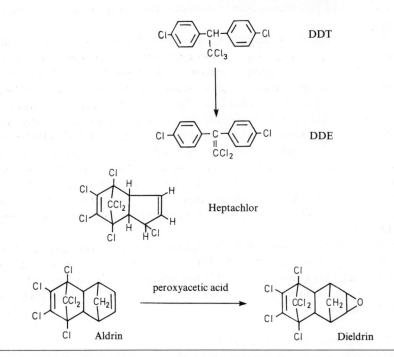

---

* E.g. the Perkin-Elmer HS 6 and the Pye-Unicam PU 4750 accessories for their own gas chromatographs.

DDT is now to be found at low levels in many kinds of environmental samples from the biosphere, along with its primary metabolite, DDE. But while low levels of DDT affect the breeding success of birds which have eaten insects killed by the pesticide, and quite low levels of Dieldrin are lethal to small mammals, it is difficult to establish at what level DDT constitutes a health hazard to humans. Workers handling the compound have been known to accumulate substantial amounts in the fatty tissues of the body and also in the blood (up to $100 \mu g\,g^{-1}$ has been recorded, and $10 \mu g\,g^{-1}$ is not uncommon) without any apparent ill effects. Small animals can also accumulate significant amounts of these pesticides, but only show some reaction to them in times of stress or starvation, when the body fat is consumed and the compounds are released into the bloodstream. The early history of the misuse of these compounds was first brought to the attention of a wider public in 1962 by Rachel Carson in her now classic work *Silent Spring*.[10]

Current estimates recommend that levels of Aldrin and Dieldrin in food should not exceed $0.1 \mu g\,g^{-1}$ (but $0.02 \mu g\,g^{-1}$ for baby foods and dried milk).[11] Before such low concentrations can be determined in foods, a separation and preconcentration procedure will be necessary—the clean-up step.

Clean-up steps for organochlorine compounds at trace levels (usually referred to as pesticide *residues*) normally make use of solvent-extraction systems.[12] Fats need special attention, and should first be dissolved in hexane, with warming, then chilled to precipitate the fat and leave the OC's in solution.[13] The compounds can then be partitioned into dimethyl-formamide (DMF) to effect a further degree of separation, and finally back into clean hexane when water is added to mix with the DMF. The hexane layer (b.p. 69°C) is evaporated to low bulk and a portion injected into a gas chromatograph for separation and determination of the individual pesticides. The recovery of such a multi-stage clean-up procedure always gives cause for worry, but this one has been shown to give better than 80 % recovery for all the common OC's (more than 90 % for most of them) at the $0.1 \mu g\,g^{-1}$ level in mutton fat.

Further discrimination against interfering compounds is achieved by using an electron capture detector (ECD) (see Section 3.10.6) which has an excellent sensitivity towards the OC's but not towards simple hydrocarbons. An alternative clean-up procedure for "wet" samples is described in detail in Ref. 4, Chapter 29.

7.8.2 *Organophosphorus pesticides*

Compounds in this class, including Dichlorvos, Malathion and Parathion, are much more toxic than those in the previous class, but are less stable and

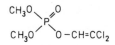

Dichlorvos

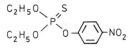

Parathion

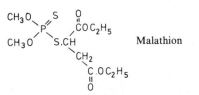

Malathion

so less persistent in the environment: Methods for their determination have been reviewed by Abbot and Egan.[14] They are likely to be encountered (and may have to be determined) at levels of 0.01 $\mu g \, g^{-1}$ or less. These very polar molecules are readily separated from aqueous samples by steam distillation[15] in a dichloromethane-water azeotrope, with the pesticides partitioning into the DCM layer as it separates on condensing. Evaporation to low bulk, which is easy with such a volatile solvent (b.p. 40°C) is followed by gas chromatographic analysis.

The detector recommended for determination of the OP's is the flame photometric detector:[16] the hydrogen flame of the FID emits light when certain elements are present, blue for sulphur (S_2 molecules emitting at 394 nm) and green for phosphorus (HPO molecules emitting at 526 nm). This light is detected by a photomultiplier after passing through an appropriate spectral filter. When a filter for the phosphorus band is used, sulphur is also detected (though with lower sensitivity) while hydrocarbons are discriminated against by a factor of about 10^4. It is convenient to run this as a dual detector FID/FPD and to record both signals on a twin-channel chart recorder: it is then easy to see which compounds contain sulphur or phosphorus and which do not.

7.8.3 Columns for gas chromatography of pesticides

As most of the compounds of interest have comparatively low volatilities it is necessary to run columns at quite high temperatures—typically at 200°C. The various silicone oils show good stability at such temperatures and also effect reasonably good separations: DC 200, a methyl silicone, has been found to give an acceptable separation of many OC's at 200°C (Fig. 7.6).

However, identification of any one compound on the basis of a retention time (bearing in mind that real samples do not consist of the standard mixture of common pesticides, all at the same concentration) is not reliable, and at least one other retention time should be determined, on another column. There is a strong temptation to use another silicone stationary

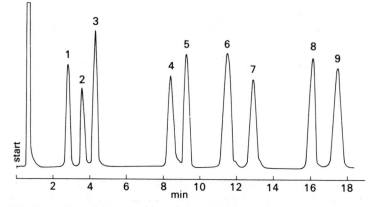

Figure 7.6   Separation of chlorinated hydrocarbon pesticides on a 6′ silicone oil gas chroma-
tograph column, OV-210 on Gas Chrom Q (by courtesy of Alltech Associates Inc.) 1, α-BHC; 2,
Lindane; 3, Aldrin; 4, Heptachlor epoxide; 5, p,p'—DDE; 6, o,p'—DDT; 7, Dieldrin; 8, p,p'—
DDD; 9, p,p'—DDT.

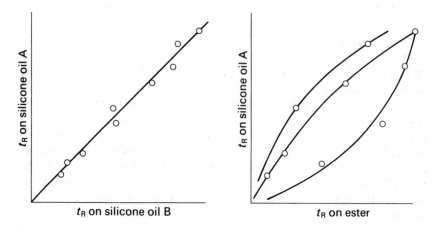

Figure 7.7   Correlations between retention times for a group of compounds on two similar
columns and on two different columns.

phase, but the order of elution for a substantial number of common pesticides
changes little from one silicone to the next, so this does not really help. But if
quite a different stationary phase is used, such as an ester (diethylene glycol
succinate has been recommended) the order of elution will be quite different
and identification is then more reliable. This effect can be demonstrated by
the correlation diagrams shown in Fig. 7.7. Thomson and Watts have
discussed the choice of columns for pesticide residue analysis, quoting
extensive tables of retention ratios of common pesticides on different
columns.[17]

7.8.4   *Standards for pesticide residue analysis*

Samples of pure pesticides can be purchased from chemical supply houses, but it may be more convenient to buy ready-prepared solutions of mixtures of common pesticides, which can be diluted further as required (e.g. BDH Nanogen analytical pesticide standards, or Supelco Inc. standard pesticide mixtures).

7.9   Fatty acids: derivatization in gas chromatography

The long-chain (C_8–C_{24}) fatty acids occur naturally, bound to glycerol (1,2,3-trihydroxypropane) as triglycerides in both plant and animal oils and fats. The acids usually have straight carbon chains, though animals fed on certain diets, such as sheep on a barley diet, can incorporate branched-chain acids. While the fully saturated acids occur widely, different oils can often be characterized by the proportions of the unsaturated acids with from one to three double bonds (the "polyunsaturates" in margarine and cooking oil). Indeed, analysis of an oil for the fatty acids can often serve to indicate its source or to detect adulteration with an alternative (and usually cheaper) material.[18] Thus rapeseed oil used to adulterate olive oil can be detected by the presence of the C_{22} unsaturated erucic acid.

As the higher fatty acids are not sufficiently volatile to be separable by gas chromatography, they must be converted into more suitable derivatives— usually the methyl esters. This is conveniently carried out in one operation along with hydrolysis of the triglyceride: one route uses dimethoxypropane in methanolic hydrochloric acid at a little over room temperature.[19] The procedure is simple, reliable, avoids the use of some hazardous reagents required in other procedures, and works at a low enough temperature to avoid other interfering reactions, particularly at the double bonds.

7.9.1   *Determination of fatty acids in edible fats and oils*

The methanolic hydrogen chloride is prepared by running 10 ml of acetyl chloride dropwise from a burette into 90 ml of methanol agitated by a magnetic stirrer, all carried out in a good fume cupboard, The reaction is lively but proceeds smoothly, a sharp pop being heard as each drop of acetyl chloride enters the solution.

Transfer about 0.2 g of oil or fat to a 30-ml glass-stoppered bottle, weighing by difference. Add 14 ml of dry benzene from a burette, then 1 ml of dimethoxypropane and 5 ml of the methanolic hydrogen chloride (each from a glass safety pipette) and leave stoppered overnight at 25°C, or for 5 hours at 40°C. Add 1–2 g of neutralizing mixture (sodium carbonate, bicarbonate and sulphate, all anhydrous, in a 2:1:2 ratio, dried at 120°C overnight), wait 15 min for evolution of CO_2 to cease and the solids to settle, then inject 5 μl on to a polar silicone stationary phase column (a cyano-silicone such as OV 225 or Supelco 2340 are suitable) in a gas chromatograph fitted with an FID. Temperature programming is very desirable for this analysis: 4 min at 80° followed by a gradient of 15°/min to 250°C with hold there for 10 min will be found to work well. A less polar silicone column will hardly resolve the unsaturated acids from the saturated ones. Figure 7.8 shows a chromatogram of a sample of coconut oil run under these conditions: it is a convenient reference standard in the absence of the individual acids. If the pure acids are available, weigh 20-mg portions of three or four of them into the 30-ml bottle and proceed as for the determination.

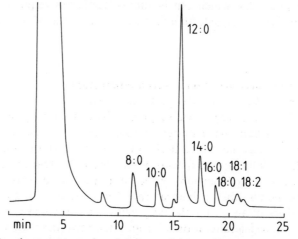

Figure 7.8 Gas chromatogram of methyl esters of fatty acids in coconut oil. Silicone oil column; 4 min at 80°C, 15°/min to 250°C. 18 : 1 denotes the C_{18} acid with one double bond.

Table 7.2 lists the approximate proportions of fatty acids found in a number of common substances.

7.9.2 Other derivatization reactions

A number of other reactions have been used to convert acids into their methyl esters, and also to convert other non-volatile compounds such as sugars, steroids and amino acids into volatile compounds. Phenols may be analysed as such by gas chromatography, but the peaks exhibit bad tailing on many stationary phases, and for this reason it is common practice to convert them to the corresponding methyl ethers before chromatographing them. Table 7.3 lists a few of the more important derivatization reactions (for a more detailed discussion see Perry[21]).

7.9.3 Capillary gas chromatography

Difficult separations would call for very long columns, demanding in turn high carrier gas input pressures. An alternative to a packed column is a capillary column: typically 25 m of glass or silica capillary with a bore of 0.25 mm coated thinly on the inside wall with the stationary phase. Because the amount of stationary phase is small these columns are easily overloaded, and most of the injected sample has to be rejected by a splitter system. However, the small amounts of sample, and in particular the very low carrier

Table 7.2 Relative percentages of fatty acids in some fats and oils*

Fatty acids	Coconut oil	Palm kernel oil	Palm oil	Peanut oil	Olive oil	Sesame oil	Corn oil	Sunflower oil	Linseed oil	Butter	Lard
Group† Oil	1		2	3		4	5		6		
8:0 Capyrylic	10	4									
10:0 Capric	8	4								1	
12:0 Lauric	55	48								1	
14:0 Myristic	15	16	1							17	2
16:0 Palmitic	6	8	44	16	19	9	16	4	10	43	30
16:1 Palmitoleic					2					4	4
18:0 Stearic	1	2	4	4	2	5	2	3	5	9	14
18:1 Oleic	3	15	40	45	63	35	26	25	21	20	40
18:2 Linoleic	1	3	10	31	13	45	54	55	16	1	9
18:3 Linolenic				2	1		2	5	48	0.5	1
20:0 Arachidic				2							

* Actual values for any one sample may vary a little from these, but not significantly.
† The classification into groups according to the major component is that used by Ullmann.[20]

Table 7.3 Some derivatization reactions for gas chromatography

Compounds	Reagent	Product
Fatty acids	HCl/MeOH/dimethoxy-propane	Methyl esters
	BF_3/MeOH	Methyl esters
Sugars	Trimethylsilylimidazole (TSIM)	Trimethylsilyl ethers
Phenols	Hexamethyldisilazane	Trimethylsilyl ethers
Phenols	Trifluoroacetic anhydride	Trifluoroacetate esters
Steroids	Acetic anhydride	Acetates
Amino acids	Acetic acid/n-propanol	N-acetyl n-propyl esters
Inorganic anions	Take to dryness as Ag^+ salts; n-butyl iodide	n-Butyl halogenides

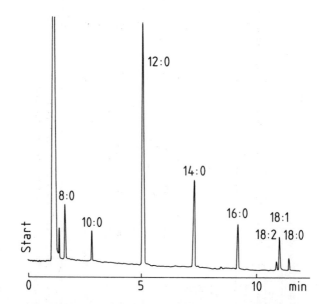

Figure 7.9 High-resolution gas chromatogram of fatty acid methyl esters from coconut oil (see Figure 7.8) run on a 25 m × 0.25 mm capillary column with low-polarity silicone oil stationary phase. The authors thank Dr. Alistair Smith of the Rowett Research Institute for running this chromatogram.

gas flow-rates which are used, make this system especially compatible with the mass spectrometer as detector. A high-resolution chromatogram is shown in Fig. 7.9, and may be compared with the conventional chromatogram shown in Fig. 7.8.

7.10 Chromatography of non-volatiles: HPLC

While GLC is an extremely useful technique for many analyses, effecting separation and quantitation of components in mixtures at very low levels, it is of no help at all for compounds which have a low vapour pressure or are unstable at elevated temperatures. Such compounds must be separated by liquid chromatography, in which the mobile phase is a solvent or solvent mixture running down a column packed with a finely divided solid absorbent such as alumina or silica gel. This is an old technique, particularly simple for coloured compounds where the separation can be watched as the compounds are carried down the column, but with the disadvantage that the resolution is very poor and good separations of even a few components are difficult to achieve.

In Section 3.10.7 the concepts of theoretical plate and HETP were introduced, along with the van Deemter equation relating HETP to the carrier gas flow-rate. A somewhat similar theory can be applied to liquid chromatography, with the differences that diffusion coefficients for solutes in the adsorbed and the mobile liquid phases are similar, and transfer between the phases is fast and requires very little energy. The equation takes the form

$$h = A \cdot v^{1/3} + \frac{B}{v} + C \cdot v \qquad (7.4)$$

where h is the reduced plate height (in terms of the number of particles end-to-end to equal HETP (HETP $= d_p \cdot h$, where d_p is the average particle diameter) and v is the reduced velocity, expressed in terms of the ratio of particle diameter to the diffusion coefficient multiplied by the linear flow-rate of the solvent, f

$$v = \frac{f \cdot d_p}{D}.$$

Equation (7.4) can be rewritten as

$$\text{HETP} = A \cdot d_p \cdot f^{1/3} + \frac{B \cdot D}{f} + \frac{C \cdot f \cdot d_p^2}{D}. \qquad (7.5)$$

The first term reflects the tortuosity—the difference in pathlength for different molecules taking different paths down the column: it is proportional to d_p. The second term represents broadening of the band by molecules diffusing in all directions, and is considerable at low solvent flow-rates, but as the diffusion coefficients are much smaller in the liquid phase than in the gas phase, this is a much smaller effect in liquid chromatography than in gas chromatography. The last term reflects the rate of transfer between the stationary and the mobile phases: its contribution to HETP is larger for bigger particles. A plot of HETP vs. v, the reduced flow-rate, is not unlike the curve for gas chromatography shown in Fig. 3.32, and for typical columns the minimum value of HETP should be found for $v = 3$, and the optimum particle size then works out at around 5 μm. The performance is also better if all the particles are of similar size, and if they are spherical rather than irregular.

However, to achieve the desired flow-rate with such small particles necessitates applying a considerable pressure—say around 20 bar (300 psi) for a 10-cm column, and double that for a 20-cm column. Solvents can be supplied to columns at such pressures, at flow-rates of a few ml min^{-1}, with the help of a reciprocating piston pump. The introduction of such high quality pumps by a number of makers has made possible the development of what became known as High-Pressure Liquid Chromatography, then as High-Performance Liquid Chromatography, both denoted by HPLC. For further details the reader is referred to the excellent introductory book by Knox.[22]

7.10.1 *The high-pressure liquid chromatograph*

Figure 7.10 illustrates schematically the main components of an instrument for HPLC.

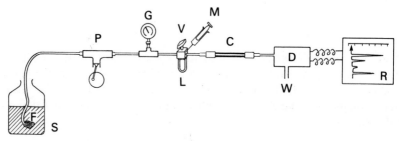

Figure 7.10 Schematic diagram of a high-pressure liquid chromatograph. *S*, solvent taken up through filter *F* by pump *P*, fed to rotary injection valve *V* fitted with sample loop *L* filled from microsyringe *M* and then to column *C* and detector *D*, then to waste *W*. Output displayed on recorder *R*, solvent pressure indicated on gauge *G*.

The *pump* is required to supply solvent at high and constant pressure (up to 4500 psi = 300 bar) and at low flow-rates of a few ml min^{-1}. Double-acting pumps give a smoother flow which helps to minimize baseline ripple with some detectors.

Sample injection by syringe directly on to the column is possible, but injection into a loop on a rotary valve (similar to the gas-sampling valve described in Section 3.10.4) is much to be preferred. Sample sizes lie in the range 1–20 μl of solution.

Columns are made of thick-walled stainless steel tubing, typically 10 or 20 cm long, and with a bore of 2–3 mm, packed with particles of diameter from 3 to 20 μm (usually 5 or 10 μm). Packings fall into three main categories:

   (i) polar solids (alumina, or silica gel) for use with low-polarity solvents,
  (ii) bonded-phase packings (silica gel to which long-chain alkyl groups are bonded (C_8 or C_{18}) by reaction of an alkyl chlorosilane with the silica) which are suitable for use with polar solvents such as aqueous ethanol, and
 (iii) ion-exchange resins, useful for the separation of amino acids or or inorganic anions.

While in GLC it is the stationary phase and the temperature which are the most important variables affecting the separation of mixtures, in HPLC it is the choice of solvent or solvent mixture which can be varied to achieve better separations, and only a few different columns will enable a large number of different analyses to be carried out. Gradient elution with a solvent of gradually changing composition is the HPLC equivalent of temperature programming in GLC.

Detectors fall into two categories—those which measure a property of the solution and those which respond only to the solutes. The former include refractive index and conductimetric detectors, and the latter include spectrophotometric and spectrofluorimetric detectors. Table 7.4 summarizes the more important detectors now being used for HPLC work, and Table 7.5 gives some examples of HPLC separations to illustrate typical combinations of columns and solvents.

7.10.2 *Preconcentration procedures for HPLC*

Solvent-extraction clean-up followed by evaporation to low bulk may be used prior to analysis by HPLC, just as in GLC, and is recommended for the determination of PAH's in water (Chapter 4, Ref. 46, method 610) or pesticide residues in food. An alternative procedure, particularly well suited to the analysis of waters, uses collection by adsorption from the water on to a solid adsorbent (a C-8 or C-18 bonded silica gel) followed by desorption in a

Table 7.4 Detectors for liquid chromatography

Type and abbreviation		Comments	Linear dynamic range	Sensitivity
Refractometer	RI	Detects anything, but sensitive to changes in temperature or solvent composition	wide	modest
Conductivity meter	Cond.	Particularly useful for ion-chromatography	wide	very good
Spectrophotometer (UV)	UV	Only for compounds (or their derivatives) which absorb in the UV, but compatible with gradient elution	restricted	good
Fluorimeter	F	Excellent for a restricted range of compounds, e.g. PAH's	wide	very good
Electrochemical detectors	Elec.	Selective, e.g. towards nitro- and quinone groups, sulphides	wide	good
Atomic absorption or emission spectrometer	AS	Detects metals after separation of organometallics. Flame or ICP atom source	restricted wide	modest good
Mass spectrometer	MS	Problems of interfacing hinge round removal of solvent, but this can now be done satisfactorily	wide	good

Table 7.5   Some typical HPLC separations

Compounds	Column	Solvent	Detector
Chlorinated hydrocarbon pesticides	silica gel	n-heptane	RI
Caffeine, codeine ephedrine	silica gel	methanol/NH_4OH	UV
Steroids	silica gel	CH_3Cl/methanol	RI
PAH's	silica gel	n-heptane	F
Fatty acids (as p-bromophenacyl esters	C-8 bonded silica gel	acetonitrile/water	UV
Dicarboxylic acids	C-18 bonded silica gel	water/methanol + 0.1 % propionic acid	UV/RI
Carboxylic acids, sulphonic acids	C-18 bonded silica gel (reverse-phase ion-pair chromatography)	water/methanol + tetrabutylammonium phosphate	UV
Monosaccharides	NH_2-bonded silica gel	acetonitrile/water	RI
Inorganic anions	ion-exchange resin (ion-chromatography)	Na_2CO_3, $NaHCO_3$ aqueous buffer	Cond.

solvent which is carried directly into an HPLC column. A solvent of much lower polarity is then used: in this case aqueous methanol gradually changing to pure methanol effects a good separation on a C-18 bonded silica gel.[23]

7.11   Some natural poisons: the mycotoxins

The reader may be forgiven if, after reading this far, he comes to the conclusion that all toxic compounds in the environment are man-made, but this would be false, and dangerously so in the case of the aflatoxins. The four compounds of this group were first isolated[24] from cultures of a fungus, *Aspergillus flavus*, which grows on groundnuts under tropical conditions, and has been found to be associated with widespread deaths of animals fed on feedstuffs derived from contaminated nuts.

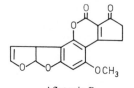

Aflatoxin B$_1$

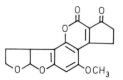

Aflatoxin B$_2$

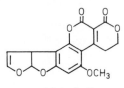

Aflatoxin G$_1$

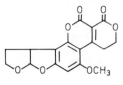

Aflatoxin G$_2$

It has been pointed out (Ref. 4, p. 427) that one contaminated nut in 10 000 good ones (about 5 kg) will give a significant level of aflatoxins in the batch, so there is a serious problem in sampling. Indeed, no other substances are routinely tested for in foodstuffs at such low levels—of the order of 10 μg kg^{-1}. Much of the investigation on levels and occurrence has been done on 10-kg batches, but for routine screening 1-kg samples are normally taken. The methodology has been reviewed by Schuller et al.[25] and acceptable levels have been recommended by an FAO expert committee.[26]

7.11.1 *Separation of aflatoxins: thin-layer chromatography (TLC)*
While the authors do not recommend that students carry out experiments with such hazardous materials as the aflatoxins (B_1 is a powerful carcinogen, and all cause damage to the liver) their separation and identification as fluorescent spots on a thin layer chromatographic plate is an excellent example of an application of this simple technique, and is especially appropriate as these compounds were named according to the colour and position of the fluorescent spots on the plate—B for blue and G for green.

In thin-layer chromatography (TLC)[27] the stationary adsorbed liquid phase is held on a thin layer of silica gel particles on a plate of glass (recoatable and so re-usable) or a piece of thick aluminium foil (disposable). The mobile phase moves upwards by capillary attraction, so no pump or irrigation system is required. Figure 7.11 illustrates the apparatus: the solvent reservoir is a pool at the bottom of a glass jar, into which one end of the TLC plate dips. Small portions of concentrated extract (say 10 μl) are spotted on to

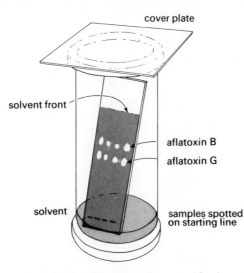

Figure 7.11 Apparatus for thin-layer chromatography, as used for the separation of aflatoxins.

the plate near the bottom, along with similar portions of a standard mixture for comparison. Development times are typically about half an hour.

Procedure.   A 50-g sample of finely chopped peanuts is extracted with 25 ml of water and 250 ml of chloroform in the presence of 25 g of diatomaceous earth to absorb the oil. The extract is filtered and the first 50 ml poured on to a glass column containing 10 g of fine silica gel which will retain the aflatoxins. Interfering substances are washed off first with 150 ml of hexane, then with 150 ml of dry ether, and finally the aflatoxins are eluted in 150 ml of 3% methanol in chloroform. This fraction is evaporated almost to dryness (on a steam bath) and the residue taken up in 1 ml of chloroform. A 10-μl portion is spotted on a TLC plate, alongside a similar portion of standard solution (concentration about $10 \,\mu g \,ml^{-1}$) and developed in 3% methanol in chloroform. The jar is closed with a glass plate to prevent evaporation of the solvent mixture. From the top down the spots are due to B_1, B_2, G_1 and G_2 respectively. Full working details are given in Ref. 7 (p. 429), along with instructions for the quantitative assay by UV spectrophotometry.

An alternative determination is by HPLC on the concentrated extract[28] — this is more sensitive than the TLC-visible fluorescence method and a little faster. Moreover, the higher resolution afforded by this technique permits the determination of other mycotoxins in the extract, including penicillic acid.

7.12   Trace metals in food

Many metals are to be found at low levels in plants and in animal tissues and therefore also in food. It would be very convenient to be able to classify them under two or possibly three headings: essential trace elements (usually bound to enzymes or in the bone structure), toxic elements (often also bound to enzymes, but irreversibly) and the others which do not appear to play any significant role in living systems. But the situation is not so simple. Several elements are now known to be essential at low levels, but are toxic at higher levels, and sometimes the level which may give rise to symptoms of toxicity may be only fifty times the desired level as an essential trace element, even less for selenium. So a table with three headings such as Table 7.6 is more helpful, leaving out those which play no important role.

Table 7.6   Trace metals in living systems

Essential	Na, Mg, K, Ca
Essential but also toxic	Cr, Mn, Fe, Cu, Zn, Sn, Se
Toxic	As, Sb, Cd, Pb, Hg etc.

There is a further complication when one has to consider levels of metals present in foods: the metal may be present to a greater or lesser extent as organometallic compounds which are likely to have very different toxicities to those of the inorganic species of the same element. The food analyst is nowadays frequently asked to distinguish between these two forms and to determine both. The determination of metals in foods has been reviewed by Crosby.[29]

7.12.1   *Determination of total trace metals*

The problems associated with the destruction of organic matter (and with the breakdown of organometallic compounds) so as to permit quantitative recovery of trace metals for their subsequent determination formed the subject of a pioneering investigation by Gorsuch.[30] In any situation where volatility is likely to cause loss of metals, wet-acid mineralization, usually with sulphuric plus nitric acids, must be resorted to. But there are simpler cases where dry-ashing is satisfactory (see Chapter 2, Ref. 16) as in the determination of copper in marmalade.

Copper may be found at easily detectable levels in home-made jams and marmalades prepared in a brass jelly pan (though the levels, at around $10\,\mu g\,g^{-1}$ give no cause for alarm as the maximum allowable concentration is $20\,\mu g\,g^{-1}$).

Procedure. Heat about 1 g of magnesium nitrate in a silica crucible at 500°C to give a protective layer of magnesium oxide on the bottom of the crucible. Add 5 g of marmalade, heat gently to dryness, then ignite at 500°C for 2 hours, or until the ash is quite white. When cool, leach with enough 6 M hydrochloric acid to dissolve the magnesium oxide (with warming) and dilute to 25 ml. Transfer 10 ml to a 50-ml separating funnel, add 5 ml of 20 % w/v ammonium citrate solution (already treated with reagent and extracted with chloroform till the extract is colourless) 5 ml of 0.1 % w/v aqueous sodium diethyldithiocarbamate and 5 ml of chloroform. Shake vigorously for 30 sec, allow the phases to settle and then filter the chloroform layer into a 10-ml standard flask and make to the mark with more chloroform. Mix well, and measure the absorbance at 440 nm in a 1-cm cell. Prepare a calibration covering the range 5–25 μg of copper.

The atomic absorption determination of copper using the line at 324.8 nm works well at the 1–10 $\mu g\,ml^{-1}$ level, using the hydrochloric acid solution corresponding to 5–50 $\mu g\,g^{-1}$ in the marmalade. Prepare standards containing the appropriate concentrations of all reagents, including a blank.

Tin is sometimes determined in canned foods (the permitted level is $250\,\mu g\,g^{-1}$) though fruit juices only attack the tin plate in the presence of air, i.e. after the can has been opened. Mineralization with sulphuric acid and hydrogen peroxide avoids the need for nitric acid which might convert the tin to insoluble SnO_2 (though whether it does so at trace level is disputed). Atomic absorption determination uses the line at 284.0 nm and works at the $10–50\,\mu g\,ml^{-1}$ level. Standards should be prepared in the same concentration of sulphuric acid as it interferes slightly.

Arsenic used to be a common hazard as it entered the food chain from impure sulphuric acid used in the production of some sugars. It is nowadays only rarely encountered, and then probably because it is still being used in some parts of the world as a weedkiller (as sodium arsenate). The AAS determination of arsenic as arsine (AsH_3) is simple and sensitive. The gaseous product is released from the sample by treatment with sodium borohydride in a similar apparatus to that used for the cold-vapour determination of mercury (Section 6.15.1) but with the difference that the optical cell is a silica tube heated in a flame to break down the arsine to arsenic atoms. Levels as low as $0.001\,\mu g\,ml^{-1}$ can be determined by this method.

Cadmium in waste waters and in sewage sludges used as fertilizers can enter the food chain via fish and vegetables respectively, and when used in coloured glazes on cooking utensils it is readily leached by natural fruit acids. Such glazes are no longer permitted for cooking utensils, but if an old one is available, the estimation of leached cadmium and lead makes an interesting investigation.[31] The spectrophotometric determination with dithizone or the stripping voltammetric determination is suitable.

Lead is present in a wide variety of foodstuffs, averaging about $0.1\,\mu g\,g^{-1}$ (as against the maximum permitted level of $2\,\mu g\,g^{-1}$ for most foods). Organic matter should be destroyed by wet-oxidation and the lead determined by the dithizone method (see Section 4.22.1, and also Pearson,[2] p. 84).

Mercury is difficult to determine for two main reasons: first, it is so easily lost by volatilization at all stages of the analysis, and second, it is easy to pick up contamination from mercury in chemical laboratories. This topic is discussed later (Section 8.10.). Wet oxidation with sulphuric plus nitric acids is frequently used, sometimes with the addition of some potassium permanganate to keep the mercury fully oxidized, but for fish samples, overnight hydrolysis at room temperature in 20% potassium hydroxide has been preferred. The cold-vapour AAS method (see Section 6.15.1) or the dithizone spectrophotometric method (Section 4.22.1) may be used to determine mercury. Methods have been reviewed by Ure and Shand.[32]

7.12.2 *Determination of organometallic compounds*

Compounds in this class have at least one metal–carbon bond: chelates of metals with organic acids are still considered to be "inorganic" species because they tend to be labile and water-soluble. Most of the organometallic compounds of interest are man-made, but some are produced by micro-

Table 7.7 Some commercially important organometallic compounds which may be present in foodstuffs

Element	Compound	Use
Tin	triphenyltin acetate	sprayed on seed potatoes to prevent blight
	bis(tri-*n*-butyltin) oxide	as fungicide in wood preservatives
	dibutyltin- or dioctyltin-di-isothioglycollate	as stabilizer in PVC for food packaging and bottles
Lead	tetramethyllead and tetraethyllead	as anti-knock additives in petrol: some remains unburned and is discharged in the exhaust gas along with inorganic lead particulates
Mercury	phenylmercury acetate	as fungicide on seed grain for winter planting
	methylmercury salts and dimethylmercury	produced by microorganisms from inorganic mercury in river sediments

organisms in the environment, starting from inorganic species. Table 7.7 lists some of the commoner compounds which may be encountered in environmental samples, including foods. Production of organo-lead and organo-tin compounds runs to several thousand tons per annum.

Methods for the determination of organometallic compounds in foods follow the same lines as those for pesticide residues: solvent-extraction clean-up followed by chromatographic analysis. Gas chromatography is applicable to the more volatile compounds such as methylmercury compounds and lead alkyls, while liquid chromatography (HPLC) is attracting increasing attention for the others. Electron-capture detection offers good sensitivity for GLC work, but for HPLC determinations a number of workers are using atomic spectroscopic methods such as atomic absorption and plasma emission. The good sensitivity of the latter is an attractive feature, but the equipment is expensive both to buy and to run.

Methylmercury compounds are particularly toxic to man, causing irreversible brain damage when they are ingested, e.g. from fish caught in polluted waters. Solvent-extraction clean-up makes use of the ease with which the anion of the water-soluble salts can be exchanged.[33] Dimethyl mercury is fat-soluble and more volatile than the salts, and also more toxic, but it is found at lower levels.

Aqueous samples are treated with potassium bromide and the CH_3HgBr is extracted into toluene. This phase is separated and washed with aqueous thiosulphate to strip the methyl mercury back as $CH_3HgS_2O_3^-$. Addition of iodide and extraction with benzene effects the final separation as CH_3HgI which is sufficiently stable and volatile to be determined by GLC on a polar column followed by electron-capture detection. Glass columns must be used since the compound can disproportionate when in contact with hot stainless steel columns:

$$2CH_3HgI \rightarrow (CH_3)_2Hg + HgI_2.$$

As little as $0.1\ \mu g\ ml^{-1}$ of mercury in the benzene extract can be determined by this method. Some aspects of the performance of this determination are discussed in Section 8.10.

References

1 Analytical Methods Committee (1974) *Official, Standardised and Recommended Methods of Analysis*, 2nd edn., Society for Analytical Chemistry, London.
2 Pearson, D. (1976) *The Chemical Analysis of Food*, 7th edn., Churchill Livingstone, London.
3 Macleod, A. J. (1973) *Instrumental Methods of Food Analysis*, Paul Elek, London.
4 Horwitz, W. (ed.) (1970) *Official Methods of Analysis*, 11th edn., Association of Official Analytical Chemists, Washington.
5 Harvey, D. and Penketh, G. E. (1957) *Analyst*, **82**, 498.
6 Morries, P. (1973) *J. Assoc. Public Analysts*, **11**, 44.

7 Brooks, C. J. and Edmonds, C. G. (1979) in *Practical Mass Spectrometry*, Ch. 3, Middleditch, B. S. (ed.), Plenum Press, New York.
8 Dilli, S. and Robards, K. (1977) *Analyst*, **102**, 201.
9 Crompton, T. R. (1979) *Additive Migration from Plastics into Food*, Pergamon, Oxford.
10 Carson, R. (1971) *Silent Spring*, Penguin Books, Harmondsworth.
11 FAO/WHO (1974) *Pesticide Residues in Foods*. Technical Report Series no. 545 of the 1973 Joint FAO/WHO Meeting, WHO, Geneva.
12 Beynon, K. I. and Elgar, K. E. (1966) *Analyst*, **91**, 143.
13 Maunder, M. J. de Faubert, Egan, H., Godly, E. W. and Hammond, E. W. (1964) *Analyst*, **89**, 168.
14 Abbott, D. C. and Egan, H. (1967) *Analyst*, **97**, 475.
15 Elgar, K. E., Marlow, R. G. and Mathews, B. L. (1970) *Analyst*, **95**, 875.
16 Natusch, D. and Thorpe, T. (1973) *Anal. Chem.*, **45**, 1184A.
17 Thomson, J. F. and Watts, R. R. (1981) in *Analysis of Pesticide Residues*, Moye, H. A. (ed.), John Wiley, New York.
18 Dickes, G. J. and Nickolas, P. V. (1976) *Gas Chromatography in Food Analysis*, Chapter 10, Butterworths, London.
19 Mason, M. E. and Waller, G. R. (1964) *Anal. Chem.*, **36**, 583.
20 Ullmann, F. (1956) *Encyclopädie der Technischen Chemie*, 3rd edn., Vol. 7, Urban and Schwartz, Munich, p. 477.
21 Perry, J. A. (1981) *Introduction to Analytical Gas Chromatography*, Chapter 12, Marcel Dekker, New York.
22 Knox, J. H. (ed.) (1978) *High Performance Liquid Chromatography*, Edinburgh University Press.
23 May, W. E., Chesler, S. N., Cram, S. P., Gump, B. H., Herz, H. S., Enagonio, D. P. and Dyszel, S. M. (1975) *J. Chromatog. Sci.*, **13**, 535.
24 Hartley, R. D., Nesbit, B. F. and O'Kelly, J. (1963) *Nature*, **198**, 1056.
25 Schuller, P. L., Horwitz, W. and Stoloff, L. (1976) *J. Assoc. Off. Anal. Chem.*, **59**, 1315.
26 WHO Report, *Environmental Health Criteria Hazards of Food: Contamination from Aflatoxins* (1979) No. 11, WHO, Geneva.
27 Stahl, E. (ed.) (1969) *Thin Layer Chromatography*, Allen and Unwin, London.
28 Hunt, D. C. (1981) *Anal. Proc.*, **18**, 471.
29 Crosby, N. T. (1977) *Analyst*, **102**, 225.
30 Gorsuch, T. T. (1970) *The Destruction of Organic Matter*, Pergamon, Oxford.
31 Dömling, H. J. (1973) *Z. Anal. Chem.*, **267**, 118.
32 Ure, A. M. and Shand, C. A. (1974) *Anal. Chim. Acta*, **72**, 63.
33 Rodriguez-Vazquez, J. A. (1978) *Talanta*, **25**, 299.

8 Competitive analytical chemistry

Analytical chemistry is such an old and long-established branch of chemistry that it is sometimes regarded as well-known, well understood, easy, and simply a service to other scientists. It has so often been taught as a collection of procedures, even of recipes, that many no longer think about the methods themselves. The many sensitive instrumental methods now available have made work easier for analysts, but they have also created new difficulties for those who believe that purchasing instruments will solve all their problems. This has meant that analytical chemists have begun to ask much more searching questions concerning methods and results, and to take part in interlaboratory tests to check their results against those obtained elsewhere; instead of fearing exposure as bad analysts, they are anxious to compare performance with others and also to try to solve the problems which may then arise. This chapter describes some examples of comparisons between laboratories and critically considers them, some of their results, and the explanations the authors have offered.

8.1 The lunar rocks

When the first American astronauts landed on the moon in 1969, they collected samples of rocks and soils for groups of analytical chemists all over the world to analyse. Geochemists were especially eager to see the analytical results, to match them against their theories of the origin of the moon. But how good *were* the results, beyond proving that the moon is not made of green cheese? This was the question which George Morrison, one of the principal investigators in the lunar programme, attempted to answer in 1971.[1]

An impressive range of techniques was employed to obtain the required answers, and it appears that the large, expensive instruments were most popular, with neutron activation (NAA), electron microprobe (EM) and mass spectrometry (MS) coming top of the list and wet chemistry rather far down. The reasoning behind this preference was quite simple: the investigators were asked to get the maximum information from as little sample as possible, and so multi-element techniques were the obvious choice. But the quality of the results was in some cases not as good as might have been

237

expected, possibly because these wide-spectrum methods were employed instead of procedures optimized for each element in turn. It is worth considering some of the results in detail.

Chromium was present in sample 12070 at about $\frac{1}{4}\%$, and should not have been too difficult to determine. However, the spread of results was actually quite large, with 13 results lying between 0.208 and 0.303 (seven of them by NAA) and $s_{rel} = 12\%$. Of particular interest was the fact that the figure of 0.270 obtained by chemical separation and mass spectrometry of the acetyl acetonate was very close to the mean value of 0.277 %: this was the only method designed and optimized for one element. There is perhaps a temptation with other techniques such as neutron activation analysis to feel obliged to report a figure because a signal has been measured, even though the precision is known to be poor.

Seventeen values were reported for lanthanum in the same sample, with a mean of $33 \mu g\, g^{-1}$ and a spread from 22 to $40 \mu g\, g^{-1}$. Morrison commented that the relative standard deviation of 15 % was too high for an element at this level, but found it very difficult to "grade" the laboratories on their scores, other than saying that some seemed to get many results close to the means while others did not. Some laboratories were determining only a few elements and sometimes difficult ones, so that lower precision was to be expected in these cases, and the "right" value was in any case unknown. The only technique which always appeared to come up with "good" results was isotope-dilution/mass spectrometry, a slow and expensive method which was used for only fourteen elements.

The investigation of the lunar samples attracted much publicity and possibly drew the attention of an unusually wide group of scientists to the quality of the analytical data, but many other detailed interlaboratory comparisons have been undertaken on mineral samples.

8.2 Trace elements in fly ash

In 1974, results from an inter-laboratory comparison of analyses of coal fly ash (the very fine ash released with the hot gaseous products from the combustion of coal or oil), oil and petrol[2] showed very large variations for trace elements: in the fly ash five elements had individual values differing by more than an order of magnitude between highest and lowest (e.g. Li, 20–300; Mg, 2200–44 000; Na, 500–6600; V, 180–2000; and Zn, 70–1000, all $\mu g\, g^{-1}$). The quality of the results for major elements such as iron (range 5.3–26 %, probably 18 %) also gave cause for concern. Heterogeneity might have been one difficulty, but one cannot help thinking that simpler single-element determinations by titration, spectrophotometry or atomic absorption, after getting the sample into solution, would have provided better results than the multi-element techniques such as spark-source mass spectrometry (SSMS), optical emission spectroscopy (OES) and NAA, all applied directly to the sample.

8.3 The 100 % fallacy—analyses of an amphibole

We are entitled to ask whether the older methods were any better. By a lucky accident, Larsen[3] in 1938 sent samples of some amphibole rocks to two analysts instead of one and found the results to be in poor agreement. "I have never believed that a very high degree of accuracy is attained for ordinary rock or mineral analysis, but the differences here are disconcerting," he wrote, comparing the results from three analysts, the last of whom used methods appropriate to a fluorine-containing silicate mineral. Larsen discussed the problems associated with sampling rocks for analysis, a factor we have mentioned several times in this book, but some of the results themselves are thought-provoking (Table 8.1).

Table 8.1 Comparison of three analyses of an amphibole.[3] Taken from a comparison of analyses by Larsen (1938) *Amer. J. Sci.*, [5] **35**, 94.

Component	Analyst A	B	G
SiO_2	37.70	37.86	40.18
Al_2O_3	12.36	14.83	14.26
TiO_2	3.10	0.60	1.79
CaO	16.86	14.96	12.88
(+others)	⋮	⋮	⋮
Total	100.04	100.09	99.86

A common guideline for acceptability is that the individual percentages should add up to $100 \pm 0.5\%$. The first two sets do, which might just suggest that the samples were very inhomogeneous. But the analyst B in fact looked for some constituents which A did not, totalling 1.8 %, and neither found fluoride, which was later found to be present at 0.8 %. Getting the total up to 100 % is probably intended to keep the customer happy rather than to guarantee the quality of results. This was borne out by the experience of one of the authors when asked to analyse a number of three-component gas mixtures (of He, N_2 and O_2). After much careful work and calibration it was possible to get figures adding up to $100 \pm 0.5\%$. The author was very satisfied with the performance but the customer wondered why the totals were not exactly 100 % (that would have been easy to achieve if the helium had been determined by difference!) Larsen commented: "Many geologists who are not familiar with the probable errors in chemical analyses draw unwarranted conclusions from small differences for different samples". Perhaps our problem is one of educating the customer, and this again emphasizes the importance of a realistic approach in teaching analytical chemistry to university students.

8.4   An extensive programme to study igneous rocks

More recent findings were those of Schlecht, who in 1951 published the results of the "first extensive program ever organized to study the composition of igneous rocks".[4] Samples were carefully prepared and distributed to 25 laboratories throughout the world specializing in rock analysis. He commented: "the great discordance in the results reflects the present unsatisfactory state of rock analysis . . . it is not possible on the basis of the present evidence to decide how much of the error in rock analysis is caused by the lack of skill in the analyst and how much is inherent in the procedures themselves. It will require laborious effort and carefully designed experiments to determine this." This last comment is particularly apt; unfortunately, there are still too many people doing analysis and publishing results who have not taken sufficient care to check their reliability and correctness. Some of the results which Schlecht reproduced are presented in Figure 8.1. Of these (for a diabase) the results for silica seem in agreement, for alumina less so (corrections have to be made for other precipitated oxides), and for minor components the disagreement is often very serious. The spread of results for FeO is large, reminding us of the importance of technique: this is not an easy determination, one that still presents problems and must be done by chemical methods. Calcium (present in larger amounts) shows better agreement. Schlecht was, however, hopeful for improvements in the future: "With

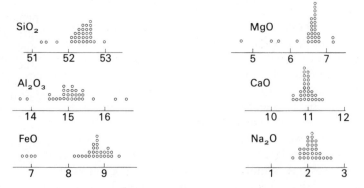

Figure 8.1   Results for analyses of a diabase, given in %. Reproduced by courtesy of *Analytical Chemistry* from Schlecht (1951).[4]

modern reagents a direct determination of alumina in rocks may be practicable. Flame photometry offers the possibility of increased accuracy and less labour in the determination of the alkalies." We have to remember that up to this time purely chemical methods were used almost exclusively.

8.5 New methods for old

It is appropriate now to ask whether modern methods have really improved the situation. Bennett[5] tried to answer this question in a recent review (1977), and came to the conclusion that the newer methods are certainly faster, taking (say) three days for a rock analysis instead of ten, and that the results are no worse for major elements and distinctly better for alkali metals and for minor elements. Table 8.2 shows the precision of results for the determinations of some elements in a sillimanite which had been the subject of investigation in two series of comparisons.

Table 8.2 Comparison of precision of results for the analysis[5] of sillimanite, done in 1953 and again in 1968, expressed as standard deviation (absolute) in %, with number of results indicated in parenthesis. Taken from Bennett, H. (1977) *Analyst*, **102**, 153, with permission.

Year	SiO_2	Al_2O_3	CaO	MgO
1953	0.20 (19)	0.29 (33)	0.17 (14)	0.06 (14)
1968	0.13 (28)	0.24 (22)	0.06 (26)	0.03 (26)
Amount present	~36%	~63%		

Sillimanite is rather a resistant mineral, difficult to decompose completely, and furnaces running at higher temperatures can certainly assist in more complete fusion decompositions. But both sets of results were still essentially from chemical analysis, and nowadays most laboratories doing routine rock analysis will use X-ray fluorescence analysis. How does this affect the situation? The instrumentation is capable of giving impressive results, but the accuracy still depends on the reliability of the standards used to calibrate the equipment. Bennett[5] wrote: "The current full range of standard referee methods, being both accurate and fast, seems likely to remain substantially unchanged, not because they have achieved perfection, but rather because they are at least adequate for current needs and are likely to be used less and less in the future."

Sidney Abbey, writing[6] in 1981 of interlaboratory comparisons of rock standards, was of the opinion that results obtained by present-day methods were certainly no better than they were 50 years ago for major components such as silica. He commented: "Application of rigorous statistical interpretation would be of highly questionable value in attempting to ascertain a correct answer since the data were more heterogeneous even than the samples". He was particularly concerned about the frequency of occurrence of highly inaccurate values rather than the spread of reasonable ones. He felt one should not compare techniques alone, e.g. AAS, XRF, NAA, but complete procedures, and concluded: "There is no such thing as a bad method—only bad analysts who fail to allow for its limitations".

8.6 Trace elements in sea water

A different kind of comparison, and one which usually gives a more encouraging picture, is that of different methods in one and the same laboratory. Sturgeon et al.[7] compared isotope dilution mass spectrometry (ID/MS), graphite-furnace AAS and inductively-coupled plasma emission spectroscopy (ICP) for the determination of trace elements in sea water. Only GF/AAS could determine Fe, Mn, Cd, and Zn directly, but with prior separation on an ion-exchange resin all three techniques gave very satisfactory agreement for elements at around $1 \, ng \, g^{-1}$. However, to analyse one sample by all four methods for the nine elements investigated took two months. Clearly, time and patience are essential ingredients of a method for trace analysis.

8.7 Analysis in archaeology

Leaving rock analysis, we may look at some other types of samples. The application of analytical chemistry to modern archaeology is a fascinating study, and is also a field where communication and understanding are not as good as they should be. Many archaeologists do not really know how chemical analysis or other physical measurements can assist them and may well get unhelpful results simply by asking the wrong questions in the first place. What can the analyst offer, and how good are the results he can supply?

W. T. Chase, of the Smithsonian Institution, Washington, wrote[8] in 1973: "While thousands of analyses of archaeological bronzes have been reported in the literature, the basis for comparing them, especially for different chemical laboratories, is shaky". He therefore organized a programme to see what sort of results could be expected, in which two ancient bronze articles—an axe-head and a spear-head—were carefully cleaned, ground up, packed and sent out to 21 laboratories for analysis.

Results for some of the more important minor elements from the larger number which were actually reported are shown in Table 8.3. It can be seen that the variation between the laboratories was large for all these elements,

Table 8.3 Trace elements in an ancient bronze. Taken from Chase, W. T. (1974) in *Archaeological Chemistry*, Beck, C. (ed.), *Advances in Chemistry*, Vol. 138, American Chemical Society, Washington, with permission.

Element	$\bar{X}$, %	Range	n	s_{rel}, %
Ag	0.025	0.01–0.05	14	47
As	0.043	0.009–0.09	8	70
Fe	0.055	0.03–0.08	10	31
Mn	0.002	0.0004–0.004	5	74
Sb	0.023	0.002–0.1	12	140

and one might well wonder just what the figures mean, if anything. The variation may be a question of lack of attention to details such as allowing for interferences, checking calibrations, or inherent error (particularly with MS, ES, and to some extent with NAA). However, some laboratories also took the trouble to look at the sample under the microscope and reported inhomogeneities: this may have been the real source of the trouble. Though the originators had tried to remove corrosion products and distribute only metal, they were not entirely successful, and as many trace elements tend to be enriched in certain solid phases of corrosion products, the variation in the published results becomes less surprising. As well as the problems inherent in the sample material was the practice of most laboratories of working with very small samples, necessitated normally by the value of items in museum collections. Five to ten milligrams were taken for many analyses, and only sometimes as much as a hundred milligrams. This affected the quality of the results for major elements also, so much so that, on the basis of the tin values, Chase concluded "six out of twenty-one laboratories failed to categorize the bronze correctly from a metallurgical point of view". Several laboratories reported copper by difference, about which approach enough has already been said, but of the remainder, fourteen "good" values gave a mean of 81.6 % with $s_{rel} = 1.8 \%$, a more encouraging set of results.

8.8 Practical limits of methods—trace iron in tungsten

The problem of sample size was discussed in Chapter 2 in connection with the determination of trace iron in tungsten. An interesting sequel to that work was a comparison[9] of three methods for the determination itself. The performances of the complete procedures are summarized in Table 8.4. It would seem that performance is determined by external factors such as contamination, reproducibility of instrumental measurements and so on. The intrinsically higher sensitivity of the atomic absorption method allows one to take smaller samples (possibly a mixed blessing) but does not give a lower limit of detection on the tungsten samples. X-ray fluorescence does, however, offer a hidden advantage in that it can also determine five other trace elements on the same sample for the same cost in effort and time.

Table 8.4   Determination of trace iron in tungsten. Taken from Ortner, H. M. and Schere, V. (1977) *Talanta*, **24**, 215, with permission.

Criterion	Spectrophotometry	XRF	AAS
Working range (μg)	6–56	10–100	0.6–5.6
Sample size (mg)	500	1000	50
Concentration range (μg g^{-1})	←——————— 10–100 ———————→		
Standard deviation (μg)	1.5	1.6	1.5
Limit of detection (μg g^{-1})	6	7	6
Time for one-off (h)	1.5	1	2
Time for ten (h)	4	4	8

8.9   Ethanol in pharmaceutical preparations

By no means all interlaboratory comparisons are concerned with elemental analysis, and from the field of organic analysis the determination of ethanol will serve as a good example. This determination is important because the amount of tax collected by governments depends on the alcohol content of drinks, for example. That determination has to be carried out with a very high accuracy (0.1–0.2%) but for pharmaceutical products the requirements are less severe. Until 1973 the British Pharmacopoeia method for the determination involved a quadruple distillation—very time-consuming and therefore very expensive even if automation could help one person to keep several determinations running simultaneously. Why not use gas-liquid chromatography? Of course, there are small problems: some columns do not like water, and some detectors give non-linear response, and so on, but the real problem lies in convincing official bodies that the new method is at least as good as the old one, if not better. Dr. Islam of the British Pharmacopoeia Commission has described the results of interlaboratory tests on some preparations containing ethanol, using the two methods.[10] The relative standard deviations ranged from 0.85 to 1.04% for GLC and from 1.07 to 1.43% for distillation, so the new method was accepted, being faster and more precise. The distinction was, however, not too clear-cut, as laboratories which normally used the distillation method tended to get better results by that technique than the laboratories which only occasionally used it. When one or two dubious results were rejected, the means obtained by the two methods were not significantly different, which gives one confidence in both of the methods.

8.10   Mercury in the environment

An example of a difficult trace organometallic analysis is the determination of alkyl mercury compounds in the environment. These compounds are quite volatile and so can be determined by gas chromatography, but not easily, since they undergo some interesting reactions on the hot columns to give corresponding dialkyl mercury compounds. However, if one takes care to work with glass columns and to follow procedures strictly, analyses are possible. In fact, if we look at some results quoted by Mary Schafer of the US Food and Drugs Administration[11] we can see that interlaboratory tests gave quite a reasonable agreement in terms of the mean value and only a slightly worse standard deviation than those reported individually by two laboratories (Table 8.5).

Table 8.5   Determination of MeHgCl in canned tuna fish. Taken from Schafer, M. L. *et al.* (1975) *J. Agr. Food Chem.*, **23**, 1079, with permission.

	Interlab. study	N.C.A. lab.	U.S. Dept. of Health FDA lab.
Number of samples	—	8	9
Mean value, $\mu g\,g^{-1}$	0.79	0.83	0.81
Standard deviation, $\mu g\,g^{-1}$	0.18	0.05	0.06
Coefficient of variation, %	23	6	8

The method for this determination is complex—an eight-stage extraction and re-extraction procedure for clean-up and preconcentration before the sample is finally injected on to the chromatograph column. As the levels were around the $1\,\mu g\,g^{-1}$ level, spikes were added to fish samples at the same level, and indicated around 80% recovery with a coefficient of variation of 14%. These results are indeed rather encouraging for such a complex procedure, but there is no room for complacency, as is illustrated by results from a round-robin organized to determine total mercury in milk powder,[12] summarized in Table 8.6.

Table 8.6   Interlaboratory investigation on the determination of mercury in dried milk powder. Taken from Tölg, G. (1977) *Z. Anal. Chem.*, **283**, 257, with permission.

Values, $ng\,g^{-1}$	10, 1, 100, 8, **0.5**, 10, 44, 1.4, 50, 1, 136, 54
Mean	$35.5\,ng\,g^{-1}$
Standard deviation	$44\,ng\,g^{-1}$ $(=124\%)$

The range of values is enormous, though in all cases the levels are lower than those just mentioned for methylmercury in fish. There could well be a problem here in deciding what the real level was (Sidney Abbey's comment[6] on the importance of statistical analysis of sets of results is particularly relevant here) but because Tölg[12] and his team were able to check each step of their essentially very simple procedure (which uses only high-purity oxygen gas as a reagent, and nothing else) they were confident that $0.5\,\mathrm{ng\,g^{-1}}$ did represent the correct value. The high values were therefore all the result of contamination, and the "correct" result was obtained by working in a special suite of clean rooms with very low dust and contamination levels, an extreme but clearly a necessary precaution, as these results bear out.

8.11　Lead in blood—success at last

In Section 1.2 we saw how difficult it was to compare figures for blood-lead levels in people living in different parts of the world, and it was clear that the quality of many results left much to be desired. This conclusion was common to several of the investigations mentioned in this chapter; these various interlaboratory comparisons failed, however, to suggest how the quality of the data might be improved.

With a view to achieving some real improvement in laboratory performance, the UK External Quality Assessment Scheme for General Clinical Chemistry was established in 1969 (as the National Quality Control Scheme). Whitehead[13] in 1973 outlined its main objectives, which included

(i) an assessment of the improvement in the precision and accuracy attained by the participating laboratories, made possible by
(ii) a fast turn-round on issuing samples, analysing samples, returning and processing the results, and finally publishing the results and sending a statistical analysis to all participating laboratories within 14 days—quickly enough for the results still to be of interest and for possible discrepancies to be investigated, and thus for the performance to be improved.

One problem has been to find a clear and simple way of presenting the results, and in particular to provide a measure of the performance of individual laboratories for the various determinations carried out. A variance index was initially used, expressing the difference between the laboratory's actual results and the mean for all the laboratories, relative to the standard deviation for all the results. More recently, a variance index score (VIS) has been used, and for blood-lead figures laboratories are also given a smoothed mean running variance index score (MRVIS) based on their ten most recent scores: if their performance is improving, then the current VIS will normally be less than the current MRVIS.

The success of the present method of presentation is shown in a plot of average MRVIS values for 1979–1981 for all the laboratories doing blood-lead determinations, shown in Fig. 8.2, where the steady decrease in the score represents a closer approach of all values to the mean value for each sample, i.e. an improvement in the performance.

The statistical analysis also compares the figures for determinations of lead by different methods. Table 8.7 shows a recent (1981) set of results for estimation of blood-lead: it is reassuring that the mean values, and also the standard deviations, are not significantly different for the five classes of methods. It is tempting to conclude that difficulties here now lie more in the methods of sample preparation and in the choice of standards than in the method of determination, not unlike the case for trace iron in tungsten mentioned earlier.

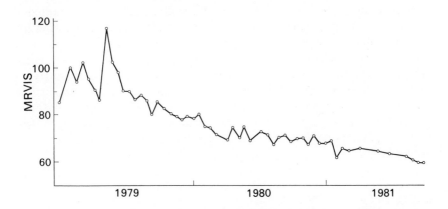

Figure 8.2 Average MRVIS for blood-lead. UK External Quality Assessment Scheme, 1979–1981. The authors thank Professor Whitehead and Mr. Bullock of the UK External Quality Assessment Scheme at the Wolfson Research Laboratories, Queen Elizabeth Medical Centre, Birmingham, for permission to reproduce this up-to-date and as yet unpublished information.

Table 8.7   Estimation of blood-lead (1981)

Method	Number of results	Mean* $\mu\,moles\,l^{-1}$	$\mu g\,l^{-1}$	Relative standard deviation (%)
AAS—Delves cup	21	1.56	323	13.2
AAS—flameless	38	1.59	329	10.6
AAS—other	6	1.63	337	12.7
Dithizone (manual)	3	1.54	319	21.7
Electrochemical	3	1.52	315	1.5

* As many of the test samples for this scheme are spiked with small amounts of substances to be determined to give a wider range of test concentrations, the mean value quoted here should not be taken as typical of British adult blood-lead levels.

The National Quality Control Scheme has shown that a true competitive spirit, safeguarded by confidentiality of the published results, can serve to stimulate and help laboratories to improve their performance and also monitor their progress as they do so.

All good stories should finish with a moral—a lesson which we might learn and remember to prevent us making the same mistakes which others have made before us. We have two suggestions: first, that in any new analytical problem we take the time to check all the steps for recovery and satisfactory performance, recording sufficient data to make this investigation genuinely useful and reliable, and second, that if at all possible we should check the results by a second completely different procedure.

Both of these recommendations cost time and therefore money, but perhaps what Larsen[3] said in 1938 is still valid: "Geologists are probably getting all they are paying for and perhaps more. Would it not be wiser for us to have fewer analyses, to pay a little more for them, and to insist on a higher quality?" The authors think this is relevant, not only in geological analysis, but also in many other applications of analytical chemistry to numerous different types of samples. We hope that our readers, whether as practitioners or as customers, will bear this in mind and strive to get the most out of their analyses in the future by taking time to think, to check, and then to analyse. We hope that for them, as it is for us, analytical chemistry will always be fun.

References
1 Morrison, G. H. (1971) *Anal. Chem.*, **43** (7) 22A.
2 von Lehmden, D. J., Jungers, R. H. and Lee, R. E. (1974) *Anal. Chem.*, **46**, 239.
3 Larsen, E. S. (1938) *Amer. J. Sci.*, [5] **35**, 94.
4 Schlecht, W. G. (1951) *Anal. Chem.*, **23**, 1568.
5 Bennett, H. (1977) *Analyst*, **102**, 153.
6 Abbey, S. (1981) *Anal. Chem.*, **53**, (4) 529A.
7 Sturgeon, R. E., Berman, S. S., Desaulniers, J. A. H., Mykytiuk, A. P., McLaren, J. W. and Russell, D. S. (1980) *Anal. Chem.*, **52**, 1585.
8 Chase, W. T. (1974) "Comparative analysis of archeological bronzes", in *Archaeological Chemistry*, Beck, C. (ed.), *Advances in Chemistry*, Vol. 138, American Chemical Society, Washington.
9 Ortner, H. M. and Scherer, V. (1977) *Talanta*, **24**, 215.
10 Islam, A. (1975) *Proc. Soc. Anal. Chem.*, **12**, 266.
11 Schafer, M. L., Rhea, U., Peeler, J. T., Hamilton, C. H. and Campbell, J. E. (1975) *J. Agr. Food Chem.*, **23**, 1079.
12 Tölg, G. (1977) *Z. Anal. Chem.*, **283**, 257.
13 Whitehead, T. P., Browning, D. M. and Gregory, A. (1973) *J. Clin. Path.*, **26**, 435.

Appendix 1

TWA-TLV's for some gases and vapours

Time-weighted average TLV's for some commoner substances, taken from the complete list in *Guidance.Note EH15/80: Threshold Limit Values 1980*, by permission of the American Conference of Governmental Industrial Hygienists.

Substance		ppm	$mg\,m^{-3}$
Acetaldehyde		100	180
Acetone		750	1780
Acetonitrile		40	70
Acrolein		0.1	0.25
Acrylonitrile	c	2	
Aldrin	s		0.25
Ammonia		25	18
Aniline	s	2	10
Arsine		0.05	0.2
Benzene		10	30
Beryllium	s	0.002	
Biphenyl		0.2	1.5
Bromine		0.1	0.7
Butanone (MEK)		200	590
Cadmium, dust, salts			0.05
Carbon dioxide		5000	9000
Carbon disulphide	s	10	30
Carbon monoxide		50	55
Carbon tetrachloride	s	5	30
Carbonyl chloride (phosgene)		0.1	0.4
Chlorine		1	3
Chloroform		10	50
bis(Chloromethyl)ether	c	0.001	
Chromates	c		0.05
Cyanogen		10	20

Substance		ppm	$mg\,m^{-3}$
Heptachlor			0.5
Hydrogen chloride		5	7
Hydrogen cyanide	s	10	10
Hydrogen fluoride		3	2.5
Hydrogen selenide		0.05	0.2
Hydrogen sulphide		10	14
Lead, dusts, salts			0.15
Lindane	s		0.5
Liquefied petroleum gas		1000	1800
Malathion	s		10
Mercury			0.05
Mercury—alkyls	s		0.01
Mercury—other forms			0.1
2-Methoxyethanol (methyl cellosolve)	s	25	80
Nickel carbonyl		0.05	0.35
Nitric acid		2	5
Nitric oxide		25	30
Nitrobenzene	s	1	5
Nitrogen dioxide		3	6
Osmium tetroxide		0.0002	0.002
Oxalic acid			1
Ozone		0.1	0.2

Appendix 1—*continued*

Substance		ppm	mg m^{-3}
2,4-Dichlorophenoxyacetic acid			10
DDT			1
Dichlorvos	s	0.1	1
Dibutyl phthalate			5
Dichlorodifluoromethane (Freon 12)		1000	5000
Dichloromethane		100	360
Dichlorvos (DDVP)	s	0.1	1
Dieldrin	s		0.25
Diethyl ether	s	400	1200
Dimethylformamide	s	10	30
Ethyl acetate		400	1400
Fluoride			2.5
Formaldehyde		2	3

Substance		ppm	mg m^{-3}
Parathion	s		0.1
Pentachlorophenol	s		0.5
Phenol	s	5	19
Phosphine		0.3	0.4
Pyridine		5	15
Stibine		0.1	0.5
Styrene	s	50	215
Sulphur dioxide		2	5
Sulphuric acid	s		1
Tellurium (compounds)			0.1
Tetraethyl lead	s		0.1
Tetramethyl lead	s		0.15
Thallium (soluble compounds)			0.1
Tin, organometallic compounds	s		0.1
Toluene	s	100	375
1,1,1-Trichloroethane		350	1900
Vinyl chloride	c	5	10

s denotes danger from absorption of vapour through the skin.   c denotes that substance is a known carcinogen.

Appendix 2

Quality of water for human consumption

Taken from the complete listing in *Official Journal of the European Communities*, (1980), L 229, pp. 16–21, Directive 80/778. Reproduced with permission.

	Guide level	Maximum admissible concentration
pH	6.5–8.5	
Conductivity	$400\,\mu S\,cm^{-1}$	
Chloride	$25\,mg\,l^{-1}$	
Sulphate	$25\,mg\,l^{-1}$	$250\,mg\,l^{-1}$
Nitrate	$25\,mg\,l^{-1}$	$50\,mg\,l^{-1}$
Nitrite		$0.1\,mg\,l^{-1}$
Fluoride		$1.5\,mg\,l^{-1}$
Calcium	$100\,mg\,l^{-1}$	
Magnesium	$30\,mg\,l^{-1}$	
Sodium	$20\,mg\,l^{-1}$	$150\,mg\,l^{-1}$
COD (permanganate)	$2\,mg\,l^{-1}$	$5\,mg\,l^{-1}$
Phenols (not natural ones)		$0.5\,mg\,l^{-1}$
Surfactants		$200\,mg\,l^{-1}$
Organochlorine solvents	$1\,\mu g\,l^{-1}$	
Pesticides (total)		$0.5\,\mu g\,l^{-1}$
PAH's		$0.2\,\mu g\,l^{-1}$
Heavy metals: Copper	$100\,\mu g\,l^{-1}$	
Arsenic		$50\,\mu g\,l^{-1}$
Cadmium		$5\,\mu g\,l^{-1}$
Mercury		$1\,\mu g\,l^{-1}$
Lead		$50\,\mu g\,l^{-1}$

Appendix 3

EPA priority pollutants*

Volatiles

Acrolein
Acrylonitrile
Benzene
Bromomethane
Bromodichloromethane
Bromoform
Carbon tetrachloride
Chlorobenzene
Chloroethane
2-Chloroethylvinyl ether
Chloroform
Chloromethane
Dibromochloromethane
1,1-Dichloroethane
1,2-Dichloroethane
1,1-Dichloroethene
trans-1,2-Dichloroethene
1,2-Dichloropropane
cis-1,3-Dichloropropene
trans-1,3-Dichloropropene
Ethylbenzene
Methylene chloride
1,1,2,2-Tetrachloroethane
Tetrachloroethene
1,1,1-Trichloroethane
1,1,2-Trichloroethane
Trichloroethene
Trichlorofluoromethane
Toluene
Vinyl chloride

Base-neutral extractables

Acenaphthene
Acenaphthylene
Anthracene
Benzo(a)anthracene
Benzo(b)fluoranthene
Benzo(k)fluoranthene
Benzo(a)pyrene
Benzo(g,h,i)perylene
Benzidine
Bis(2-chloroethyl)ether
Bis(2-chloroethoxy)methane
Bis(2-ethylhexyl)phthalate
Bis(2-chloroisopropyl)ether
4-Bromophenylphenylether
Butylbenzylphthalate
2-Chloronaphthalene
4-Chlorophenylphenylether
Chrysene
Dibenzo(a,h)anthracene
Di-n-butylphthalate
1,3-Dichlorobenone
1,4-Dichlorobenzene
1,2-Dichlorobenzene
3,3'-Dichlorobenzidine
Diethylphthalate
Dimethylphthalate
2,4-Dinitrotoluene
2,6-Dinitrotoluene
Dioctylphthalate
1,2-Diphenylhydrazine
Fluoranthene
Fluorene
Hexachlorobenzene
Hexachlorobutadiene
Hexachloroethane
Hexachlorocyclopentadiene
Indeno(1,2,3-cd)pyrene
Isophorone
Naphthalene
Nitrobenzene
N-Nitrosodimethylamine
N-Nitrosodi-n-propylamine
N-Nitrosodiphenylamine
Phenanthrene
Pyrene
2,3,7,8-Tetrachlorodibenzo-p-dioxin
1,2,4-Trichlorobenzene

Appendix 3—*continued*

EPA priority pollutants*

Acid extractables

4-Chloro-3-methylphenol
2-Chlorophenol
2,4-Dichlorophenol
2,4-Dimethylphenol
2,4-Dinitrophenol

2-Methyl-4,6-dinitrophenol
2-Nitrophenol
4-Nitrophenol
Pentachlorophenol
Phenol
2,4,6-Trichlorophenol

Pesticides

Aldrin
α-BHC
β-BHC
γ-BHC
δ-BHC
Chlordane
4,4′DDD
4,4′DDE
4,4′DDT
Dieldrin
Endosulfan I
Endosulfan II
Endosulfan sulfate

Endrin
Endrin aldehyde
Heptachlor
Heptachlor epoxide
Toxaphene
PCB-1016
PCB-1221
PCB-1232
PCB-1242
PCB-1248
PCB-1254
PCB-1260

* Full details are given in Chapter 4, Ref. 46.

Appendix 4

Commonly used abbreviations in analytical chemistry

Abbreviation	page	Abbreviation	page
AAS	168	HETP	88, 227
AOAC	211	HPLC	226
APDC	199	ICP	179
ASTM	63	IR	70
ASV	141	LD	69
BHA	215	LIDAR	75
BHT	215	MAC	109, 251
BOD	107, 121	MIBK	199
COD	107, 121	MS	86, 237
DCM	221	NAA	237
DDE	219	NAPS	55
DDT	219	OC	219
DO	106	OES	239
DTA	18	OP	219
ECD	86, 220	PAH	68
EEC	109	PIT	54
EIA	7	SSMS	239
EM	237	TCD	86
EPA	111	TCDD	69
FAO	231	TISAB	133
FES	176	TLC	231
FID	86	TLV	56, App. 1
FPD	86, 221	TOC	114, 145
GC/MS	151, 214	UV	76
GLC	83	VIS	246
GSC	83	WHO	54, 210

Index

absorbance 72
absorption systems, for gases 80, 146
accuracy 14, 19
adsorption, use of 43
    losses due to 25
aerosol 52, 64
aflatoxins 230
airborne solids 57
aluminium, in soil 174
ammonia, in soil 158, 166
    in water 122
amphiboles 239
anaerobic bacteria, gases from 107
AnalaR reagents 31
anodic stripping voltammetry 141
apparatus, materials for 25
arcs, for spectroscopy 179
aromatic hydrocarbons 92, 150
arsenic, in food 233
    in hair 23
ascorbic acid (vitamin C) 216
aspiration, of plants 170
atomic absorption spectrometry 137, 168
atomic fluorescence spectrometry 137
automatic analysis 20, 127
available nutrient elements 157

barium, in soil 174
benzoic acid, in food 212
beryllium, GC determination 48
biochemical oxygen demand 107, 121
biogeochemical prospecting 184, 185
biphenyl, on fruit skins 212
blanks 19
blood, lead in 5
boron, in metals 45
    in plants 194
bones, lead in 6
butylated hydroxyanisole, in food 215

cadmium, in food 234
    in hair 23
    in soil 2, 175
    in water 137, 242
calcium, in plants 192, 194
    in soil 174
calibration graphs 15
    curvature of 17

capillary gas chromatography 224
carbon dioxide, in air 34, 52, 89
carbon monoxide, in air 93
carbon, organic 145
carbon rod atomizer 23, 204, 242
cascade impactor 57
catalytic reduction of CO 94
cation exchange, in soil 159, 175
charcoal adsorption tubes 79
chemical interferences in flame spectroscopy 172
chemical oxygen demand 107, 121
chloride, electrode for 131
chloride, in water 130, 136
chromium, in soil 174, 238
chute splitter 151
citrus fruit, fungicides on 213
Clean Air Act 54
clean bench and room 24
clean-up 37
cleaning glassware 28
cobalt, in plants 198
    in soil 174
coins, analysis of 23
cold traps 79
cold-vapour AAS 206
columns, for GC 85, 221
comparison of results 18
condensation, trapping by 42
conductivity, electrical 116, 159
    detector, thermal for GC 86
containers, materials for 25
contamination 27, 34, 113
copper, in jam 233
    in soil 175
    in water 145

DDT 219
deficiency, in feeds 185
    in plants 184
    in soil 159, 183
depreciation 21
derivatization, for GLC analysis 223
detection, limit of 14
detectors, for GC 85
    for HPLC 229
determination, limit of 14, 19
diesel oil 149

differential pulse stripping analysis   144
differential thermal analysis   181
diffusion   42
  samplers for gases   80
dioxin   69
dissolution of samples   35, 162, 192
  selective   44
dissolved oxygen in water   116
distillation   43
  isothermal   31
distribution coefficient   39
dithizone   137
Draeger tubes   77
dropping mercury electrode   117
dry-ashing   191
dust, composition of   70
  particle sizes of   52
  measurement of   57

electrodes, for pH   115
  ion-selective   131
electron-capture detector   87, 152, 220
electron microprobe   66, 237
electrothermal atomization   23, 204, 242
emission spectrography   179, 200
environmental impact assessment   7
Environmental Protection Agency   146, 152
  priority pollutants   App. 3
enzymes   201
errors, classification   12, 13
  sources of   24, 47
ethanol, in pharmaceuticals   244
ethylene blue   95
evaporation, concentration by   150, 220
exchangeable cations in soil   159, 175
extractants, in soil analysis   157

fats, determination of   211
fatty acids   223
fertilizer requirement   157
fish, analysis of   2
  oxygen requirements of   106
flame emission spectroscopy   176
flame ionization detector   87, 101, 152, 221
flame photometric detector   87, 221
flame photometry   178
flames for atomic spectroscopy   170
fluoride, in airborne solids   66
fluoride electrode   132
fluorimetry   195
fly ash   238
foliage, trace elements in   184
food, composition of   211
freon   73

fungicides on fruit peel   213
fusion in molten salts   36, 162, 193

gallium, in soil   174
gamma-ray spectroscopy   45
gases, as reagents   32, 36
gas-liquid chromatography   69, 79, 82, 146, 148, 151, 214, 221
geochemical prospecting   156
graphite furnace, for AAS   205
grinding, of dried plants   162, 191
grit, particle sizes of   52

hair, analysis of   23, 191
half-wave potential   140
head-space analysis   43, 217
Health and Safety at Work Act   56
heavy metals, in food   232
  in water   136
heterogeneity   33
hollow-cathode lamp   169
homogenization   191
HPLC   226
hydride generation, in AAS   206, 233
hydrocarbon fuels, boiling ranges   148
hydrogen sulphide, in air   50, 95
  in sediments   96
hydrological cycle   104

incomplete volatilization, interference by   173
inductively-coupled plasma   179, 201
infra-red absorption   70, 97, 148
  emission   74
  gas analyser   74
  spectra of gases   73, 98
injection systems for GC   85
interferences   20
  in AAS   172
  in FES   177
  with ion-selective electrodes   134
inter-laboratory comparisons   237
ion chromatography   136
ion exchange   44, 136
ionization interferences   173
ion-selective electrodes   131
iron, in air   67
  in plants   192
  in soil   174
  in tungstic oxide   243
  in water   242
isothermal distillation   31

katharometer detector   86, 93
kerosene   149

kinetic methods of analysis   201
Kjeldahl digestion   21, 168, 192

Lambert-Beer Law   72
lanthanum, in lunar soil   238
laser remote sensing   75
lead, in air   5, 6, 59, 66
  in the body   5, 6, 190
  in blood   6, 246
  in food   234
  in Arctic ice   53
  in soil   174
  in water   5, 137, 139, 143
legislation, on air   54, 56
  on food   209
  on rivers etc.   108
  on water   147
lime requirement of soil   165
limit of detection, determination   14, 19
liquid chromatography—HPLC   226
liquid-membrane electrodes   134
losses of analyte, by adsorption   25
  by volatilization   29
lunar rocks   237

Mackereth oxygen cell   118
magnesium, in plants   192, 194
  in soil   174
manganese, in plants   192
  in soil   174
  in water   242
mass spectrometry   69, 76, 151
materials for apparatus   25, 214, 237, 238
mean   10
mercury, in food   234, 245
  in urine   207
  in water   137, 139
microbial degradation   191, 193, 212
molecular spectra, in AAS   172
molten salts, fusion with   36, 162, 193
Mount St. Helens, ash from   63
mycotoxins   230

nebulization   170
neutron activation analysis   45, 237
nickel, in soil   174
nitrate, in soil   158, 166
  in water   125, 129, 136
nitrite, in soil   124, 129, 158
nitrogen, total, in plants   192
  in soil   158, 166
nitrogen oxides, in air   97, 99
non-dispersive IR gas analyser   74

odour threshold   53
oils, plant and animal   223, 225
optical microscopy   60
organic acids, GLC determination   26
organochlorine pesticides   219
organometallic compounds   234
organophosphorus pesticides   43, 220
oxides of nitrogen, in air   97
  IR spectra   98
oxygen in water   106, 116, 119
oxygen-flask combustion   199

particle-size distribution   60, 158
partition coefficient   39
permeation tubes   81
pesticides   219
petrol, aromatics in   93, 149
pH, of soil   163
  of waters   115
phenols, in water   147
  nitration of   125
phosphorus, in plants   192
  in soil   4, 166
  in water   126
plants, analysis of   183
plastics for containers   29
plasmas for emission spectroscopy   179, 201
pneumatic nebulizer   170
polarography   117, 139
pollutant, definition of   50
  priority   App. 3
polymer membrane electrodes   118, 133
polynuclear aromatic hydrocarbons   68,
  150, 153, 229
potassium, in plants   192
  in soils   174, 194
potentiometric titrations   135
powder diffraction patterns   63
precipitation, for separations   44
precision   14, 19
preconcentration, from food   229
  from water   150
preservatives, in food   212
profile of soil   156
prospecting, using plants   185
protein, in food   211
pump, peristaltic   128
purge-and-trap methods   146
pyrex, composition of   28
pyrohydrolysis   37

Q values, table of   14
qualitative analysis   1
quality control   3
quantitative analysis   1

radioactivity   69
rain water, composition of   112
range, of results   11
readability   46
reagents   30
regression analysis   16
releasing agents   173
river quality   107
Rome, ancient water supplies of   114
routine testing   4

sampling, planning   33
   of animals   189
   of airborne solids   58
   of gases   78
   of nuts   231
   of plants   187
   of rocks and soils   160
   of waters   111
scale of working   23
selectivity   19, 134
sensitivity   19
separation methods   37, 42
sewage sludge   185
silica, fused, for glassware   27
silicon, in soil   174
smoke   52, 57
sodium, calibration for flame photometry   17
   in plants   192
   in soil   174
soil formation   155
solubilities, of hydrocarbons in water   150
   of oxygen in air-saturated water   119
solvent extraction   38, 137, 145, 148, 150,
   174, 198
speciation   144
speed of analysis   20
   response   47
specific gravity   43
spectrofluorimetry   69, 195
spectrophotometry UV, visible   69, 75, 96,
   101
   IR   70, 97, 101
spinning riffler   161
standard deviation   10, 15
statistics   9
steam distillation   147, 167, 213
storage of samples   35, 113
stripping of dissolved volatiles   43

strontium, in soil   174
subsampling   161
sulphate, in rain water   136
sulphur cycle   5
sulphur dioxide   55, 75, 95
sulphur, in plants   199
swans, lead in   6
synchronous demodulation   171

t values, table of   18
teeth, lead in   6
Teflon, for containers   29
temperature programming, for GC   90,
   149, 213, 223
thermal conductivity detector   85, 93
thermal methods of analysis   159, 181
thiamine (vitamin B_1)   215
thin-layer chromatography   231
Threshold Limit Values   8, 56, App. 1
tin, in food   233
total organic carbon, in water   145
toxicity, in soils   159, 183
trace metals, in food   232
tracers, isotopic   190
transmittance   72
tungstic oxide, iron in   23, 243
turbidimetry   199

ultraviolet absorption spectrometry   69, 75,
   96
urine, lead in   5
   mercury in   207

van Deemter equation   88, 227
vitamins, in food   215
volatilization, losses due to   29
vycor, composition of   28

washing of samples   189, 191
water, purification of   32
   legislation on   107
   quality, Directive on   App. 2

X-ray diffraction   60, 61, 156, 159, 180
X-ray emission   65
X-ray fluorescence   65

zinc, in soil   2, 174
   in water   242